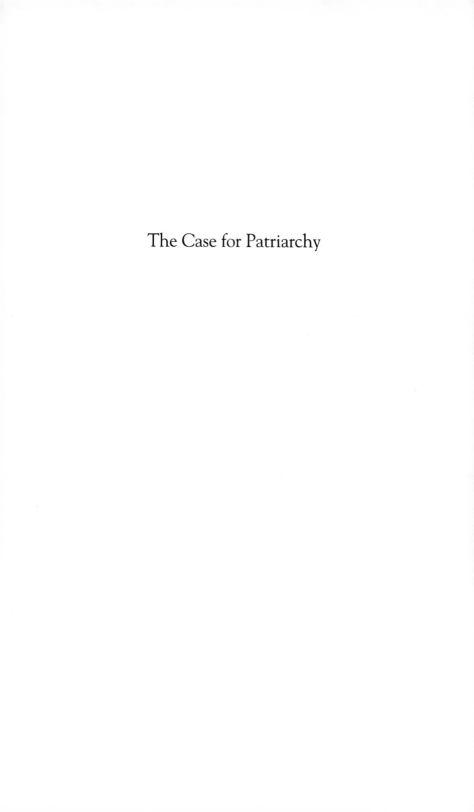

The Case for Patriarchy

Also by Timothy Gordon

Catholic Republic
Why America Will Perish without Rome

Timothy J. Gordon

The Case for
Patriarchy

CRISIS PUBLICATIONS

Manchester, New Hampshire

Crisis Publications
Box 5284, Manchester, NH 03108
1-800-888-9344

www.CrisisMagazine.com

paperback ISBN 978-1-622828-401
ebook ISBN 978-1-622828-418

Library of Congress Control Number: 2021942955

First printing

Contents

Acknowledgments

Here below, in AD 2021, amidst globalist Luciferianism and feminism, God's spies experience enhanced difficulty discharging our tasks. Such a state of affairs renders battle-ready allies all the more valuable. Accordingly, I wish to thank heartfully the love of my life — my wife and best friend, Stephanie Carissa; my six children; my publisher (specifically Charlie McKinney and Michael Warren Davis, both of whom kept this book alive); and all the good folks at Church Militant. Thank you all for doing your part in making this book possible. I would like to dedicate this book to the Seat of Wisdom, Most Holy Virgin Mary.

The Case for Patriarchy

1

What Household Revolution Looks Like

Have you ever proposed a plan to a married male friend who, with a desperately contrived laugh, responded by saying, "Let me go check with my boss"? The phenomenon proves common enough, so I will refer to it in the present tense. Your friend was and is referring to his wife, who is *not* his boss. In fact, although he doesn't know it, the situation is quite the opposite.

Nor is your friend merely making a meaningless joke or being ironic, notwithstanding the desperately precalculated laugh mixed into his disturbing announcement: "Maybe my friend is mostly joking ... hopefully," he wants you to think. Of course, the laugh has been peppered in such as to help him to "save face" via ambiguation, or at least to add a bit of doubt to your scorn. He — the head of a household, theologically subject only to God — actually believes, through the habituation of erroneous custom, that he requires *permission* from his helpmate to do something simple or small. That is, your friend, a household patriarch, actually and literally confesses the lunatic belief that a boss must in ordinary circumstances seek permission from his help.

Obviously, I've presented the reader a silly question, and one not truly needing to be asked. Virtually all of the friends of virtually all of my readers regularly respond to proposed male plans or propositions with precisely this emasculated refrain. If so, this indicates that I've opened with a strictly rhetorical question geared toward showing my reader just how disordered society has everywhere become.

Imagine, at a routine physical, presenting your doctor with a symptom you've long assumed to be innocuous and asking him as an afterthought, "but isn't this normal, doc?" Imagine further receiving the stern reply, "No, it is not. Let's run a battery of tests."

Fear then strikes at the heart of man.

That's precisely what this book is oriented to do: run a battery of tests at the outset of which one already knows that the prognosis looks quite grim. Nothing about the perversion, inversion, and subversion of Western civilization's household patriarchy turns out to be "normal" or innocuous. And this much is true, even if 90 percent of the men out there insist on chuckling loudly and almost convincingly at their malady. Judging by symptoms alone, this malady already seems to have proven fatal to Western civilization.

Just look at the metastasized forms of super-feminism that beset the West and even Christianity today: homosexualism and transgenderism. As I will argue countless times in these pages, the worldview of feminism, which fooled your friend into cashing in his "patriarch card," is none other than a Christian precursor to transgenderism. It, too, is based on the fallacy that men and women can mutually agree to swap roles.

But they cannot. This book will show you why this much is the case. It will also provide something of a "path" out of the woods for Christians.

Although most Christians will find the thesis of this book shocking, it would actually make a very poor dissertation. Why? Because when we examine the particulars of Christian teaching, the issue of "Christian feminism"—or alternately, the presumption *against* ubiquitous household patriarchies within Christendom—turns out to be such a self-evident first principle that it is an utter nonstarter, an intellectual zero. In these pages, I will show the reader that there's no reasonable argument against the moral and anthropological brute fact of Christian patriarchy. Accordingly, Christianity simply cannot coexist with the anti-patriarchal worldview of feminism. For just under two millennia, Christianity straightforwardly formulated, with almost startling specificity, that married laymen are patriarchs relating to their wives as Christ relates to His Bride, the Church.

Indeed, what could be more thematically central to a first day at a new job than identifying who is boss? Nature and nature's God have rendered it utterly clear who is the boss of the family! Yet the fact that no reasonable means to argue otherwise exists has not stopped Christianity's feminist infiltrators, wolves in sheep's clothes, from bending, censoring, and contorting this key central fact of the married vocation. And like Adam before them, Western society's men have been astoundingly swift in their shameless forfeiture of their vocational birthright to familial headship.

Given its painstakingly obvious impropriety, the widespread mistaking—via presumptive sexual fungibility—of wives for husbands and vice versa cannot have happened but for a sweeping diabolical disorientation, enveloping nearly all the denizens of our age. After all, identifying one's boss is not supposed to be the hard part of a job; adequately and artfully obeying the boss is!

I will suggest that Christianity has lost its way because Christianity has lost its sense of the literality of the household patriarchy.

In parish after parish around the United States, the sexual revolutionaries, for one instance, have even *censored* one of the most explicit scriptural marital instructions—Ephesians

5:21–24 — in the Catholic Missal! *They censored the Bible, folks!* That's how monomaniacal the Marxist feminists are. While it sounds like the fatuous exaggeration of some shoddy parody, it is true: the following lines are actually bracketed in many Catholic missals: "Be subject to one another out of reverence for Christ. Wives, be subject to your husbands, as to the Lord. For the husband is the head of the wife as Christ is the head of the church, his body, and is himself its Savior. As the church is subject to Christ, so let wives also be subject in everything to their husbands."

Considering that countless more passages of Scripture attest to the exact same truth of human life, one can easily see why the feminists did it. The Word of God singlehandedly foils all the plans laid by twentieth- and twenty-first-century radicals. Reading such passages honestly and without redactions at Mass would only reinforce the household patriarchy that these radicals sought so desperately to topple within Christendom. This book will suggest that the feminists and Marxists needed Christian patriarchy neutered, or dead, in order to succeed in all their *other* machinations. So they simply hijacked the patriarchy by muting or editing all the countless Christian teachings reinforcing it.

After showing in this first chapter the toxic methods and ramifications of the hijacking, this book will evidence in the second chapter that Christ established not only a clerical patriarchy — an all-male episcopate and priesthood, which proves far more obvious to most readers than the lay patriarchy — but also a lay patriarchy of male householders who act as domestic priest, prophet, and king. As I will show, the Old Testament, the New Testament, the Patristics (West and East), the Scholastics, the Roman Catechism, and even the nineteenth- and twentieth-century popes all tell the *exact same tale*, without a whisper of variation: husbands are the indispensable bosses of families, and wives are husbandly helpmates with the primary charge of dignified obedience.

Following that, a pithy third chapter will study the history of the so-called waves of feminism to evince the subtle tricks and gambits early feminists employed to obviate the true gospel with a false gospel, a would-be "matriarchy." After all, if the true Christian domicile under a patriarch is an *ecclesiola*, a mini-Church led by a priestly and prophetic king, then the false Christian household created by feminist machination proves to be an anti-Church under so-called matriarchs.

In the latter half of the book—chapters 4, 5, and 6—I will consider the feasibility of a patriarchal restoration project. Those chapters will examine what that restoration of the Christian lay vocation should look like in society at large, if it were to succeed. These final three chapters will explicate right-minded Christian patriarchal virtue in chapter 4, the proper remedial course of action in chapter 5, and, in chapter 6, the telltale marks of the polity composed of a virtuous patriarchy—a theoretical society joyfully surviving the death of feminism, the evil regime of the Wicked Witch of the West.

The Toppling of the Patriarchy as the World's First Color Revolution

Sadly familiar to too many American readers in a post-2020 universe is the subversive tactic of *color revolution*: furtive yet forcible regime change implemented through a combination of unpopularity of the standing regime, swift actions by usurpers (known as color revolutionaries), speciously discrediting the tenuous legitimacy of the already unpopular standing regime, and carefully curated manipulation of popular opinion about the regime change through an ongoing disinformation campaign, by elites or media propagandists.

In this short section, I will show how shockingly close the feminist toppling of the patriarchy hued to a world-historically inaugural instance of color revolution. Chapter 2 will demonstrate why and how household patriarchs are, in fact, fully legitimate — and even theologically necessary — according to the dictates of Christian Scripture and Tradition. Chapter 3 will demonstrate the historical and philosophical methodology comprising how feminists made the opposite seem to be the case. But for now, it suffices to show how closely the feminist propaganda campaign described in this chapter (and again in chapter 3) appears to mimic the phases of color revolution.

As the reader will see below, the only aspect of the toppling of the household patriarchy that *doesn't* perfectly match up with color revolution's seven phases, or pillars, is the slow-burning century or so it required to effectuate it: from the mid-nineteenth century to the mid-twentieth century. (Usually, as Americans now well know, color revolutions typically occur swiftly, and in the dead of night, as the polity sleeps.) In the age of revolution, the subjugation of the lay patriarchy has proven the most devastating of all the many subversive revolutions waged upon Christendom by the radical, secular Left *apparatchiks*. In this section, I will describe the world's most momentous regime change — a household "sexual revolution." Then, in the next, I will give its toxic effects, which the reader should recognize as the checkpoint symptoms described by the doctor to his patient during diagnosis: "Your symptom ought to feel like this; does it?"

Michael McFaul identifies the following as the seven pillars, or phases, of color revolution.[1] I will show how each aptly applies to the feminist subversion of the household patriarchy.

The First Pillar

A semi-autocratic — not a fully autocratic — regime is susceptible to color revolution.

Color revolution is, according to McFaul, most efficient when the regime being revolted against is semi-autocratic rather than fully autocratic. Think of the delicate hierarchical nature of Christian matrimony. It consists of a best friendship between unequals,[2] as Aristotle will describe marriage even prior to the Church's elevation of the holiest human relationship to a sacrament. As the reader will see in chapter 2 — because we live after the color revolutionaries' toppling of the patriarchy — many folks no longer understand that the husband of the home is autocratic or monarchical *at all*. In reality, the Christian patriarch is, of course, a very literal kind of monarch — along with a domestic priest and prophet. But for Christians, the household patriarchy turns out to be a hairsbreadth less than absolute monarchy, since, under the dignified sacramental heading of spousal charity, the Christian wife relates to her patriarch in what can only be called an "advisory-plus" role, even as obedience remains her charge. The *Catechism of the Catholic Church* (CCC) is quite specific to distinguish her deference from the less dignified type of obedience by the family's children.

---

[1] Michael McFaul, "Transitions from Postcommunism," *Journal of Democracy* 16, no. 3 (July 2005): 5–19.

[2] Aristotle, *Nicomachean Ethics* 9.

The Case for Patriarchy

As the reader can guess, color revolution would not thrive under absolute autocracy since it requires the "breathing room" afforded by a semi-autocratic regime. Color revolution requires something like what the American colonials called "salutary neglect" by England in 1775. How else would even furtive subversion operations get off the ground? This requires semi-autocracies rather than autocracies proper. In precisely this way, chapter 3 will show how the feminists were able to create more space for themselves by adverting constantly to the nuanced, dignified role of the wife, then exaggerating the power endemic to the wife's lieutenant role between father and children, and then simply excising altogether the wifely requirement of obedience. In other words, Western civilization's husband was a semi-autocrat who suffered the incremental aggrandizement of the domain of the female advisory role until that role swallowed the husbandly prerogative it was supposed to be advising. Rue the tale of how the first phase of the world's most terrible color revolution came to pass.

The Second Pillar

The representative of the regime must be somewhat unpopular.

Color revolutions build on extant momentum. They cash in opportunely on frangible political capital already existing, or not existing, within polities. Accordingly, such revolutions are not typically waged against extremely popular incumbent candidates, but, rather, quite selectively against regimes already flagging in popular enthusiasm. Imagine taking a tenuous cultural and political arrangement within some society — macroscopic or microscopic, a small republic or a family — and playing it against the regime in precisely the way that its unruly subordinates were already itching to do.

The household patriarchy was a subtle arrangement all along, as will be discussed at greater length in chapter 3, in reference to Eve's subversion of the patriarchy in her act of Original Sin. As every married man knows, even when his household is in good order, sustained wifely obedience necessarily involves the lifegiving grace of the sacrament, even in the case of a good wife. Concupiscence ceaselessly tempts disobedience. Human nature relentlessly threatens subversion of righteous authority. Relationships—even the most intimate human type, the marital one—are complicated. Acquainted with and emboldened by Eve's inclination toward rebellion against the patriarchy, which altered human nature for the worse going forward, all that the feminist color revolutionaries of the nineteenth century had to do was nudge women a bit with propaganda.

Add to this delicate state of affairs the fact that, in concrete particular situations around the world, day in and day out, many husbands hang on to their household authority by just a thread. Many are not "popular" with their wives. Many are not admirable leaders. Many are enslaved to sin and self-service. Just as concupiscence played on female nature in a certain degrading way, it mitigates and outstrips male nature and male leadership in a different way. Given the revolutionary conditions of the time, the mediocre husband's house has been a "house of cards" ever since the mid-nineteenth century.

The Third Pillar

The color revolutionaries must present a united, organized opposition to the standing regime.

When the color revolution is a "go," it's a go. After the necessary conditions—namely, an unpopular regime in a weak, transitional moment—are in play, its players must present a wholly united front through actions in concert. As we will see in the fourth phase of color revolution, perfectly concerted actions by revolutionaries usually amount to non-self-contradicting and constant propaganda. If they can pull this off, they can fool almost everyone in a given society.

Since the Fall of mankind, through Eve's rebellion, any destroyers or usurpers of familial fabric acting under diabolical agency or inspiration will perennially understand the weak spot in family unity: obedience. As noted above, concupiscence provides a fallible human inclination upon which to play. Since the will and intellect of all men and women were darkened at the Fall, obedience is a difficult charge even to faithful servants and lordly stewardship is a difficult charge even to good-willed leaders.

In 1848—the same year that Marx and Engels published the identically themed *Communist Manifesto*—feminist operatives signed Elizabeth Cady Stanton's *Declaration of Sentiments*, which memorialized the deliberations of the Seneca Falls Convention, inaugurating what we today call "feminism." (Chapter 3 will investigate this document in great detail.) Playing on the canny breath of death Eve had insinuated into the Garden—and into human nature thereafter—the feminist revolution against the patriarchy was officially a "go." Ever since this juncture in the mid-nineteenth century, the feminist revolution has been raging on. In one aspect, its crawling incrementalism, the feminist color revolution would be unlike any of the color revolutions of the twentieth or twenty-first century.

The Fourth Pillar

Having ousted the previous regime, color revolutionaries drive home the point that, in light of current popular opinion, that regime holds a delegitimized right to rule.

In the case of the electoral color revolutions of the twentieth and twenty-first centuries, regime delegitimization tended to occur through the gross mischaracterization or direct manipulation of whatever happened on election night. As Americans now know only too well, this initial pulse of electoral delegitimization happens suddenly and violently, as the electorate sleeps.

But in the century-long case of the toppling of the patriarchy, which was underway most actively from the 1850s through the 1960s, the feminist delegitimization of male headship was transmitted primarily by protracted usage of the "perfectionist fallacy." The fallacy posits that a proposition is wholly invalid unless its efficacy is wholly efficient. In other words, the feminists have popularized the erroneous notion that a husband's rule over his household is not secure or legitimate unless he is *perfectly* lordly, like Christ Himself (which, of course, is impossible). On the other hand, Christianity *actually* professes that wives must obey their husbands' directives in *all* things except explicit orders to commit grave sins. A wife cannot disobey her husband on strictly prudential grounds—not even on the hypothetical basis that his order might possibly, at some later time, contribute to the development of a bad habit that could theoretically lead to sin. Yet this is precisely what the "Christian feminists" began teaching, during that century, in order to claim compliance with scriptural passages such as Ephesians 5, yet without actually admonishing any wives to obey any husbands. After all, no husbands will actually come anywhere close to meeting Christ's mark.

Once more, the genuine Christian teaching is that a wife can disobey only if her husband clearly orders her to do (or not to do) something she must not (or must). For instance, if a husband orders his wife to consume a contraceptive pill or not to attend Mass on Sunday, she can and must disobey him. But the feminists convinced Christian wives—seemingly from within the Faith—that their wifely paths to "conscientious objections" were far more numerous, broad, and prudential than they, in fact, are. This is how the delegitimization phase of the patriarchy-toppling color revolution worked.

The Fifth Pillar

There must be enough independent media to "inform" citizens about the "illegitimate" right to rule by the incumbent regime.

Here, the secular Left well knows they are fish in water. For many decades, they've monopolized both news and entertainment media, burying and fabricating ledes wherever necessary or convenient to the cultural revolutions they're fomenting. In the last decade, their position has been strengthened in the only way they were conceivably "weak" before: powerful, multinational corporations now run at commercial breaks concomitant ads that support the revolution being advocated in the news, sitcom, or drama programming.

In the case of the feminist color revolution, popular messaging of recent decades has transmitted a crystal-clear message: men's time is up; the Age of Women has arrived. The citizens might as well be informed directly of the illegitimacy of men's right to continue ruling the homeplace and society. Talking heads on the TV screen might as well be chanting, "Out with the old and in with the new!"

As we will see below, the most potent "one-two punch" for the effectuation of this message has been the intermittent refrain of television shows, alternating with four-minute commercial "breaks." The entertainment media apparatus has, over the course of my lifetime, squeezed almost all male protagonists out of heroic plots and conflicts. If male characters make any sort of appearance whatsoever—which is by no means a guarantee—it will certainly come in the form of a supportive, traditionally effeminate role, flanking a female lead who fights fires, gets bad guys, kicks down walls, or flies to the moon. (Sometimes, semi-masculine roles have been preserved for male villains, although even this seems to be going by the wayside.) This shift has been thematically reinforced by concomitantly repositioned contexts and subtexts in commercials that advocate alternative domestic situations, such as men staying home to cook or clean, wearing aprons or robes, as their wives carry their briefcases out the front door to work.

Counterinsurgency is forestalled primarily through psychological means. The "illegitimacy" of men's right to reclaim their natural and traditional role is usually forefended against by the mechanism of insinuated ridicule. Radical advertising has mastered the art in a very short span of time. If a husband in a television commercial asks his wife, pseudo-humorously, if he can reclaim (even briefly) the remote control as they sit in front of the television, she will shoot him a single glance that signals his abjectly impoverished station. Often, in these commercials, the too-thin or too-fat husband, always non-threatening and utterly emasculated, will then drop his head in shame or look at the screen like a sideshow clown who has just been hit with a pie. Typically, the camera will then pan to the wife, who shoots her own expressive look at the camera. Her expression always bespeaks one proposition: "My husband is a hapless idiot." The psyop that virtually all of these commercials effectuate seems to be ruthlessly efficient at establishing the message—"Don't even try it"—to men who would mount a restoration effort.

The Sixth Pillar

The color revolutionaries mobilize a sizable political opposition to the standing regime, up to tens of thousands of demonstrators and protesters.

After the media propaganda has been promulgated in the previous phases, the color revolution must organize thousands of planted "protesters" in order to whip up tens or (if all goes well) hundreds of thousands of additional nonplanted ones. In other words, the propaganda comes first; then comes the color revolution–generated "support" shown publicly by planted operatives, who "demonstrate" to the broader public that the propaganda is working. Finally comes genuine support from the public, in cases of success. This sixth phase is oriented toward convincingly falsifying grassroots support for the color revolution until *actual* grassroots support kicks in. The watchword is *fake it 'til you make it*. Eventually, a successful color revolution will host a mix of planted and nonplanted demonstrators against the regime.

In the case of the sex revolution against the patriarchy, the support shown for media propaganda was transmitted largely through … more media propaganda. Unlike other color revolutions, the toppling of the patriarchy proceeded vastly more slowly, as noted above, which meant that protest in the streets was not nearly as important. Instead, the feminist movement proceeded by adding to news and entertainment media messaging a sideshow of real-life play actors — celebrities who lived out the feminist prescriptions in ways that the public could regularly keep up with and consume. Actresses and journalists such as Jane Fonda, Barbara Walters, Gloria Steinem, and Melanie Griffith gave American women a reasonable public basis, in tabloid format, for believing that the living out of feminist fantasies could actually be successfully navigated. The modern term for this *fashionable lifestyle modeling* is "live-action roleplaying," or LARPing.

The sixth phase of color revolution relied heavily on glamorized celebrity LARPing in full public view, because household wives of the 1950s and 1960s needed to see that "this feminism stuff actually works out in real life" before they began to try it out themselves in the 1970s. Little did they know that lifestyle modeling fails to qualify as "real life" and that the feminist way of life did not veritably "work out" morally or spiritually for its practitioners. Nonetheless, the psyop successfully enlarged the number of feminists—moving the revolution from a fringe 1960s radical or hippie way of life to one that became popularly viewed as stable and practicable in the 1970s. Indeed, on the basis of such lifestyle modeling, the protestors and demonstrators against the patriarchal regime swelled from a few thousand to several hundred thousand within one generation.

The Seventh Pillar

Divisions continue to exist among the standing regime's coercive forces.

Finally, in their seventh phase, successful color revolutions propagate the fractionalization of the regime's would-be defenders. Just as we saw in phase two, that the susceptible standing regime was already unpopular prior to the onset of the revolution, the purpose of the color revolution is to discredit, shame, and then silence the regime. The goal is not only to defeat the regime, but, rather, to defeat and then permanently disable and *silence* it.

This explains why the feminists, like all radicals, never take their foot off the accelerator. Firstly, allowing a more reasonable regime to debate a less reasonable one would favor the former.

The patriarchy, if allowed by media outlets the breathing room to remount an offensive, would certainly prevail. Secondly, radicals are trained well to "shoot to kill." Like any good opponent, they have habituated the practice of completely incapacitating their rivals whenever they have the chance. In the realm of feminism (and other recent instances we've seen of color revolution), this involves the total silencing—until kingdom come—of retrogrades who would stick up for the *ancien régime* on media and social media. Censorship is accordingly total.

The Toppling of the Patriarchy

The widespread supplantation of the lay patriarchy of the household with a sort of feminist "matriarchy" has engendered both demand-side and supply-side failures in Christian matrimony. And it has done so *both* for Christian men and women, and *both* before and during marriage. Each type of failure, demand side and supply side, has proven generally devastating to the Church and the world. The proto-transgender, anti-patriarchal culture of feminism inchoately permeating Christianity in the 1960s increasingly malformed and misinformed the young practitioners of marriage in the twenty-first century. Accordingly, even most of Christian marriage's well-meaning practitioners and advocates of today have unknowingly absorbed many feminist presuppositions and slanders into their own defenses of the institution. Unmarried onlookers, especially young men, observe the situation and figure marriage is not for them.

By our own day, the nonpatriarchal family proves to be a *tabula rasa* long since wiped clean of its elements of true Christianity and real vocation. As we saw above (and will see in far more detail below), it was a manufactured ignorance. By design, the most important attributes of Christian family have been vituperated, and the feminists will do whatever they can to ensure the permanence of our popular dementia.

The primary demand-side failure of the popular repudiation of the patriarchy has been the proliferation of the ostensible unattractiveness of marriage. Making something look ugly affects popular desire for it, of course. Since young men simply dismiss out of hand the possibility of finding wives who would qualify under the classical Christian model, they don't know what they're missing. Accordingly, young men are, on the average, unwilling to marry as young as they did in all previous ages.

This proves highly similar to a classic demand-side economics problem. Marriage has been gravely slandered and misrepresented in such a sweeping way. Think, for instance, of its only partly caricatured portrayal in the sitcom *Married with Children*. Very few young men look forward with relish to it, as they should. A properly ordered marriage furnishes practically the most beautiful life a man can possibly have—second in rank only to a life of religious celibacy. So we should find ourselves all the more shocked that most young men of our age have abandoned that first fact of young male life: the happy hunting for a wife at eighteen or nineteen years of age. But we understand the cause: twenty-first-century marriage couldn't possibly look *less* sexy.

From the perspective of a masculine young Christian who knows better, contrast the attractive properties of veritable vocational marriage—a genuinely sexy thing—with its unattractive, pseudo-Christian foil today. The latter is but a wraith of the former, and yet the vast majority of young men assume that the cheap copy, rather than the genuine article, awaits them inevitably on their wedding day. One wonders: Does this frightening new feminist arrangement represent *art imitating life*, or the opposite? Throughout all of human history up until a few decades ago, marriage's natural desiderata paid dividends every day in the life of a husband. The daily and weekly routine of life continuously incentivized him to become a better and more lordly patriarch. The wife paid her honor to her husband in ways that rendered the entire arrangement well worthwhile, and the husband enthusiastically reciprocated in equal but opposite ways.

But in their diabolically ingenious color revolution against the patriarchy, clever feminists devolved and deteriorated matrimony's most sought-after male prizes. The devolving, deteriorating substitution occurred on (at least) five levels.

Firstly, men are naturally attracted not just to beautiful women *generically*, but more especially to the finely crafted beauty of wives who make themselves beautiful *specifically* for their husbands' tastes. The traditional model of marriage encourages such narrow tailoring to tastes (which men, of course, should reciprocate wherever applicable). Conversely, on the current, beauty-less model of marriage, men are scorned for all indicia of any expectation of physical beauty or preference-specific "sexiness" in their wives. Moreover, husbands are scorned for even the slightest expression of approval of or desire for the natural wifely virtue of not "letting oneself go" physically. (Meanwhile, women who complain that their husbands are putting on weight are applauded for their candor!)

Secondly, men are naturally attracted by the notion of wife as cook, cleaner, and caretaker. Of course. For all of human history, husbandly expectations were indulged with cooking, cleaning, and caretaking. Yet, on the absurd current model of marriage as nonspecialized labor, husbands are everywhere scorned for their attraction to this natural (and practical) desideratum of the actual vocation.

Thirdly, men are by their nature and function *hobby horses*: the acquisition of heightened strength, skill, hand-eye coordination, or *nous* befits their role as householder. By his very job title, a husband and father must teach, preach, earn, encourage, inspire, and protect. This is to say, the cultivation of hobbies benefits each of the members of the family under the father's headship. Accordingly, unlike other members of the household not charged with holistic leadership, husbandly pastimes and hobbies prove fundamentally and uniquely valuable to the common good of the family. Therefore, the good wife should lead her children in cheering or watching or joining the recreational interests (to some reasonable extent) of the father.

Until the color revolution by the "matriarchy," husbands were historically indulged in this area as well. Yet, on the current egalitarian model of marriage, husbands spend their time supporting the pastimes of their wives and children instead of tending to their own, and thereby neglect to better themselves. According to the popular culture, it seems that whenever married men do engage in some male hobby or other, it is usually relegated to the dank, untouchable ignobility of the "man cave," where — by design — none of the family pays them any attention as they do it.

Fourthly, men are naturally and even biologically inclined toward leading others, a noble impulse that vocational marriage encourages, emplaces, and accommodates. For healthy, functioning Christian families, husbandly leadership is indispensable. Of course, this is the central theme of the book you are reading: until a few decades ago, husbands were always and everywhere presumed to be the family leaders. Yet on the current leaderless model (or even that of the wifely-leader model) of marriage, men seek to exercise their headship elsewhere, via some species of careerism, local politics, or through being recreational "weekend warriors" with other fathers who should be with *their* families — spending *far* too much time away from the wife and kids. Yet, instead of planning to spend even more time away from the family to flex this natural yet modernly unused muscle, men should spend intentional and fun time at home, with special emphasis on reclaiming domestic leadership in the domain of team-building family activities. On the current state of affairs, they think this return to tradition is outside the realm of possibility. They must be disabused of this notion.

Fifthly, human beings mutually desire one another's desire. Accordingly, men are attracted not to headstrong, officious women but rather to the supportive, submissive ones who will appreciate (rather than covet) male strength and leadership. The traditional Christian designation for this natural fact is "complementarity." Supply does not create its own demand in this case; nature bestows the demand that men and women have for each other, since we bear opposite natures. As this book's Christian anthropology and theology will show, men are active, while women are passive. Males represent the expressive principle, while females represent the receptive one. Yet, on the current egalitarian model of marriage, men have often retrofitted the female qualities they claim attraction to — through a widespread cultural gaslighting — as those of "strong women" who don't actually fit as well within the married vocation.

In short, the true married vocation invites women who are loyal, docile, supportive, faithful, lovely, and encouraging *believers* in their husbands. Chapter 2 will substantiate this bold Christian claim. These are women who *own* their role as helpmates and who will do anything in their power to aid the husband's mission: make his favorite meal, wear his favorite outfit, shower him with kisses and hugs, guard his heart from the slings and arrows of the workaday world. But today's matrimonial pretenders and its feminist architects have served up wives who decry loyalty as cultish; faithfulness as spiritlessness; loveliness as servility before unhealthy body imaging; and belief in the husband's dreams and goals as the wifely abandonment of dreams and goals altogether. (This last is an utter lie. Wives are simply wired to have dreams and goals by *adoption* of their husbands'!).

At school functions like basketball games or field days, my male high school students used to witness my wife's grace and loveliness in action and later remark to me that they never knew marriage could be so pleasant, comfortable, fun, and exciting for the husbands living out the vocation properly. Most of them came from modern "matriarchal" households. I would respond, "This is what it's *supposed* to be! But you must make something kingly, self-sacrificial, and moral for your future wives to trade for."

This exclamation, a *cri de coeur*, of the young says it all. The attack on the family was engineered, preternaturally, to set and maintain marital expectations *low*, which enslaves us all to sin and ultimately to Hell. We need fathers, after all, to train us in the ways of Heaven. We may conclude upon the demand-side effects of the repudiation of the patriarchy today that almost no young men want to get married at all. And who can blame them? Simply, the conditions for the possibility of marriage's desirability have been vituperated, vanished from the face of the earth.

We must not forget the identity of the author of this banishment. The intelligence that designed this overthrow is, by necessity, far superior to the individual feminist's. In 1981, a poignant clue was given about the nature of this impending attack on the Christian family. The Fatima seer Sr. Lucia dos Santos wrote an unexpected letter to Cardinal Carlo Caffarra, imploring him: "Father, a time will come when the final battle between the Kingdom of Christ and Satan will be over marriage and the family. And those who will work for the good of the family will experience persecution and tribulation. But do not be afraid because Our Lady has already crushed his head."[3] The recipient of this letter, Cardinal Caffarra, said in 2017 that "what Sr. Lucia wrote to me is being fulfilled today."[4]

The good cardinal's observation rings true, especially in light of the ongoing overthrow of the household patriarchy, all but consummated in our day. The proliferation of homosexualism, and more recently transgenderism, adds force to his remark. But the vast majority of the diabolical firepower against society belongs to the attack on the family through the attack on the father. While most conservatives and Christians apprise the grim situation's root cause oppositely — that the proliferation of the LGBT movement most starkly denotes the veracity of Sr. Lucia's words — it is rather the ubiquitous demotion of the father that has enabled that proliferation.

While an examination of the root causes of the patriarchy's susceptibility to feminist hijacking will be offered in chapter 3's historiography of feminism, the following short list of the supply-side failures of the current family structure should suffice for now. Unlike the family's demand-side failures, the supply-side

---

[3] Dorothy Cummings McLean and Pete Baklinski, "Abortion, Homosexuality Show 'Final Battle' between God and Satan Has Come: Cardinal," LifeSiteNews, May 23, 2017, https://www.lifesitenews.com/news/abortion-homosexuality-show-final-battle-between-god-and-satan-has-come-car.

[4] Diane Montagna, "Cardinal Caffarra: "What Sr. Lucia Wrote to Me Is Being Fulfilled Today," Aleteia, May 19, 2017, https://www.google.com/amp/s/aleteia.org/2017/05/19/exclusive-cardinal-caffarra-what-sr-lucia-wrote-to-me-is-being-fulfilled-today/amp.

counterparts beset us on all sides, such that most people — not only conservative Catholics — can and do spot them quite readily. Even Leftists and non-Christians bemoan certain aspects of them.

Downstream of the sex revolution and female-run households, the casual observer notes that families in the West have grown nonsustainably small. In fact, most Western countries are not even replacing their own populations.[5] The most deficient of these low-birth-rate countries mount constant national campaigns to raise birth rates, even against the good interest of their feminist lobby, which opposes life initiatives as anathema to female "liberation." Generally speaking, they aim to raise the fertility rate to roughly two babies born to each wife, such as to obviate the dreaded "dying" demographical status. Europe is currently in its demographical death throes and has been for some time. Folks in the United States have historically felt insulated against Europe's low numbers, but more recently, as the nation has secularized more aggressively, we have joined in Europe's demographical concern as our birthrate has dropped to its lowest in a century.[6]

No country can serve two masters, as the United States (and European countries) presently attempts to do. Birth rates will not rise significantly after Americans have been propagandized so ceaselessly and effectively about the need to contracept. The statistics show that the contraceptive mindset has all but preponderated in society.

---

[5] "EU Births: Decline Continues, but Not from Foreign-Born Women," Eurostat, March 23, 2021, https://ec.europa.eu/eurostat /web/products-eurostat-news/-/ddn-20210323-2.

[6] Mike Stobbe, "US Birth Rate Falls to Lowest Point in More Than a Century," AP News, May 5, 2021, https://apnews. com/article/birth-rates-science-coronavirus-pandemic-health-d51571bda4aa02eafdd42265912f1202.

The Case for Patriarchy

Almost all women who identify as religious have used contraceptive methods—99 percent of mainline Protestants, evangelical Protestants and Catholics, and 96 percent of people with other religious affiliations. Among sexually active women who were not seeking pregnancy, 88 percent were using a contraceptive method in 2016, and this proportion has remained steady since 2002.[7]

What these American and European liberals clamoring for higher birth rates *don't* understand is that the contraceptive mindset depleting census numbers is doing something far more grave to society as well: it is embittering and dividing spouses against each other. Denying marriage's procreative impulse equates to a denial of its first and best reason for being—its *telos*, purpose, or goal. This is none other than Aristotle's function argument, applied to marriage and family: the best and happiest iteration of X is represented by an X that serves its goal most efficiently. The family's first goal is procreation, and its second is the unity and virtuous happiness of its spouses. So, the healthiest instance of a family is a thriving, actively procreative family.

The implicitly feminist Left, along with politically moderate casual observers, seem to want rectification of the problem of microscopic family size only after the problem has reached the point of devastating demographic crisis. The faithful Catholic pleads for greater sanity. In other words, the "dying demographics" story turns out to have more depth and breadth than that which those simply wanting higher birth rates imagine: the analysis in these pages urges a more careful view of the *spiritual* and *psychological*

---

[7] "Contraceptive Use in the United States by Demographics," Guttmacher Institute, May 28, 2021, https://www.guttmacher.org/fact-sheet/contraceptive-use-united-states#.

problems of contraception, which easily outrank demographic depletion in their need for urgency of redress. Demographic depletion proves only a tertiary crisis, whereas contraception's primary manifestation is as a spiritual problem and secondarily presents as a psychological one.

It must not be forgotten that contraception's impetus was the selfsame sex revolution that toppled the patriarchy and shamefully pressured wives into the workplace.

Because husbands and wives around the West aren't tending to matrimony's first goal (procreation), they are generally failing in its second goal: mutual happiness and intimacy between spouses. C. S. Lewis's adage about the importance of prioritization comes to mind: "Put first things first and we get second things thrown in: put second things first and we lose both first and second things." Noncontracepting couples who stand for a culture of life tend to capture both desiderata mentioned in the previous section: big families and intimate, loving interspousal rapport. Contracepting couples who stand for a culture of death tend to capture neither.

Thus, a pandemic that seeks out and destroys marital intimacy has ravaged Western countries since the inception of the feminist assault on the patriarchy.

Psychologically, the inevitable signal a contracepting wife sends to her husband is one of preemption: "I don't want what you offer; what you offer, which I reject, is the most fundamental expression of yourself." The law of averages being what it is, it would be absurdly unreasonable to expect that—on a massive scale, anyway—marriages operating on this preclusive dictum can sustain emotional intimacy between spouses. Generally speaking, they cannot. In turn, marriages that lack emotional intimacy tend to end in divorce: the modern divorce rate perennially borders on 40 percent among first marriages and above 50 percent among "remarriages."[8]

Accordingly, while it is difficult to produce statistics that substantiate the common observation that turbulence is the watchword in today's "matriarchal" household, the staggering divorce rate helps a commonsense Christian to connect the dots. At any rate, it requires no special expertise to note the acrimony, resentment, role reversal, and palpable daily power struggles occurring in the average marital situation in 2021.

The most emblematic vice of the modern failed marriage and the toppled patriarchy is pornography: it stands for the twin propositions of shrill wifely rejection and enervated husbandly submission to vice. In 56 percent of divorces, at least one spouse has an "obsessive interest in porn."[9] When one spouse is using porn, 68 percent of couples report a decrease in their sex life, which hardly shocks the imagination. A staggering 70 percent of men report looking at porn at least once a month. Unsurprisingly, 98 percent of all men report having looked at pornography at least once, but far more surprisingly, 98 percent of all men also report having looked at pornography in the past six months.[10]

Res ipsa loquitur: by pornography statistics alone, one notes that there exists an obvious problem with the patriarchy. Instead of being honorable, chaste, restrained, protective, and highly

8   "Marriage and Divorce," American Psychological Association, https://www.apa.org/topics/divorce-child-custody.
9   "26 Shocking Porn Statistics Most Men Don't Know," Husband Help Haven, https://husbandhelphaven.com/porn-statistics/.
10 Grant Hilary Brenner, "When Is Porn Use a Problem?," *Psychology Today*, February 19, 2018, https://www.psychologytoday.com/us/blog/experimentations/201802/when-is-porn-use-problem.

attracted to their wives, today's household men are furtive, perverted, unrestrained, unprotective, and ostensibly not attracted to their wives.

Although the secular left has long claimed that rearing fewer children ensures the parental ability to pool mental and economic resources such as to raise them better, we do not see history or sociology bearing out this bald assertion. We see quite the opposite. Our age of small, unhappy, contraceptive families produces, at unprecedented levels, youth beset by prominent moral crises of all sorts: the opioid epidemic; a precipitous rise in the out-of-wedlock birthrate; widespread youth purchase in the pop cults of homosexualism and transgenderism; low church attendance; and high rates of depression and suicide. With such a violent sea change over the last two generations, our questions about root causes must always bring us back to the Catholic necessitation for the patriarchal family. Everything boils down to the family, which experienced a shocking regime change *at the exact same moment in which all these crises erupted.* Obviously, the events must be causally related.

Mothers began "running" families and outsourcing, at alarming rates, the duties of mothering to day-care workers. Then the offspring of the family grew anxious and miserable: maternal absence from the household had negatively impacted the offspring in such households.[11]

---

[11]   Scott Boylan, "Optimal Early Childhood: The Effects of a Stay-at-Home Parent on Child Development" (private paper, 2021). Boylan writes: "In response to research regarding the importance of a stress free environment for young children, it is important to evaluate the stress responses to non-maternal child care. A study conducted by researchers Megan Gunnar, Eric Kryzer, Mark Van Ryzin, and Deborah Phillips focuses on the biological analysis of the effects that day care has on children. The

The Case for Patriarchy

But no one in the family grew more depressed than mothers themselves, a fact that the feminists cannot explain subsequent to their widely celebrated toppling of the patriarchy: "By many objective measures the lives of women in the United States have improved over the past 35 years, yet we show that measures of subjective well-being indicate that women's happiness has declined both absolutely and relative to men."[12] Of course, hapless lines of feminist prose such as this reflect the unfounded presupposition that the measures of female life enhancement over the past thirty-five years being referenced were indeed *objective*. They weren't. Instead, they presumed what they set out to prove. Like women who errantly believe they can become "transgendered," the feminists' presumption that acting more masculine would make them happy was a doomed errand from the outset. It is a sad tale. Such persons deserve our prayer and love and gentle correction.

---

quantitative research involved examining the increase in salivary cortisol from mid-morning to mid-afternoon in 151 children (3–4.5 years old) in full-time home-based daycare ... due to existing evidence that children's cortisol levels rise at daycare, the researchers hypothesized that their results would show the same, and that the time spent and quality of care would be the strongest determining factors. Confirming their hypothesis, the results revealed that cortisol increases were noted in the majority of children (63%) at day care, with 40% classified as a stress response." Boylan connects these maternal-deprivation stress statistics (above) to the theory that "continual disruption of the attachment between infant and primary caregiver could result in long term cognitive, social, and emotional difficulties for that infant [inclusive of] delinquency, reduced intelligence, increased aggression, depression, and affectionless psychopathy."

[12] Betsey Stevenson and Justin Wolfers, "The Paradox of Declining Female Happiness," NBER, May 15, 2009, https://www.nber.org/papers/w14969.

Generally speaking, each of these failures by "matriarchal" homes demonstrates what nature already implies: doing things "backward" yields unhealthful results.

Manipulating Demand, Manipulating Supply

How did feminists so effectively diminish the popular male demand for Christianity-required marital roles and natural sex-based virtues? Aren't such robust natural drives all but impossible to supersede via social engineering? Don't the supply-side failures of today's presumptive marital arrangement tell on the dysfunctionality of the arrangement itself?

To each of these questions, one must answer: evidently not. Somehow, popular messaging by feminism maintains a morally unstable but politically stable balance. As noted in the section above on color revolution, the messaging is the lynchpin of the successful psyop.

Accordingly, I decided to take a random, nonscientific sampling of the commercial messaging oriented toward male consumption. I chose the primetime male programming taking place during this year's NBA Playoffs as my sample. Here's what the actual, nonmanipulated first attempt turned up.

In the first advertisement I watched, the setting was a "heads up" automobile race on an oval track between a man and a woman. As one can guess, the woman handily beat the commercial's male protagonist, even though no woman has ever won the Indianapolis 500 and "since the F1 World Championship began in 1950, only two women have qualified for Grands Prix."[13] If

---

[13] Joe Saward, "Formula 1 Still Waiting for Next Woman to Conquer the Road to the F1 Grid," *Autoweek*, January 22, 2021, https://www.google.com/amp/s/www.autoweek.com/racing/formula-1/

the skills and hand-eye coordination requisite for motor sports are so empirically and demonstrably masculine as these cursory facts show, why pretend? Since most professional female drivers cannot even *qualify* for — let alone win — an F1 Grand Prix, why does an advertiser try to depict one who obliterates a male driver in a one-on-one race? The answer is, of course, that the truth hasn't got much to do with advertising. And this axiom of life becomes exponentially truer in the case of feminist advertising.

Anyway, this first ad rang true to my expectations.

In the next advertisement — another commercial involving cars — a woman again controlled the scene and the setting. But in this commercial, a household mother, rather than a professional racer, operated the family car down a suburban avenue, as her husband sat in the passenger seat and faithfully took her orders. Her husband submissively tended to the children in the backseat, as mothers customarily used to do. He navigated for her, as wives customarily used to do. If someone from thirty-five or even twenty-five years in the past would have seen this commercial, they would have been brought up to date on the functional transgenderism that has been at work in society between their time and ours: this commercial's man and woman simply *swapped places*.

Again, this commercial sequence was wedged right in the middle of primetime male programming: the NBA Playoffs. Shouldn't one expect to witness an advertising tendency that positions its rhetoric toward male protagonists, since advertisers typically want to maximize sales by *sating* rather than challenging consumers' cultural assumptions? Not after the feminist color

---

amp35246612/formula-1-still-waiting-for-next-woman-to-conquer-the-road-to-the-f1-grid/.

revolution. The only answer seems to be that advertisers today have abandoned their commercial goals for ideological ones.

In the third advertisement I watched, a female teacher instructed a group of adult men from a whiteboard. She chastened, encouraged, corrected, guided, and lectured them. The men appearing in the commercial acted just as traditional females would be expected to do: they were docile, obedient, eager to please, and submissive.

There was nothing scientific about my little experiment. I hereby publish no methodology associated with it. I make no special guarantees about it. Yet, since that night, nearly identical commercial results have been consistently yielded evening after evening, and every one of my readers recognizes the results as perfectly characteristic of our day. So, why are my conclusions so shocking to read, and why do the feminists establish themselves in *especially masculine* bastions of the world, such as sports?

In order to commandeer the patriarchy, the feminists had to venture wherever patriarchal impulses were strongest.

I recall with poignant feeling my first personal encounter with the unjust, bitter feminist impulse to "take down" significant aspects of the patriarchy.[14] Coincidentally, perhaps — or perhaps not — the incident from my young life relates to sports. One of my eighth-grade teachers, Mrs. H, baselessly and loudly announced

---

[14] Specifically, I recall the sting of feminism's self-righteous and blithe injustice. The feminist with whom I interacted on that occasion, my teacher, was infinitely assured of the righteousness of her worldview's rectificatory force: she conceived of her assaults on our patriarchal assumptions as the first act of reclamation of some sort of crusader's civil right. I recollect the calculated gravity, in my imagination, of the mob's hypothetical ridicule of me, if I had spoken up that day, in eighth grade. I did not.

in class that, in her estimation, the best female basketball player, Mia, could "easily" defeat any of the best male basketball players at our school. This was quite an ambitious claim: our boys' team won the league championship later that year, and we were famously good. More pointedly, I was our school's celebrated basketball player, and her comment was, not all that obliquely, aimed squarely at me, along with one or two other male players sitting in class at the time. More broadly, of course, Mrs. H's comment was aimed at *all* of the boys who played seriously or even recreationally in P.E. class: Mia had tried to "run" in our four-on-four games during P.E. once or twice and, of course, could not match even the eighth-best male player on the court (not that Mrs. H cared to check her facts).

Like a good feminist, Mrs. H was grievously incorrect in her voluble, moralizing declaration. Yet, if I had responded in class, in the name of justice, by substantiating—even assiduously and dispassionately—the reasons for my discomfort, then I would have been made to appear small-souled and petty. More important to me at the time, I would have been ridiculed as a "chauvinist" or whatever the 1990s' "woke" term for defenders of the patriarchy would have been.

My point, of course, is not to beat up on females, who are genuinely superior to males at female endeavors. It is rather to defend masculinity from encroachments into it by non-males. It follows that males are genuinely superior to females at male endeavors. Moreover, men find themselves in my situation every day of the year in their very places of work. Instead of confronting a single thoughtless, misled teacher who might actually have apologized (had I been braver), workplace men who dare to speak out would certainly confront an army of radicalized workforce females who have been diligently drilled by popular

messaging—and, more specifically, by human-resources depart-
ments—to search out and destroy *precisely* the sort of defensive
commentary made by men on their own behalf. As a professional
speaker and author, I make my living by spending hours and
days crafting arguments in defense of masculinity; conversely,
men in the ordinary workplace cannot cash in in similar ways,
given their job titles. Nor do they hone the skill set requisite for
making such arguments compelling.

In this way, please receive this book as an article of civil rights
—a voice for the voiceless.

Sports Wars

Remember as you read: the greatest nondivine human being ever
to walk our planet was a woman. She ranks the greatest of all the
saints. She is the Queen of Heaven. But notably, she managed to
glorify the Lord with her immaculate soul, *without* bearing any of
the trappings of leadership or headship. This proves that, for half
the population out there anyway, discharging one's God-given
duties with extreme honor—even perfection—need not involve
leadership. (In fact, for females, it precludes it: the Virgin Mary's
boss and household head, St. Joseph, ranks second in holiness
only to her in spite of the fact that he was her boss.)

The Virgin Mary did not beat up bad guys, play sports, give
orders, get a formal education, or even preach the gospel. None
of these tasks—duties associated exclusively with effective male
headship of a household—were intended for her. It should not
insult a right-minded Christian woman to read statistics that
evince that, by male standards, women are putatively unskilled
at sports, strength contests, or certain types of gamesmanship.
Since these categories reside comfortably outside of the woman's
domain, assessment evincing her low performance therein cannot

or should not threaten her. She retains the confidence that she is, of course, vastly superior to her husband in all tasks veritably falling under her own charge, if that aspect of competition matters.[15]

Even to men, these skills of athleticism and hand-eye coordination prove mere means to a meaningful end—that of being an efficient household patriarch. In fact, they prove to be but trifles in all ways unrelated to that end.

Sports—motor sports, martial arts, tennis, basketball, and the like—constitute training for household leadership. Naturally, the nonpropagandized public lacks the inclination to view female sports because they intuit, without understanding intellectually, the teleological discomfiture inherent in the proposition. In response, the feminist lobby has recently employed and enjoyed a stranglehold on a shockingly aggressive guerilla advertising campaign that goes like this: "You don't consume this recreative male activity or pastime done by females because you're a jerk."

One would be tempted to call this marketing strategy a total failure or a last resort but for the fact that, say, the WNBA already cannot conceivably be in a worse marketing position. With or without its guilt-tripping commercial advertising campaign, no one watches WNBA games. At any rate, one can say confidently that the whiny ad campaign is not harming the league. And although no WNBA ads ran during my nonscientific test described above, many of their resentment-filled commercials regularly and perennially pop up during NBA Playoffs. Decidedly, according to the professionals responsible for popularizing

---

[15] In some nuanced but real sense, the Virgin Mary reminds us that woman is above these categories (perhaps this removes the sting!). Ever instructive, the unimposing figure of the Virgin reminds us that she is the greatest of all saints precisely because she was such a perfectly obedient follower, not a leader.

the league, the WNBA's best marketing pitch, its most alluring "siren song," constitutes league players sounding off about the ostensible reasons as to why virtually no one wants to watch their televised or in-person games.[16] This is hardly exaggeration: in what amounted to an *improved* outing compared with other years, "WNBA games averaged about 7,716 in-person fans per game in 2017."[17] Conversely, the NBA enjoyed excellent turnout in that year, more than doubling WNBA per-game attendance (remember: the NBA ticket sales are inclusive of more than two-and-a-half times the amount of franchises being averaged, over the course of a season that is almost three times longer): "[In 2017] attendance for regular season games increased for the fourth straight season, reaching 22.1 million. Average attendance per game was 17,978, with a record high 741 sellouts. By the end of the season, the league had sold 95% of all tickets available."[18]

Notably, never included amongst their catalogue of "reasons" for the public's abject disinterest is the single, true one designated above: by God's design, women lack the *teleological design* corresponding with the modicum of skill requisite for the popular consumption of professional basketball. That is, without surpassing

---

[16]   This is an actual commercial. I'm not making it up.

[17]   Matt Bonesteel, "Adam Silver: One of the WNBA's Problems Is That Not Enough Young Women Pay Attention to It," *Washington Post*, April 29, 2019, https://www.washingtonpost.com/news/early-lead/wp/2018/04/20/adam-silver-one-of-the-wnbas-problems-is-that-not-enough-young-women-pay-attention-to-it/#:~:text=WNBA%20games%20averaged%207%2C716%20fans,was%20the%20WNBA's%20second%20season.

[18]   Brad Adgate, "Why the 2017–18 Season Was Great for the NBA," *Forbes*, April 25, 2018, https://www.forbes.com/sites/bradadgate/2018/04/25/the-2017-18-season-was-great-for-the-nba/.

a minimal skill level, the viewing of one's sports match remains a chore or an obligation, rather than a pleasurable activity. It's not rocket science: you pay to go to a Celtics game, while you feel as if someone should pay you to watch his nephew's soccer match. Ask any casual defender of the women's league, after they've extolled its allegedly dazzling crop of professional talent for a few minutes: "So, do *you* watch?"

The negative reply will always be and sound the same. And this reply provides a key to the understanding of the popular psychology that affirms feminism as a nonfalsifiable proposition. Almost no one watches the league, yet its existence is magically and presumptively justified in the popular mind, no matter what. For each of the league's twenty-five seasons on the books now, it "has turned an average $10 million net loss (revenue – costs) per year, since its inception in 1996,"[19] not once turning a profit. And no, this isn't accountable to the "jerkiness" of basketball viewers but, rather, to the fact that even the considerably "woke" American public bears no sustainable interest in paying money to watch a female perform a male pastime.

By way of another rhetorical question: Why is anyone surprised by the popular ascendancy of transgenderism in the culture of Western civilization when female UFC fighters now populate almost every single UFC undercard? This is none other than *functional transgenderism*. Even if the female fights lack the commercial draw of the male fights in similar proportion to ticket sales for WNBA and NBA games, respectively, the same unreasoned, existential defenses of female fighters abound. "Those WNBA

---

[19] "Does the WNBA Make Money?," Self Improvement Base, December 2, 2020, https://selfimprovementbase.com/does-the-wnba-make-money/.

girls are great ballers," they'll tell you. "Those UFC girls are tough," you'll hear. Disagreeing politely, you'll reasonably ask why the respective leagues' commercial statistics are so low. To be sure, you'll receive a muffled, unsatisfying answer.

The irony proves to be stupefying. Just as I felt the smarting sting of outrageous irony on that middle-school day — being sermonized by an authority figure that our school's *male* basketball players like me were speciously "talked up" and that a *female* basketball player who couldn't compete was somehow the unsung hero — professional male athletes have felt the same injustice at a more public level (even if the male players are multimillionaires enjoying five thousand times more fans than the female players). Happily, some dauntless NBA players have begun to resist all the hand-biting *ressentiment* frequently heard from the WNBA.[20] After all, the WNBA is parasitic upon the NBA from a business and marketing perspective, yet the players in the former

---

[20] The Golden State Warriors' Draymond Green intrepidly made the case, against female athletes in the WNBA, for meritorious pay, which favors male athletes: "But [WNBA players] *are* [complaining], because they're not laying out steps that they can take to change [the general lack of interest in their league]. So, it's coming off as a complaint. Because the people that can change it, they're just going to continue to say, 'Well, the revenue isn't there. The revenue isn't there. So, if you don't bring in the revenue, we can't up your pay.' They're going keep using that. But the reality is, as true as that is, it's an excuse. Because everyone says, 'We support women. We support women empowerment. We support women in the workplace. We do this for women, we do X for women, blah blah blah.' And everyone uses it to their advantage. Yet these women (athletes) are not using these people who are saying those very things to their advantage. So, then, it just becomes a complaint that falls on deaf ears because they're going to use the same excuse."

association incredibly allege just the opposite: without the NBA to prop up the WNBA, female salaries would be far lower than what they currently are: they'd be zero.

And this sporting new little sister–big brother relationship turned sour, which is emblematic of today's feminist-patriarchy feud more widely.

For centuries, men and women played sports together only as a sort of tongue-in-cheek, romantic "show me," like a lady of the court teaching one of the king's knights to do calligraphy. Thus, what in privacy between husband and wife might otherwise be harmless, flirtatious faux-competition ("Anything you can do I can do better") becomes a matter of injustice when it transacts publicly between players in a female league making false claims against their counterparts in a male league of the same sport. Such idle talk immediately grows into scandal requiring correction. This is precisely the state of affairs we behold today, which proves uniquely telling.[21]

For another example, imagine being Karsten Braasch, the male tennis player "ranked around the 200-mark in the [men's tennis] world"[22] who in a single day in 1998 defeated back-to-back

---

[21] As a general matter, society's historically and anthropologically attenuated attachment to justice proves shamefully weak: Why would society's "record" be any better in its reception of fashionably mouthy female athletes whose slanderous "trash talk" against male athletes requires a public straightening of the record? Society proves especially inept at vigilantly guarding justice as counter-cyclical balance: for example, when female athletes become fashionable, without even realizing it, society encourages the relentless dogpiling on any and all dissenters.

[22] "When Serena and Venus Lost to a Male Tennis Player at Australian Open," EssentiallySports, January 19, 2021, https://

both Venus and Serena Williams, two of the presumptive all-time greats in women's tennis. Bear in mind, these two giants of the female tennis world possess more than thirty Grand Slam titles between them. Braasch must have felt a bit like I felt on that day back in middle school, knowing with practical certitude that, as roughly the two-hundredth-best male tennis player in the world, he could handily defeat the two best female tennis champs. Obviously, he had to let his playing do all the talking—which he did—since he would be ruthlessly vilified for even the most temperate verbal defense of his superior skill. He defeated Serena first, 6-1, and then Venus, 6–2.

The impetus for the impromptu matches makes Serena, at least, sound a bit cocky, according to the article that initially broke this sporting news. Braasch recently spoke about the event and recalled how it came to be.

"It was [the] 1998 Australian Open," he said, "and the Williams sisters, Venus and Serena, had seen some of the male players practicing. On the basis of what they saw, they were convinced that they could beat a man ranked around 200 in the world and wanted to set up a game. I didn't take much persuading, it seemed like a fun thing to do."

The German player reflected on the match he played against Serena and stated, "My first game of the afternoon, just a one-set match, was against Serena. We were out on one of the backcourts at Melbourne Park, No. 17 I think it was. I felt so relaxed that I didn't even warm up properly. We started playing and I raced into a 5–0 lead."

---

www.essentiallysports.com/when-serena-williams-and-venus-williams-lost-to-a-male-tennis-player-at-australian-open-wta-tennis-news/.

"At this point, Venus turned up to watch," he continued. "She had just finished a press conference after a quarter-final loss against Lindsey Davenport. In the end, I won my game against Serena 6–1 but by the time we were at the net shaking hands, Venus was on the court, ready to have a go against me as well." He agreed to the match. "The game against Venus was very similar," he said. "I ended up winning 6–2."[23]

Now, even if neither of the Williams sisters *themselves* "trash talked" Braasch—maybe what Serena and Venus said qualifies, maybe it doesn't—today's feminist social configuration is arranged such that virtually all the Leftists in the world (and even most moderates) find themselves, without any rational basis, rooting for the females who picked the fight. And when Braasch prevailed over both female champs—by *any sort of* sex-blind standard, a number-two-hundred beating a couple of number-ones *ought* to be a lead story—he wouldn't even have been permitted to celebrate much. The story was quietly released and then dropped.

Moreover, if society were veritably sex-blind, as it claims to be, Braasch would have been celebrated as a David figure, prevailing not only over a pair of higher-ranked Goliaths (albeit in the female league), but moreover so doing with all the world's jeers aimed squarely at him for an act the world ambivalently—schizophrenically, even—regards as unchivalrous.

Embarrassing to all involved, this situation continues to replicate in the world of feminist-manufactured sports androgyny. As in "The Emperor's New Clothes," society's universalized performative lie proves embarrassing to all involved, but especially the female athletes who insist on challenging males. In 2017, a fact pattern

[23]   Ibid.

highly similar to the Williams-Braasch situation played out in soccer, when the best women's team in the country unsuccessfully challenged an *under-fifteen* high school boys' squad. CBS News reported that "the U.S. women's national team played the FC Dallas U-15 boys academy team … and fell 5–2, according to FC Dallas' official website. This friendly came as the U.S. looked to tune up before taking on Russia on Thursday night in a friendly."[24] Again, it appears that the proverbial gauntlet had been thrown down not by the male but rather the female athletes. And again, the male victors wound up with no reasonable or dignified means of characterizing their own victory.

Ordinarily, apart from the feminism-patriarchy issue, even the popular culture typically embraces the undeniable allure inherent in the unadorned, businesslike silencing of voluble braggarts who "talk the talk but cannot walk the walk." Society usually acknowledges that such a braggart, even if smaller and less physically capable — like many of today's female athletes — *becomes* the respective bully in the situation simply because she so unjustly convinces all the world to scorn her rival. But in the twenty-first century, this is evidently only the case if both the braggart and the silent hero are male.

Consider the now-infamous Charlie Zelenoff–Deontay Wilder confrontation. Internet troll Zelenoff filmed himself calling on the telephone heavyweight boxing champ Wilder, publicly insulting his honor and insisting in outrageous terms that he could beat him and take his title. Zelenoff's outrageous insults to and

[24] Roger Gonzalez, "FC Dallas Under-15 Boys Squad Beat the U.S. Women's National Team in a Scrimmage," CBS Sports, April 8, 2017, https://www.cbssports.com/soccer/news/a-dallas-fc-under-15-boys-squad-beat-the-u-s-womens-national-team-in-a-scrimmage/.

about Wilder were sufficiently odious and public to render immaterial the fact that Wilder is clearly the bigger, stronger man: in the concern of justice, the taciturn guy (Wilder) became the underdog, just as the weak, mouthy guy (Zelenoff) became the bully. Eventually, the two met at a gym in Los Angeles, where Wilder gratifyingly beat Zelenoff into a cowering silence.

To the point, we all cheered when Wilder taught Zelenoff a practical lesson of pugilism and shut him up. It was a poetic exercise in the virtue of justice: such an act set to rights the proportion between "talking the talk" and "walking the walk." But one strongly intuits that far fewer observers would cheer (or do cheer) for male athletes who, in evidentiary contests of skill, prove—with similar verve to Wilder silencing Zelenoff—their utter superiority to female athletes in their sport. This is because society has been brainwashed by feminists against patriarchy. Presciently, all these sentiments raced through my young mind that day in the eighth grade.

Springing the Two-Income Trap

Sports, however, represent only the most recent incursion by females into a previously male-dominated workforce of sorts. It is but one species of a broad genus. Since 1970, household wives have been shamed, guilt-tripped, and peer-pressured (by feminists) into the workforce with alarming aggression. Make no mistake: *forcing women out of the homeplace and into the workplace was the crown gem of the feminist color revolutionaries.*

Flooding the workplace with females proved feminism's most potent single attack against the patriarchy, since wifely homeplace absence destroys every other aspect of the fabric of the family. In the next chapter, we will see that Christianity explicitly proscribes it for generating these moral and vocational toxicities, which is why the feminist sex revolutionaries first had to pervert the teachings from within Christianity. But here, we will briefly examine the statistical approach to the amoral, practical problems with wives in the workplace. In short, even many of the theoretical fans of working wives wind up condemning it for its pragmatic difficulties — but they cannot condemn it efficaciously.

Even radical feminists today, like Elizabeth Warren, not very long ago admitted that encouraging the concept of working wives generates a "two-income trap."[25] According to *Vox* magazine:

> The "two-income trap," as described by Warren, really consists of three partially separate phenomena that have arisen as families have come to rely on two working adults to make ends meet: a) the addition of a second earner means, in practice, a big increase in household fixed expenses for things like child care and commuting; b) much of the money that American second earners bring in has been gobbled up, in practice, by zero-sum competition for educational opportunities expressed as either skyrocketed prices for houses in good school districts or escalating tuition at public universities; c) last, while the addition of the second earner has not brought in much gain, it has created an increase in downside risk by eliminating an implicit insurance policy that families used to rely on.[26]

[25] Elizabeth Warren and Amelia Tyagi, *The Two-Income Trap: Why Middle-Class Mothers and Fathers Are Going Broke* (New York: Basic Books, 2004).

[26] Matthew Yglesias, "Elizabeth Warren's Book, The Two-Income Trap, Explained," *Vox*, January 23, 2019, www.vox.com/policy-and-politics/2019/1/23/18183091/two-income-trap-elizabeth-warren-book.

Also according to *Vox*, Warren's almost sensible views expressed in her book would likely end up "hurting her [political popularity] with feminists"[27] since it marshaled so very much compelling evidence against the household addition of wifely second incomes and basically encouraged traditionalism. After all, the far-Left Democrat Warren extolled in the book's pages the practical virtue of stay-at-home wives, writing that "a stay-at-home mother served as the family's ultimate insurance against unemployment or disability—insurance that had a very real economic value even when it wasn't drawn on."[28]

Entering the workforce springs a trap for wives because once enticed there, by cultural or aesthetic means, it becomes difficult—almost but not quite impossible—to leave. In a recent survey, only 30 percent of married moms (it is unclear whether the survey excluded childless wives) idealized full-time employment;[29] in a different survey, it was ascertained that "53% of married mothers prefer to have one full-time earner and one stay-at-home parent while raising children under the age of five."[30] Yet far greater numbers of women than these preference statistics indicate go to work outside the home. Why? Because they got caught in the two-income trap.

---

[27] Ibid.

[28] Ibid.

[29] Robert VerBruggen and Wendy Wang, "The Real Housewives of America: Dad's Income and Mom's Work," Institute for Family Studies, January 23, 2019, https://ifstudies.org/blog/the-real-housewives-of-america-dads-income-and-moms-work.

[30] American Compass Research, *2021 Homebuilding Survey* (Washington, DC: American Compass, 2021), 8, https://americancompass.org/wp-content/uploads/2021/03/American-Compass_2021-Home-Building-Survey_Final.pdf.

The long and the short of it is that the feminists weaponized the workforce effectively enough to capture in it even those wives who don't object to it in principle, but who begin *a posteriori* to note the pragmatic problems described earlier in this chapter (that is, "supply-side failures"). In other words, once the wifely workforce's practical (or amoral) objectors take notice of the toxic practical effects of their absence from the homeplace—which are actually *moral* effects in the last analysis—it already proves too late for many of them to make a timely departure.

We saw above a list of those practical problems: spousal lack of intimacy, lack of meal preparation and homeplace maintenance, and resultant anxiety and depression in undercared-for household children. The veritable Christian teaching on family—patriarchy—is accordingly the only worldview engineered to obviate the wily, feminist two-income trap since it categorically forbids all married women (not only mothers) in ordinary situations to enter the workforce. In this case, as happens frequently, principle is more practical than the amoral approach: principle cautions household wives before they fall into the trap, whereas practical experience requires that such wives fall into the trap before noting its toxins and dangers.

While chapter 2 will offer the full extent of the Christian prohibition against working wives, chapter 3 will demonstrate how historical feminism made gains with housewives who once repudiated the feminist notion that they ought to be away from the homeplace by day.

Conclusion

In this chapter, we have seen that the same popular feminist messaging that rendered marriage unappealing during the earlier single years of men's lifespans belies the disquiet existence of so-called matriarchy within those same men's households in the later married years. After all, a piece of propaganda—a commercial, say—depicting an emasculated, unfit husband being barked at by an officious, scowling, Nurse Ratchet–like wife simultaneously wards off the unmarried from the vocation just as it reinforces and further dispirits the malformed conception of the vocation within the already married. It has proven to be a weird but effective cycle.

Evidently, since the onset of the feminist "matriarchy" some decades ago, men have grown predictable and typecast: they avoid marriage in the early years until unenthusiastically submitting to an unhappy, unnatural, perfunctory, undersexed married life sometime in the late twenties or early thirties. From the wedding day forward, too many men have been content—in lieu of heroically taking back their households for God, country, and family and setting Christendom to rights—quietly and bitterly to resent their "matriarchal boss." As underlings, men have grown accustomed to take sinful, fleeting, unhealthy pleasures wherever they can get them.

A good wife is the greatest consolation—morally, intellectually, amicably, sexually, soteriologically—to a good husband (and, in a different way, vice versa). Yet generally, we see everywhere that husbands today do not enjoy their wives, nor wives their husbands. Indeed, how could anyone enjoy one another? Wives have been radicalized, and husbands have been all but deactivated. This was the diabolical goal of the toppling of the patriarchy: the universalization of human misery.

Accordingly, too many Christian men are scratching out a vermin-like existence in the Internet underworld of pornography and other lonesome, illicit pleasures. Instead of laughing joyfully with their wives and kids, these men wheeze out the alienated, mirthless laughter of the doomed. Certainly, they're leading no one to Heaven. These wayward men are leading no one *anywhere*, for that matter. As we've already seen, their wives are "leading" their families, but not to Heaven. All cultural, statistical, and commercial indicia are consistent with this same scheme. We've even seen in this chapter that the Virgin Mary communicated as much to Sr. Lucia at Fatima.

Look at the unhappy children of Western civilization. Turn on the TV for thirty seconds. Visit three of your married friends at their homes. Go out to eat, and watch the other couples. If you have eyes to see, it will smack you in the face.

Here is the question this book will return to time and again: Why don't these young men insist on higher, traditional, Christian standards for wifely behavior within households? Why don't they take back what is rightfully theirs?

Two answers will recur throughout this book's analysis. The first is ignorance. Men don't know the actual Christian standard and therefore what is their birthright. (This book should remedy that!) The second is bad habit. Men have wallowed unhappily in the low station afforded them by the color revolution for too long. Instead of lordly kings, society's men became morally corrupt sluggards via recreational drug usage, pornography, idle or whimsical activities away from the bosom of family, non-pornographic smut of other sorts, escapist or sinful indulgences in television and movies, and so on.

The feminists morally spoiled what they dominated, which is a favorite tactic of insurgents and tyrants: flooding unhappy dominated peoples in sinful habitual enslavements, especially sexual ones. The color revolution is on, and it is up to the men of society to reclaim the patriarchy. The color revolution is on, and the insurgents will not admit what they've taken or the means by which they took it. The color revolution is on, and the bimillennial Tradition, Scripture, and Magisterium of Christianity alone can undo it.

This book's next chapters will show you how.

2

The Christian Requirement of Household Patriarchy

Just as Christianity requires an ecclesiastical patriarchy—comprising exclusively male priests and bishops succeeding Jesus' all-male apostles—it requires a lay patriarchy comprising male householders who double as priests of the home, the *ecclesiola*. This much is no overstatement: the Church literally requires the latter as strictly as it requires the former (even if the former proffers far more daily and weekly reminders in church).

In support of such a claim, this chapter has amassed all the best evidence of the Church's absolute insistence on the lay patriarchy. The simple truth shown here in chapter 2 is that so-called Christian feminists cannot rightly exist. Fundamentally, feminism seeks to topple "the patriarchy," and the patriarchy they seek to topple is Christianity itself.

The more militant among the feminists have occasionally attacked the ecclesiastical patriarchy, and increasingly so in the last century. This attack goes at least as far back as 1848, which I will discuss in some detail in the next chapter. But this book mainly concerns itself with the necessity of the *lay* patriarchy, which has been the target of vastly more pervasive attacks by popular feminism. Leadership and fatherhood have been anointed and equated with one another by nature's God. Household fathers outnumber ministerial fathers by five-hundred-fold, making the lay patriarchy considerably more statistically relevant to the feminist attack, not to mention the anti-feminist counterattack.

According to this logic, the lay patriarchy, comprising household male leadership, proves far more central to what today's pop feminists mean when they chant, "End the patriarchy." Idiotic as this secularist goal is in the secular arena, its practice proves to be outright impossible for any and all observant Christians. That is, a Christian cannot self-consistently challenge the rectitude of the household patriarchy. Straightforwardly, this is due to the fact that Christianity establishes what St. Paul calls a body of Christ wherein each "cell" of the body is a family — the "original cell of social life," according to the *Catechism* (2207) — headed and led by precisely one father.

Using Scripture, Tradition, and the Magisterium, this chapter will demonstrate the Christian fact of the needfulness of the household patriarchy, in five sections. I will let the Catholic teachings do their own talking here in chapter 2. They are so numerous that I struggled to fit them all into a single chapter. Scripture, Tradition, and the Magisterium will show clearly that the household patriarchy (a) exists necessarily, not optionally; (b) involves nontransferable, vital husbandly powers, such as leading and teaching, that, if supplanted by the wife, will destroy the moral fabric of the family; (c) requires the wife to reside at home in ordinary circumstances, as a domestic second-in-command; (d) demands the husband's payment of unconditional love to the wife; and (e) offsets the distinctiveness of Christian marriage compared against all other worldviews, religions, and philosophies.

These five aspects of the Christian lay patriarchy will be treated in the five sections of this chapter.

Patriarchy Is Mandatory

The following, helpful, multi-scriptural synopsis by John Fulton makes embarrassingly clear this chapter's thesis statement — that is, basic Christian teaching requires husbands to act as beneficent patriarchs to obedient wives and children.

The husband is the head of the wife (Ephesians 5:23), the woman being made for the man and not the man for the woman (1 Corinthians 9:8); therefore, the woman is not to usurp authority over the man (1 Timothy 2:12), but to be obedient (Titus 2:5; 1 Peter 3:6), submitting herself (Colossians 3:18) with reverence (Ephesians 5:33) and in subjection to her husband (1 Peter 3:5). Meanwhile, the husband is to love his wife as his own body (Ephesians 5:28), even as Christ loved the Church and gave Himself for her (Ephesians 5:25), and he is especially to honor his wife because of her weakness and dependence (1 Peter 3:7).

Across multiple contexts, the reader will certainly note how frequently these few New Testament passages, mentioned by Fulton, will recur in this chapter's analysis and in the analysis of Church commentators.

From another angle, the Christian requirement of patriarchy may be rendered quite clear by apprising the duties of wives, specifically. The only universal catechism, ever, to teach on the specific household duties of the Christian wife — not changed or abrogated in the slightest by the more recent universal catechism from the 1990s — reads as follows:

> On the other hand, the duties of a wife are thus summed up by the Prince of the Apostles: Let wives be subject

to their husbands, that if any believe not the word, they may be won without the word by the conversation of the wives, considering your chaste conversation with fear. Let not their adorning be the outward plaiting of the hair, or the wearing of gold, or the putting on of apparel: but the hidden man of the heart in the incorruptibility of a quiet and meek spirit, which is rich in the sight of God. For after this manner heretofore the holy women also, who trusted in God, adorned themselves, being in subjection to their own husbands, as Sarah obeyed Abraham, calling him lord. To train their children in the practice of virtue and to pay particular attention to their domestic concerns should also be especial objects of their attention. The wife should love to remain at home, unless compelled by necessity to go out; and she should never presume to leave home without her husband's consent. Again, and in this the conjugal union chiefly consists, let wives never forget that next to God they are to love their husbands, to esteem them above all others, yielding to them in all things not inconsistent with Christian piety, a willing and ready obedience.[31]

Once more, this is the only universal catechetical teaching ever issued by the Roman Catholic Church on the matter. The total wifely subjection before the husband in all things except grave sin establishes precisely what twenty-first-century feminists pinpoint when they designate "patriarchy" as an article of Christianity to be eviscerated. Indeed, as we saw above, the Roman Catechism

---

[31] *The Catechism of the Council of Trent*, trans. John A. McHugh and Charles J. Callan (Rockford, IL: TAN Books, 1982), 352.

teaches the holiness of this total wifely subjection, which is decried as "psychologically abusive" by the feminists.

Let's see why the Roman Catechism teaches thusly. By way of itemizing the specific Scripture and commentary that the above summary comprises, let's begin with the elephant in the room: Ephesians 5:22–24 — which, as mentioned in chapter 1, most Catholic missals today bracket and censor! As we will see, the great Patristic and Scholastic commentators on this passage labor to show its undeniable connection to Christology, thereby rendering it heretical to deny or diminish. Inerrant Scripture leaves no question whatsoever regarding the mandatory leadership of household fathers:

> Wives, be subject to your husbands, as to the Lord. For the husband is the head of the wife as Christ is the head of the church, his body, and is himself its Savior. As the church is subject to Christ, so let wives also be subject in everything to their husbands.

Before we look at the teachings on Ephesians 5 of the ancient commentators, such as Chrysostom and Augustine, or at the medieval commentator Thomas Aquinas, let's look at the coextensive teaching of the first modern pope, Leo XIII, who was famous for his high regard for Aquinas:

> The husband is the chief of the family and the head of the wife. The woman, because she is flesh of his flesh, and bone of his bone, must be subject to her husband and obey him; not, indeed, as a servant, but as a companion, so that her obedience shall be wanting in neither honor nor dignity. Since the husband represents Christ, and since the wife represents the Church, let there always

be, both in him who commands and in her who obeys, a heaven-born love guiding both in their respective duties. For "the husband is the head of the wife; as Christ is the head of the Church.... Therefore, as the Church is subject to Christ, so also let wives be to their husbands in all things."[32]

Note how neither of the more modern comments on Ephesians 5 — that by Leo XIII and that by the *Catechism of Trent* — do anything at all to mitigate or moderate the literality of the total subjection of all Christian wives before household patriarchs, their husbands.

Obviously, the further back in time we delve, the more likely it becomes that we shall find a literal interpretation of the Scriptural passage, which is why it was important to jump forward in time and show that even a twentieth-century pope such as Leo XIII interpreted the teaching literally. In his own commentary on this famed scriptural passage, Chrysostom reminds us that man's headship orients his wife and family at their very salvation. In other words, the father's leadership is vocationally and soteriologically indispensable:

Then after saying, "The husband is the head of the wife, as Christ also is of the Church," he further adds, "and He is the Saviour of the body." For indeed the head is the saving health of the body. He had already laid down beforehand for man and wife, the ground and provision of their love, assigning to each their proper place, to the one that of authority and forethought, to the other that of submission. As then "the Church," that is, both husbands

32 Leo XIII, encyclical *Arcanum* (February 10, 1880), no. 11.

and wives, "is subject unto Christ, so also ye wives submit yourselves to your husbands, as unto God."[33]

The connection between patriarchy and salvation cannot conceivably be any clearer, for Chrysostom: authority is laid down to the husband and submission to the wife in order to serve the health and salvation of the family. As much is consistent with the vocational end of the family: Holy Matrimony is a sacrament because marriage and family are a vocation. And while this spousal submission is anything but *mutual*—except in some vague or analogous way that, if taken too literally, would swallow the force of the passage—it most certainly informs a relation of reciprocity between man and wife. Spousal reciprocity well serves both parties, and also the offspring, in a way that cannot be reversed or replaced under any other arrangement.

For St. Thomas Aquinas, on the other hand, the Ephesians 5 familial taxonomy represents a microcosm of the structure of the well-ordered *polis*. Both political societies—family and civil society—are structured like a well-ordered soul. Indeed, St. Thomas proves to be surgical in his treatment of three specific relations a happy home requires; these three relations total the necessity of the household patriarchy:

> According to the Philosopher in his *Politics*, a home must possess three relationships if it is to be complete, namely, that of the husband and wife, of the father and the children, and that between the master and his servants. Hence these three are dealt with when the

---

[33] John Chrysostom, *The Complete Works of Saint John Chrysostom,* ed. Philip Schaff and George Barker Stevens, trans. John Albert Broadus, loc. 120417-120419, Kindle.

Apostle instructs: First, the husband and wife; second, the father and child, at "children obey" (6:1); third, the servants and masters, at "slaves, be obedient" (Eph 6:5). The first has two divisions: First, he cautions the women to be subject; Second, he admonishes the men to love, at "husbands, love".[34]

St. Thomas further subjects the family to the analysis of the happy *polis*. For St. Thomas, moreover, the family as the original society of man should be considered even more important than the well-ordered city itself, a kind of "politics-plus." Thomas shows this by emphasizing the topics of the common good—always a signal that he is talking about *natural* political and governing structures—and wifely subjection, which always signals Thomas's reference to the household patriarchy:

> Hence [St. Paul] states: "Let women be subject to their husbands because a woman, if she have superiority, is contrary to her husband" (Sir. 25:30). So he especially warns them about subjection. This is "as to a lord" since the relation of a husband to his wife is, in a certain way, like that of a master to his servant, insofar as the latter ought to be governed by the commands of his master. The difference between these two relationships is that the master employs his servants in whatever is profitable to himself; but a husband treats his wife and children in reference to the common good. Thus he mentions "as to a lord"; the

---

34 Thomas Aquinas, *Commentary on the Letters of Saint Paul to the Galatians and Ephesians*, trans. F. R. Lacher, O.P., and Matthew Lamb (Lander, WY: Aquinas Institute for the Study of Sacred Doctrine, 2012), 318.

husband is not really a lord, but is "as a lord." Let wives be subject to their husbands.[35]

So, the husband should be treated *as* a lord, while not *being* a lord *simpliciter*. St. Thomas establishes a spousal relationship that mirrors the hierarchy of the ruler to the ruled within the *polis*, but one transcending the political relations borne between even the best king and his subjects, in terms of the degree of love and commitment between spouses.

St. Thomas continues to identify headship with patriarchy, in no uncertain terms: "The reason for this subjection [described by St. Paul] is that the husband is the head of the wife, and the sense of sight is localized in the head—the eyes of a wise man are in his head (Eccl. 2:14)—and hence a husband ought to govern his wife as her head. The head of the woman is the man."[36]

Plainly, St. Thomas assures us, there is no Christian feminism. If any conceivable doubt remains—as if St. Paul has not been sufficiently clear in Ephesians 5—St. Thomas puts the theological necessity of the household patriarchy beyond all doubt by stipulating that the wife is subject to her husband's dominion "in all things not contrary to God":

> Then he brings in his example when he says: "as Christ is the head of the church." God has made him head over all the church, which is his body (Eph. 1:22–23). This is not for his own utility, but for that of the Church "since he is the saviour of his body." For there is no other name under heaven given to men, whereby we must be saved (Acts 4:12). Behold, God is my saviour; I will deal confidently

35 Ibid., 318–319.
36 Ibid.

and will not fear (Isa. 12:2). From this he draws the con-clusion he intended, saying "therefore, as the church is subject to Christ." As though he said: it is not proper for an organ to rebel against its head in any situation; but as Christ is head of the church in his own way, so a husband is the head of his wife; therefore the wife must be obedient to her husband "as the Church is subject to Christ." Shall not my soul be subject to God? (Ps. 62:1), "so also let the wives be to their husbands." And you shall be under your husband's power (Gen. 3:16), in all things which are not contrary to God, for Acts 5 (29) affirms: "We ought to obey God rather than men."[37]

The last two lines of this passage make St. Thomas's point all too clear.

So, the very meaning of the household patriarchy—the head-ship of husband—subsists in the headiness (if I may) of his most important lessons and requirements. The husband articulates these to his wife via his teaching authority, demonstrating at least the partial purpose of his leadership as constituting a teaching patriarchy. And the man's primacy comes from being made liter-ally and chronologically *before* woman. This is to say that man comprises the stuff out of which she was made. St. Paul captures this thoroughly in 1 Timothy 2:11–15:

Let a woman learn in silence with all submissiveness. I permit no woman to teach or to have authority over men; she is to keep silent. For Adam was formed first, then Eve; and Adam was not deceived, but the woman was deceived and became a transgressor. Yet woman will be

[37] Ibid.

saved through bearing children, if she continues in faith and love and holiness, with modesty.

Anticipating and responding to 1 Corinthians 11's connection to 1 Timothy 2, St. John Chrysostom connects the concept of male primacy with that of male moral instruction. Things went wrong when Eve tried to "teach" Adam as if she were a priest. Conversely, things go well when Adam uses his headship to teach Eve:

> If it be asked, what has this to do with women of the present day? It shows that the male sex enjoyed the higher honor. Man was first formed; and elsewhere he shows their superiority. "Neither was the man created for the woman, but the woman for the man." (1 Cor. xi. 9.) Why then does he say this? He wishes the man to have the preeminence in every way; both for the reason given above, he means, let him have precedence, and on account of what occurred afterwards. For the woman taught the man once, and made him guilty of disobedience, and wrought our ruin. Therefore because she made a bad use of her power over the man, or rather her equality with him, God made her subject to her husband. "Thy desire shall be to thy husband." (Gen. iii. 16.) This had not been said to her before.[38]

Accordingly, St. Paul firmly warns man against the figurative and literal covering (or veiling) of his own headship, while unequivocally exhorting woman to cover her head, that is, to deny her headship. If this can be proven true, just consider the

---

[38] *Complete Works of Saint John Chrysostom*, loc. 132419-132426.

import for the broader thesis of this book! No passage more clearly demonstrates the vocational, nontransferable mandate of male headship, which is natural to man and forbidden to woman. Consider the passage in its entirety:

> But I want you to understand that the head of every man is Christ, the head of a woman is her husband, and the head of Christ is God. Any man who prays or prophesies with his head covered dishonors his head, but any woman who prays or prophesies with her head unveiled dishonors her head—it is the same as if her head were shaven. For if a woman will not veil herself, then she should cut off her hair; but if it is disgraceful for a woman to be shorn or shaven, let her wear a veil. For a man ought not to cover his head, since he is the image and glory of God; but woman is the glory of man. (For man was not made from woman, but woman from man. Neither was man created for woman, but woman for man.) That is why a woman ought to have a veil on her head, because of the angels. (Nevertheless, in the Lord woman is not independent of man nor man of woman; for as woman was made from man, so man is now born of woman. And all things are from God.) Judge for yourselves; is it proper for a woman to pray to God with her head uncovered? Does not nature itself teach you that for a man to wear long hair is degrading to him, but if a woman has long hair, it is her pride? For her hair is given to her for a covering. If any one is disposed to be contentious, we recognize no other practice, nor do the churches of God. (1 Corinthians 11:3–16)

Commenting on 1 Corinthians, Chrysostom makes quite a strong case for female veiling, which winds up conceptually far closer to the issue of male headship than most readers assume. The covering of the head before the leader (or "head") of the tribe helps to signify the absolute dominion of the leader, which, in the case of male household leaders, Chrysostom calls "natural":

> This is again another cause. "Not only," so he speaks, "because he hath Christ to be His Head ought he not to cover the head, but because also he rules over the woman." For the ruler when he comes before the king ought to have the symbol of his rule. As therefore no ruler without military girdle and cloak, would venture to appear before him that hath the diadem: so neither do thou without the symbols of thy rule (one of which is the not being covered), pray before God, lest thou insult both thyself and Him that hath honored thee. And the same thing likewise one may say regarding the woman. For to her also is it a reproach, the not having the symbols of her subjection. "But the woman is the glory of the man." Therefore the rule of the man is natural.[39]

St. Thomas makes a nearly identical comment on the same passage of Scripture.[40] Also, St. Thomas robustly defends the precision of the notion of man as God's glory and woman as

---

[39] *Complete Works of Saint John Chrysostom*, loc. 67791-67800.

[40] Thomas Aquinas, *Commentary on the Letters of Saint Paul to the Corinthians*, trans. F. R. Lacher, O.P., B. Mortensen, and D. Keating (Lander, WY: Aquinas Institute for the Study of Sacred Doctrine, 2012) 226. St. Thomas says, "Then when Paul says, 'but the woman,' he presents that which is on the part of the woman, saying, 'but the woman is the glory of man,' because: She shall be called woman, because she was taken out of man (Gen 2:23)."

man's glory.[41] It is anything but an idiosyncratic, one-off interpretation by an offbeat or outlier interpreter of Scripture. Thomas defends the literality of the Scriptural passage in the following terms:

> Furthermore, in regard to what is within, man is more especially called the image of God, inasmuch as reason is more vigorous in him. But it is better to say that the Apostle speaks clearly here. For he said of man that he is the image and glory of God; but he did not say of the woman that she is the image and glory of man, but only that she is the glory of the man. This gives us to understand that it is common to man and woman to be the image of God; but it is immediately characteristic of man to be the glory of God.[42]

For Person A to be the "glory of" Person B is to be the teleological helpmate or dignified servant thereof. Person A's goals are the shared or *adoptive* goals of Person B. Every word of this analysis justifies and indicates the household patriarchy: Person A must, by the force of such descriptions, be the wife of Person B.

---

[41] Thomas Aquinas, *Commentary on the Letters to the Corinthians*, 226. Thomas writes: "Some object that because the image of God in man is regarded with respect to the spirit, in which there is no difference between male and female (Gal 3:28), therefore, there is no more reason why man is called the image of God than a woman is. The answer is that man is here called the image of God in a special way, namely, because man is the principle of his entire race, as God is the principle of the entire universe and because from the side of Christ dying on the cross flowed the sacraments of blood and water, from which the Church has been organized."

[42] Ibid.

In what might otherwise be speciously dismissed as merely a throwaway 1 Corinthians 11 passage on the historical conditions of veiling, St. Thomas makes perhaps the most robust argument against what today is called (by feminists who attempt to reconcile their anti-patriarchalism with Christianity) "mutual submission" between man and wife. He recounts that man is subject to God alone, yet woman is subject to God via the mediation of her husband's patriarchal dominion:

> We must consider why man should not veil his head, but the woman. This can be taken in two ways: first, because a veil put on the head designates the power of another over the head of a person existing in the order of nature. Therefore, the man existing under God should not have a covering over his head to show that he is immediately subject to God; but the woman should wear a covering to show that besides God she is naturally subject to another. Hence a stop is put to the objection about servant and subject, because this subjection is not natural.[43]

Moreover, on the topic of 1 Corinthians 11, Thomas adds the following important connection to our analysis between the binary notions of veiling/submission and nonveiling/nonsubmission:

> But it pertains to man's dignity not to wear a covering on his head; consequently, he says that every man praying or prophesying with his head covered disgraces his head, i.e., does something unbecoming to a man.[44]

---

[43] Thomas Aquinas, *Commentary on the Letters to the Corinthians*, 226–227.

[44] Ibid., 223. In a nearby location on the same page, St. Thomas expounds the issue a bit further: "Then when St. Paul says, 'but

Noteworthily, both St. Thomas (a Western Doctor in the thirteenth century) and Chrysostom (an Eastern Father in the comparably distant fourth century) take seriously the connection between the figurative and literal headship of household patriarchs. Note how, for St. Thomas, disrupting the connection between figurative and literal headship—presumably by the horrifying prospect of male veiling—proves "unbecoming to a man" in a similar way to that in which female supplantation of male leadership would accomplish. Also, on 1 Corinthians 11, St. Thomas merges his analysis of Ephesians 5 and other Scripture verses, showing at least three reasons why the man must be recognized as the head of the woman within the family. He writes that man must lead the household

> because man is naturally superior to the female: Wives, be subject to your husband as to the Lord. For the husband is the head of the wife (Eph 5:22). Thirdly, because the man exerts an influence by governing the wife: Your desire will be for your husband, and he shall rule over you (Gen. 3:16). Fourthly, the man and the woman are alike in nature: I will make him a helper like to him (Gen. 2:18).[45]

---

every woman,' he gives an admonition as it applies to women, saying, 'but every woman praying or prophesying with her head not covered, which is unbecoming, considering her condition, disgraces her head,' i.e., does something unsuitable in regard to covering her hair. But against this is the Apostle's statement: 'I permit no woman to teach in church' (1 Tim. 2:12). How, then, does it befit a woman to pray or prophesy in public prayer or in doctrine? The answer is that this must [be] understood of prayers and readings which women say in their own groups."

[45] Thomas Aquinas, *Commentary on the Letters to the Corinthians*, 220.

To put it plainly, as between man and wife, there is simply no scriptural doubt—not even a whiff of uncertainty among the most prominent Patristics or Scholastics—as to who is the help-mate of whom. Remember in this book's opening lines when I recurred to the image of a first day at a new job: discovering the identity of one's boss is not taken to be the hard part! A candid Christian could not reasonably ask for a jot of greater reader's clarity as to the matter of household bosses.

Finally, St. Thomas distinguishes between man and woman by the order of their priority within nature:

> For the man is not of the woman but the woman of the man (1. Cor. 11:8). In regard to the first it should be noted that, as was stated above, the woman is called the glory of man through something derived. Consequently, to prove this St. Paul says: "For the man in the original condition of things is not of the woman, namely, formed out of the woman, but the woman of the man." For it is said: and the rib from with [sic] the Lord God had taken from the man he made into a woman (Gen. 2:22). About man it is said that the Lord formed man of dust from the ground (Gen 2:7).[46]

St. Thomas does nothing to mute or mitigate the force of his comments on man's higher perfection than wife according to the order of nature.[47] On the contrary, his comments are rather unabashed.

---

[46] Ibid., 228.

[47] Ibid., 228–229: In the following passage, this point is driven home with extreme prejudice: "Then when St. Paul says, 'for the man was not created,' he assigns the reason for what he had said. To understand this it should be noted that the order of the perfect and of the imperfect is such that in one and the

The Case for Patriarchy

Similarly, 1 Peter 3:1–6 establishes that the submission of the wife—she being the "hidden person of the heart," obedient like Sarah before Abraham—is a first principle of household patriarchy:

> Likewise you wives, be submissive to your husbands, so that some, though they do not obey the word, may be won without a word by the behavior of their wives, when they see your reverent and chaste behavior. Let not yours be the outward adorning with braiding of hair, decoration of gold, and wearing of fine clothing, but let it be the hidden person of the heart with the imperishable jewel of a gentle and quiet spirit, which in God's sight is very precious. So once the holy women who hoped in God used to adorn themselves and were submissive to their husbands, as Sarah obeyed Abraham, calling him lord. And you are now her children if you do right and let nothing terrify you.

I've included this short scriptural passage without Patristic or Scholastic commentary for the simple reason that none is needed.

---

same subject the imperfect precedes the perfect in the order of time. For one is a boy, before he is a man. Absolutely speaking, however, the perfect precedes the imperfect in the order of time and of nature. For a boy is produced from the man. *This, therefore, is the reason why the woman was produced from the man, because he is more perfect than the woman, which the Apostle proves from the fact that the end is more perfect than that which is for the end;* but man is the woman's end. And this is what he says: For the man was not created for the woman: but woman for the man, as a helper, namely, in reproduction, as the patient is for the sake of the agent and matter for the sake of form: it is not good for man to be alone: let us make him a helper like unto him" (Genesis 2:18).

A woman's "gentle and quiet spirit" is called very precious in God's sight in this passage. Needless to say, God's tastes do not change. They are immutable. One contrasts this sharply with the perverse characterizations of female desiderata of the so-called Christian feminists.

Up to this point in our analysis, the most important Patristic Father, St. Augustine of Hippo, has been conspicuously absent from all the Magisterial evidence of the mandatory nature of household patriarchy. Let us rectify this.

St. Augustine makes the following commentary on Genesis 3 (which connects conceptually to 1 Corinthians 11): "'And thy turning shall be to thy husband, and he shall rule over thee.' What is said to Cain about his sin, or about the vicious concupiscence of his flesh, is here said of the woman who had sinned; and we are to understand that the husband is to rule his wife as the soul rules the flesh."[48] St. Thomas makes a highly similar body-soul analogy on this the spousal relationship.[49]

In another minor work, *On Marriage and Concupiscence*, Augustine continues to develop the natural and supernatural theme of

---

[48] Augustine, *The City of God* (New York: Random House, 1993), 487.

[49] Thomas Aquinas, *Commentary on the Letters to the Galatians*, 322. Thomas writes: "A husband and wife are somehow one; hence, as the flesh is subject to the soul, so is the wife to the husband; but no one ever held his own flesh in contempt, therefore neither should anyone his wife. Whence he states: he who loves his wife loves himself. Therefore, now they are not two, but one flesh (Matt. 19:6). Just as a man sins against nature in hating himself, so does he who hates his wife. With three things my spirit is pleased, which are approved before God and men: the concord of brethren, and the love of neighbors, and man and wife that agree well together (Sir. 25:1–2)."

the patriarchy: "Nor can it be doubted, that it is more consonant with the order of nature that men should bear rule over women, than women over men."[50]

In another work, *Of the Good of Marriage*, Augustine describes the conditions for the possibility of what today we call "complementarity," a concept describing a fittingness between husband and wife predicated on their natural inequality and mutual interdependence. While Aristotle describes the relationship between husband and wife as an intimate friendship between unequals,[51] Augustine baptizes this concept by holding that true union of flesh comes from one *ruling* lovingly and the other *submitting* lovingly: "Then follows the connection of fellowship in children, which is the one alone worthy fruit, not of the union of male and female, but of the sexual intercourse. For it were possible that there should exist in either sex, even without such intercourse, a certain friendly and true union of the one ruling, and the other obeying."[52] St. Augustine has thus described the household patriarchy in complementarian terms.

Needless to say, the most important Patristics and scholastics, commenting on the most important patriarchal Scriptural passages, leave no doubt about the needfulness of the patriarchy for the healthfulness of Christian society.

The Church's Warning against Feminism

As further proof that the household patriarchy is mandatory for Christians, one must simply look at the baleful circumstances that occasion the patriarchy's repudiation. While I recounted some

---

[50] Augustine, *On Marriage and Concupiscence* 10.
[51] Aristotle, *Nicomachean Ethics* 13, 9.
[52] Augustine, *Of the Good of Marriage*.

of these negative results from a twenty-first-century perspective in chapter 1, this section will proffer the perennial Catholic perspective of Scripture, Tradition, and the Magisterium. That is, just what tragedy follows—according to Scripture, Tradition, and the Magisterium—when the father's headship is ignored or denied? Worse still, what will happen when the wife commandeers partial or entire leadership over the household?

We should begin to answer by pointing out the reason for Eve's first sin, according to the formulation of the Church. Eve erred on account of her active subversion of the household patriarchy, insofar as she chose to interact with a third party (in the place of her husband), the serpent. Such a patriarchal subversion led, obviously, to sin and death. As is often said in the Church, "Death through Eve; life through Mary."

Consider the following cautionary example of the subversion of household patriarchy, from the Old Testament book of Sirach (25:16–26). It describes in detail the disastrous results of this proto-feminist subversion:

> I would rather dwell with a lion and a dragon than dwell with an evil wife. The wickedness of a wife changes her appearance, and darkens her face like that of a bear. Her husband takes his meals among the neighbors, and he cannot help sighing bitterly. Any iniquity is insignificant compared to a wife's iniquity; may a sinner's lot befall her! A sandy ascent for the feet of the aged—such is a garrulous wife for a quiet husband. Do not be ensnared by a woman's beauty, and do not desire a woman for her possessions. There is wrath and impudence and great disgrace when a wife supports her husband. A dejected mind, a gloomy face, and a wounded heart are caused by

an evil wife. Drooping hands and weak knees are caused by the wife who does not make her husband happy. From a woman sin had its beginning, and because of her we all die. Allow no outlet to water, and no boldness of speech in an evil wife. If she does not go as you direct, separate her from yourself.

Most important in this passage is the basic, palpable fact of life that the home loses all its cheeriness and its "heart" at the very moment in which even a good woman turns dour, even temporarily. On the other hand, the curse becomes permanent when the household's wife and mother turns to permanent bitterness: everyone in the home suffers, especially the husband, who begins to dine with neighbors as marital conditions worsen. Note also how this passage details that "there is wrath and impudence and great disgrace when a wife supports her husband," financially speaking. I will discuss this in greater detail in the next section.

St. Thomas remarks on this passage from Sirach that "the Philosopher says that the dominion of women is the death of a family, as tyrants of a commonwealth."[53] Additionally, as noted in the previous section, Thomas cautions that St. Paul "states: 'Let women be subject to their husbands' because a woman, if she have superiority, is contrary to her husband (Sir. 25:30). So he especially warns them about subjection."[54] In other words, the family's common good is thwarted when the wife rules over the

---

[53] Thomas Aquinas, *Commentary on the Letters of Saint Paul to the Philippians, Colossians, Thessalonians, Timothy, Titus, and Philemon*, trans. F. R. Lacher, O.P. (Lander, WY: Aquinas Institute for the Study of Sacred Doctrine, 2012), 272.

[54] Thomas Aquinas, *Commentary on the Letters to the Galatians*, 318–319.

husband. It immediately becomes a grave situation, mimicking the gravity of the tyrant's rule over the commonwealth. The common good of the household suffers badly in such a case because it reflects an objective situation of a willful reversal of nature by the wife.

Now, consider the same question—the disastrous results of commandeered household authority—from John Chrysostom's perspective on the repudiation of Ephesians 5. If a woman won't submit to her husband, in other words, everything in the household and society goes sideways, as the family is subjected to a sort of constitutional crisis:

> But if [the dominion of home] be otherwise, all is turned upside down, and thrown into confusion. And just as when the generals of an army are at peace one with another, all things are in due subordination, whereas on the other hand, if they are at variance, everything is turned upside down; so, I say, is it also here. Wherefore, saith he, "Wives, be in subjection unto your own husbands, as unto the Lord."[55]

Chapter 1 described the familial constitutional crisis promised by Chrysostom and St. Paul in rather specific terms. They were utterly correct: by our day, the feminists have done everything to show that by turning the *family* upside down, hierarchically, they could turn *morals* upside down.

In the previous section on the needfulness of patriarchy, we noted that 1 Timothy 2 bears, in addition to important implications for the necessity of household patriarchy itself, meaningful indications regarding the fatal consequences of female commandeering of headship. Chrysostom draws out many of these implications by examining the specific consequences of putting

---

[55] *Complete Works of Saint John Chrysostom*, loc. 120396-120399.

the wifely pupil in charge of the husband's domestic classroom. Under a patriarchal teacher, mistakes happen far less easily than under a "matriarchal" one. Chrysostom traces this ban on female teaching to its very origin, Eve's gullibility:

> Now it is not the same thing to be deceived by a fellow-creature, one of the same kind, as by an inferior and subordinate animal. This is truly to be deceived. Compared therefore with the woman, he is spoken of as "not deceived." For she was beguiled by an inferior and subject, he by an equal. Again, it is not said of the man, that he "saw the tree was good for food," but of the woman, and that she "did eat, and gave it to her husband": so that he transgressed, not captivated by appetite, but merely from the persuasion of his wife. The woman taught once, and ruined all. On this account therefore he saith, let her not teach."[56]

In a nearby location within his commentary, Chrysostom articulates the motivation and logic of St. Paul's admonition against female teaching. While perusing this, the reader should consider the sharp contrast it cuts to today's typical parish pedagogy, which is circumscribed by female leadership:

> "I do not suffer a woman to teach," St. Paul says. What place has this command here? The fittest. He was speaking of quietness, of propriety, of modesty, so having said that he wished them not to speak in the church, to cut off all occasion of conversation, he says, "let them not teach, but occupy the station of learners." For thus they will

[56] Ibid., loc. 132429-132433.

show submission by their silence. For the sex is naturally somewhat talkative: and for this reason he restrains them on all sides.[57]

In what amounts to a partly humorous exhortation, Chrysostom suggests that women have been *punished* with the revocation against teaching, ostensibly due to their talkative nature. (Nevertheless, he certainly and seriously upholds the scriptural admonition.)

In his commentary on Timothy 2:11–15, St. Thomas restates the critical distinction that because Eve was seduced—not Adam—henceforth women should not teach men. This admonition must, by St. Paul's reasoning, as well as St. Thomas's, carry forward into the future. Indeed, as we have seen, pedagogy informs a healthy portion of the functional rationale for male headship, which resides in the less gullible intellect of the household patriarch:

> But sin is the ceasing to be of a nature. Therefore, coming to be first begins from Adam, and ceasing to be from the woman. Hence St. Paul says, "Adam was not seduced," i.e., first, because he was the stronger; but the tempter approached the weaker in order that the stronger be seduced more readily. Here he alludes to Adam's words in Genesis. For when the Lord rebuked Adam, he said: the woman whom you gave me to be my companion, gave me of the tree and I did eat (Gen. 3:12). That is why he says, Adam was not seduced; but the woman.[58]

---

[57] Ibid., loc. 132413-132417.
[58] Thomas Aquinas, *Commentary on the Letters to the Philippians*, 272–273.

The Case for Patriarchy

So both the eminent Patristics and the best of the Scholastics —Aquinas lived closer to our day than Chrysostom's, remember—viewed pedagogical role reversal between husband and wife as a *prima facie* catastrophe.

Likewise, in a commentary on Titus 2:2–5, Chrysostom equates the womanly instruction of men with the bold usurpation of male authority by a female. Chrysostom's (and St. Paul's[59]) warnings turn out to be quite severe:

> And yet thou forbiddest a woman to teach; how dost thou command it here, when elsewhere thou sayest, "I suffer not a woman to teach"? (1 Tim. ii. 12.) But mark what he has added, "Nor to usurp authority over the man." For at the beginning it was permitted to men to teach both men and women. But to women it is allowed to instruct by discourse at home. But they are nowhere permitted to preside, nor to extend their speech to great length, wherefore he adds, "Nor to usurp authority over the man."[60]

St. Thomas proffers, in regard to the same passage in Titus 2, a similarly austere expression of the rationale for the patriarchy. He proffers it in terms of articulating the natural effect of female

---

[59] The passage from St. Paul reads: "Teach the older men to be temperate, worthy of respect, self-controlled, and sound in faith, in love and in endurance. Likewise, teach the older women to be reverent in the way they live, not to be slanderers or addicted to much wine, but to teach what is good. Then they can urge the younger women to love their husbands and children, to be self-controlled and pure, to be busy at home, to be kind, and to be subject to their husbands, so that no one will malign the word of God."

[60] *Complete Works of Saint John Chrysostom*, loc. 126535-126541.

dominion: under this unfortunate circumstance, the wife will necessarily put herself at cross-purposes with her own husband:

> First, St. Paul states what should be entrusted to their care; second, how to exercise care; third, the reason behind this advice. In regard to the first he says, "having a care of the house": the wisdom of a woman builds her house, but folly with her own hands tears it down (Prov 14:1). But in exercising care a woman should observe two things, for women are easily angered: there is no anger above the anger of a woman (Sir 25:23); therefore, he says, "gentle". As if to say: let them govern in meekness. The other thing she must observe is subordination, because when a woman has power she tries to oppose her husband's plans: a woman, if she have superiority, is contrary to her husband (Sir 25:30). Therefore, he says, "obedient to their husbands"; hence it is said: your desire shall be for your husband, and he shall rule over you (Gen 3:16). And this, "that the word of God be not blasphemed," i.e., that their disobedience not be an occasion for blasphemy.[61]

Against those who reply that extraordinary women in the Bible, such as Deborah, engaged in counsel, St. Thomas preempts via the following ready-made retort:

> Consequently, he forbids women to teach. Against this, the vision wherewith his mother instructed him (Prov 31:1), I answer that some teaching is public, and this does not belong to woman, and thus he says in the church, some is private, and by this a mother teaches her son. But

---

[61] Thomas Aquinas, *Commentary on the Letters to the Philippians*, 437.

we read that Deborah taught the people of Israel (Judg. 5:7). The answer is that her learning came through the spirit of prophecy, and the grace of the Holy Spirit does not distinguish between man and woman; furthermore, she did not preach publicly, but gave advice under the influence of the Holy Spirit.[62]

Note how St. Thomas distinguishes ordinary circumstances for female teaching from extraordinary ones. This proves to be a distinction that will also obtain in the next section on the necessary domesticity of the wife except in extraordinary circumstances. Thomas also distinguishes public from private female pedagogy, for that matter. Even Deborah (says Thomas) taught the people of Israel not publicly, but under the influence of the Holy Spirit, which reflects a privacy in her pedagogy.

The Wife as Lieutenant

Although it may be preferable to proceed chronologically from Scripture to the Patristics or Scholastics, and then on to recent Magisterial teachings, this section should begin by repeating the relevant passage from the clearest Catholic teaching on the necessity of wifely domesticity: the Catechism of Trent. After all, this section may be the most controversial one in the entire book you are reading. It runs most directly foul of the feminist project against the lay patriarchy, insisting on the domesticity of wives. Christian wives must, in ordinary circumstances, remain at home. It bears repeating (after we first produced this catechetical quotation in section one) that the Roman Catechism teaches the following:

---

[62] Ibid., 272.

On the other hand, the duties of a wife are thus summed up by the Prince of the Apostles: Let wives be subject to their husbands, that if any believe not the word, they may be won without the word by the conversation of the wives, considering your chaste conversation with fear. Let not their adorning be the outward plaiting of the hair, or the wearing of gold, or the putting on of apparel: but the hidden man of the heart in the incorruptibility of a quiet and meek spirit, which is rich in the sight of God. For after this manner heretofore the holy women also, who trusted in God, adorned themselves, being in subjection to their own husbands, as Sarah obeyed Abraham, calling him lord. To train their children in the practice of virtue and to pay particular attention to their domestic concerns should also be especial objects of their attention. The wife should love to remain at home, unless compelled by necessity to go out; and she should never presume to leave home without her husband's consent. Again, and in this the conjugal union chiefly consists, let wives never forget that next to God they are to love their husbands, to esteem them above all others, yielding to them in all things not inconsistent with Christian piety, a willing and ready obedience.[63]

The foremost reason for this teaching is not a practical one at all, but rather a moral-psychological one. Recall from sections above that even the Old Testament (in Sirach 25) touches on the evil of women in the workplace, except in extraordinary circumstances: "There is wrath and impudence and great disgrace

---

[63] *Catechism of the Council of Trent*, 352.

when a wife supports her husband." Here we witness an interesting psychological profile of the phenomenon occurring when husband and wife swap economic places: the change in roles breeds inevitable spousal resentment. At any rate, it is comforting to note the concomitance between the ancient Old Testament and the modern Roman Catechism on the matter.

Once more, in Titus 2:3–5, St. Paul repeats his admonition to women to be "domestic," meaning they should love to stay at home (moreover, he repeats the wifely admonition to be submissive): "Bid the older women likewise to be reverent in behavior, not to be slanderers or slaves to drink; they are to teach what is good, and so train the young women to love their husbands and children, to be sensible, chaste, *domestic*, kind, and submissive to their husbands, that the word of God may not be discredited."

On this passage, John Chrysostom draws out the practical implications by equating the wifely despising of her husband with the utter neglect of the home:

> "To be discreet, chaste, keepers at home, good." All these spring from love. They become "good, and keepers at home," from affection to their husbands. "Obedient to their own husbands, that the word of God be not blasphemed." She who despises her husband, neglects also her house; but from love springs great soberness, and all contention is done away. And if he be a Heathen, he will soon be persuaded; and if he be a Christian, he will become a better man. Seest thou the condescension of Paul? He who in everything would withdraw us from worldly concerns, here bestows his consideration upon domestic affairs. For when these are well conducted, there will be room for spiritual things, but otherwise, they too will be

marred. For she who keeps at home will be also sober, she that keeps at home will be also a prudent manager, she will have no inclination for luxury, unseasonable expenses, and other such things.[64]

From his own commentary on Titus 2, St. Thomas offers a more specific gloss on what it means for women to honor *domesticity*: governing the home as a dignified yet obedient second-in-command, running affairs "on the ground" in the fashion desired and dictated by the husband. Thomas writes: "All these points are mentioned in Tobit 10:13, where it is stated that Raguel and Sarah admonished their daughter to honor her father- and mother-in-law, to love her husband, to take care of the family, to govern the house and to behave herself irreprehensibly."[65]

As we jump forward chronologically to the papally dominated period of the Church's modern teaching on Catholic social doctrine, the teachings on wifely work outside the home — or on the patriarchy, for that matter — don't change by a jot. This historical fact proves critically important because, on this point, the feminist and radical infiltrators of the Church nowadays attempt to characterize ancient and modern Church teaching dichotomously. As you will see below, such infiltrators are outright lying. The modern popes (excluding only two modern popes who went against two thousand years of Catholic teaching on the matter) all teach precisely what Chrysostom, Augustine, and Thomas taught.

Pope Leo XIII teaches in multiple places that wives belong at home. First and most widely known, in *Rerum Novarum*, he

---

[64] *Complete Works of Saint John Chrysostom*, loc. 126558-126568.

[65] Thomas Aquinas, *Commentary on the Letters to the Philippians*, 438.

writes: "Women, again, are not suited for certain occupations; a woman is by nature fitted for home-work, and it is that which is best adapted at once to preserve her modesty and to promote the good bringing up of children and the well-being of the family."[66] Also in *Rerum*, Pope Leo makes a sort of argument for the domesticity of wives by presupposition (within a seemingly unrelated argument) against the dual-income trap: "If a workman's wages be sufficient to enable him comfortably to support himself, his wife, and his children, he will find it easy, if he be a sensible man, to practice thrift, and he will not fail, by cutting down expenses, to put by some little savings and thus secure a modest source of income."[67]

In a different encyclical, *Sapientiae Christianae*, Leo makes it clear that homeschooling (which he strongly urges Christians to practice) relates as corollary to the necessary domesticity of wives — since, as we've seen, Leo presupposes husbands to be the single wage-earners and wives to be the ones remaining at home. In other words, if homeschooling is the best option for familial education, then household wives must be the ones to implement it in ordinary circumstances:

> This is a suitable moment for us to exhort especially heads of families to govern their households according to these precepts, and to be solicitous without failing for the right training of their children. The family may be regarded as the cradle of civil society, and it is in great measure within the circle of family life that the destiny of the States is fostered. Whence it is that they who

---

[66] Leo XIII, encyclical *Rerum Novarum* (May 15, 1891), no. 42.
[67] Ibid., no. 46.

would break away from Christian discipline are working to corrupt family life, and to destroy it utterly, root and branch. From such an unholy purpose they allow not themselves to be turned aside by the reflection that it cannot, even in any degree, be carried out without inflicting cruel outrage on the parents. These hold from nature their right of training the children to whom they have given birth, with the obligation super-added of shaping and directing the education of their little ones to the end for which God vouchsafed the privilege of transmitting the gift of life. It is, then, incumbent on parents to strain every nerve to ward off such an outrage, and to strive manfully to have and to hold exclusive authority to direct the education of their offspring, as is fitting, in a Christian manner, and first and foremost to keep them away from schools where there is risk of their drinking in the poison of impiety. Where the right education of youth is concerned, no amount of trouble or labor can be undertaken, how great soever, but that even greater still may not be called for.[68]

Other popes made it equally or more explicit in non-Magisterial teachings that mothers—not fathers—will almost always be the home educators of offspring. Pope Pius XII taught:

If the mother devotes herself to her mission as educator, giving suitable instruction and guidance, the life-cell of society will be healthy and strong. Mothers must acquire the elementary knowledge necessary for the government

---

[68] Leo XIII, encyclical *Sapientiae Christianae* (January 10, 1890), no. 42.

of the family, the art of keeping a house in order, of dealing with statements of accounting, useful ideas about bringing up children, and, above all, enough understanding of the rules of pedagogy, to profit by the experience of others, without placing too much confidence in their mother instinct, which, of itself, will not always and surely keep them from harmful mistakes.[69]

Following increasingly upon the teachings of Leo XIII as he often did, Pope Pius XI goes even further than Leo in his encyclical *Quadragesimo Anno*. He declares that wifely work outside the home—an "intolerable abuse"—must be "abolished at all cost." This twentieth-century document leaves absolutely no doubt as to the matter of whether wifely work outside the home should be allowed as even an economically required exception:

In the first place, the worker must be paid a wage sufficient to support him and his family. That the rest of the family should also contribute to the common support, according to the capacity of each, is certainly right, as can be observed especially in the families of farmers, but also in the families of many craftsmen and small shopkeepers. But to abuse the years of childhood and the limited strength of women is grossly wrong. Mothers, concentrating on household duties, should work primarily in the home or in its immediate vicinity. It is an intolerable abuse, and

---

[69] Pius XII, "Discourse to the Pupils and Teachers for Adult Education," in *Papal Pronouncements on Marriage and the Family: From Leo XIII to Pius XII 1878–1954*, ed. Alvin Werth and Clement S. Mihanovich (Milwaukee: Bruce, 1955), 129.

to be abolished at all cost, for mothers on account of the father's low wage to be forced to engage in gainful occupations outside the home to the neglect of their proper cares and duties, especially the training of children. Every effort must therefore be made that fathers of families receive a wage large enough to meet ordinary family needs adequately. But if this cannot always be done under existing circumstances, social justice demands that changes be introduced as soon as possible whereby such a wage will be assured to every adult workingman. It will not be out of place here to render merited praise to all, who with a wise and useful purpose, have tried and tested various ways of adjusting the pay for work to family burdens in such a way that, as these increase, the former may be raised and indeed, if the contingency arises, there may be enough to meet extraordinary needs.[70]

Even Pope John XXIII, who convened the Second Vatican Council, repeats the need for a single household income and to avoid the abusive practice of wifely work outside the home. In the encyclical *Pacem et Terris*, he writes: "The worker is likewise entitled to a wage that is determined in accordance with the precepts of justice. This needs stressing. The amount a worker receives must be sufficient, in proportion to available funds, to allow him and his family a standard of living consistent with human dignity."[71] In another encyclical, *Mater et Magistra*, John describes the horrific conditions of political economy that once required women and children to become laborers:

---

[70] Pius XI, encyclical *Quadragesimo Anno* (May 15, 1931), no. 71.
[71] John XXIII, encyclical *Pacem in Terris* (April 11, 1963), no. 20.

Wages were insufficient even to the point of reaching starvation level, and working conditions were often of such a nature as to be injurious alike to health, morality and religious faith. Especially inhuman were the working conditions to which women and children were sometimes subjected. There was also the constant spectre of unemployment and the progressive disruption of family life.[72]

Whereas some popes (such as the ones mentioned above) responded to past abuses of working women, others presciently prefigured the future abuses that would surely follow upon the feminists' urgings—not to mention the rhetoric that would prop them up. The popes' predictive accuracy will shock the reader! Anticipating and preempting the modern feminist argument that, in regard to the needful domesticity of wives, "times have changed," Pope Benedict XV argued the following:

> The changed conditions of the times have conferred upon woman functions and rights which were not allowed her in former times, but no change in the opinions of men, no novelty of circumstances and events, will ever remove woman, conscious of her mission, from her natural center, which is the family. At the domestic hearth she is queen.... Hence, it may be justly said that the changed condition of the times have enlarged the field of woman's activity. An apostolate of woman in the world has succeeded that more intimate and restricted action which she formerly exercised within the domestic walls, but this apostolate must be carried out in such a manner as to make it evident that woman, both outside and within

[72] John XXIII, encyclical *Mater et Magistra* (May 15, 1961), no. 13.

the home, shall not forget that it is her duty, even today, to consecrate her principal cares to the family.[73]

Similarly, Pope Pius XII taught the following about the horrors of women in the workplace:

Has woman's position been thereby improved? Equality of rights with man brought with it her abandonment of the home where she reigned as queen, and her subjection to the same work strain and working hours. It entails depreciation of her true dignity and the solid foundation of all her rights which is her characteristic feminine role, and the intimate co-ordination of the two sexes. The end intended by God for the good of all human society, especially for the family, is lost sight of. In concessions made to woman one can easily see not respect for her dignity or her mission, but an attempt to foster the economic and military power of the totalitarian state to which all must inexorably be subordinated. To restore as far as possible the honor of the woman's and mother's place in the home: that is the watchword one hears now from many quarters like a cry of alarm, as if the world were awakening, terrified by the fruits of material and scientific progress of which it before was so proud.[74]

Just as Benedict XV anticipated and nullified the "times have changed" argument, Pope Pius XII preempts and rebuts, in an

---

[73] Benedict XV, "Woman's Mission in Modern Society", in *Papal Pronouncements*, 131–132.

[74] Pius XII, "Woman's Duties in Social and Political Life," in *Papal Pronouncements*, 43–44.

especially impassioned plea, the "we need more family income" argument:

> We see a woman who in order to augment her husband's earnings, betakes herself also to a factory, leaving her house abandoned during her absence. The house, untidy and small perhaps before, becomes even more miserable for lack of care. Members of the family work separately in four quarters of the city and with different working hours. Scarcely ever do they find themselves together for dinner or rest after work — still less for prayer in common. What is left of family life? And what attractions can it offer to children?

To such painful consequences of the absence of the mother from the home there is added another, still more deplorable. It concerns the education, especially of the young girl, and her preparation for real life. Accustomed as she is to see her mother always out of the house and the house itself so gloomy in its abandonment, she will be unable to find any attraction for it. She will not feel the slightest inclination for austere housekeeping jobs. She cannot be expected to appreciate their nobility and beauty or to wish one day to give herself to them as a wife and mother.

This is true in all grades and stations of social life. The daughter of the worldly woman, who sees all housekeeping left in the hands of paid help and her mother fussing around with frivolous occupations and futile amusements, will follow her example, will want to be emancipated as soon as possible and — in the words of a tragic phrase — to "live her own life." How could she conceive a desire to become one day a true lady who is the mother of a happy, prosperous, worthy family?

As to the working classes, forced to earn daily bread, a woman might, if she reflected, realize that not rarely the supplementary wage which she earns by working outside the house is easily swallowed up by the other expenses or even by waste which is ruinous to the family budget.... It is clear that woman's task thus understood cannot be improvised. Motherly instinct is in her a human instinct, not determined by nature down to the details of its application. It is directed by free will and this in turn is guided by intellect. Hence comes its moral value and its dignity but also imperfection which must be compensated for and redeemed by education.[75]

By way of conclusion, it should be noted that even Pope John Paul II, a pontiff with a position at times running dangerously close to the one attempting to reify a "Christian feminism," admitted that in the economic context, only fathers should work, while mothers should remain at home. In *Centesimus Annus*, John Paul II writes: "A workman's wages should be sufficient to enable him to support himself, his wife and his children. If through necessity or fear of a worse evil the workman accepts harder conditions because an employer or contractor will afford no better, he is made the victim of force and injustice."[76]

Likewise, in *Laborem Exercens*, he writes:

Such remuneration can be given either through what is called a family wage — that is, a single salary given to the head of the family for his work, sufficient for the needs

---

[75] Ibid., 129–131.

[76] John Paul II, encyclical letter *Centesimus Annus* (May 1, 1991), no. 8.

of the family without the other spouse having to take up gainful employment outside the home—or through other social measures such as family allowances or grants to mothers devoting themselves exclusively to their families. These grants should correspond to the actual needs, that is, to the number of dependents for as long as they are not in a position to assume proper responsibility for their own lives.[77]

Clearly, the need for wives to remain at home qualifies among the very clearest and most amply evidenced of the papally repeated, habitual (and therefore perennial) teachings of the Catholic Church. In fact—notwithstanding the fiery opposition the basic teaching receives from so-called Christian feminists—an honest observer would be hard-pressed to find a social or cultural topic more consistently and perennially taught by the Church.

Patriarchal Love

After reading everything above, it may be too easy to forget that Christian patriarchy involves higher duties for husbands than for wives. The husbandly Christian standard is one of near-infinite patience and near-perfect protectivity toward wives. It is a standard wrought of total self-sacrifice.

When husbands meet this high standard, it conduces to the general happiness of both spouses, along with the children. All the family, rather than the husband alone, shares in the glory of a well-ordered household. Even compared with Judaism, which situates the husband's comfort as the metric for good order, the

---

[77] John Paul II, encyclical *Laborem Exercens* (September 14, 1981), no. 19.

motivation for such a high Christian standard of marriage renders Christianity utterly unique. This ought to be our expectation since, after all, Christianity alone elevates matrimony to a sacrament. Consider what Pope Leo XIII writes on the matter in *Arcanum*:

> Not only, in strict truth, was marriage instituted for the propagation of the human race, but also that the lives of husbands and wives might be made better and happier. This comes about in many ways: by their lightening each other's burdens through mutual help; by constant and faithful love; by having all their possessions in common; and by the heavenly grace which flows from the sacrament. Marriage also can do much for the good of families, for, so long as it is conformable to nature and in accordance with the counsels of God, it has power to strengthen union of heart in the parents; to secure the holy education of children; to temper the authority of the father by the example of the divine authority; to render children obedient to their parents and servants obedient to their masters.[78]

Time and again, Christian teaching prevails upon husbands to bestow happiness and honor upon wives. This requires a peaceable spousal coexistence, without much squabbling, constituted of reciprocal (rather than male-exclusive) enjoyment of benefit. In his lengthy Homily X, on Colossians 3:18–25, Chrysostom teaches profoundly on this topic:

> See how again [St. Paul] has exhorted to reciprocity. As in the other case he enjoineth fear and love, so also doth he

---

[78] Leo XIII, *Arcanum*, no. 26.

here. For it is possible for one who loves even, to be bitter. What he saith then is this. Fight not; for nothing is more bitter than this fighting, when it takes place on the part of the husband toward the wife. For the fightings which happen between beloved persons, these are bitter; and he shows that it ariseth from great bitterness, when, saith he, any one is at variance with his own member. To love therefore is the husband's part, to yield pertains to the other side. If then each one contributes his own part, all stands firm. From being loved, the wife too becomes loving; and from her being submissive, the husband becomes yielding. And see how in nature also it hath been so ordered, that the one should love, the other obey. For when the party governing loves the governed, then everything stands fast.[79]

Moreover, the inspiring spousal admonition of 1 Peter 3:2–6, seen in a section above, concludes in its seventh verse: "Likewise you husbands, live considerately with your wives, bestowing honor on the woman as the weaker sex, since you are joint heirs of the grace of life, in order that your prayers may not be hindered." Husbands are required to honor loving wives.

Along similar lines, the famed Ephesians 5:22–24 passage above concludes with the following verses (25–30):

Husbands, love your wives, as Christ loved the church and gave himself up for her, that he might sanctify her, having cleansed her by the washing of water with the word, that he might present the church to himself in splendor, without spot or wrinkle or any such thing, that she might be holy and without blemish. Even so husbands should

---

[79] *Complete Works of Saint John Chrysostom*, loc. 114292–114311.

love their wives as their own bodies. He who loves his wife loves himself. For no man ever hates his own flesh, but nourishes and cherishes it, as Christ does the church, because we are members of his body.

Chrysostom exegetes this particular "positive" admonition for husbandly love in Ephesians 5 by asking rhetorically why any Christian husband would even *want* to treat his wife as a slave. A master does not look after the well-being of the slave, nor does the master enjoy the company of a slave. Contrary to what Machiavelli believed, for Chrysostom, it is indeed better to be loved than feared:

Though thou shouldest undergo all this, yet wilt thou not, no, not even then, have done anything like Christ. For thou indeed art doing it for one to whom thou art already knit; but He for one who turned her back on Him and hated Him. In the same way then as He laid at His feet her who turned her back on Him, who hated, and spurned, and disdained Him, not by menaces, nor by violence, nor by terror, nor by anything else of the kind, but by His unwearied affection; so also do thou behave thyself toward thy wife. Yea, though thou see her looking down upon thee, and disdaining, and scorning thee, yet by thy great thoughtfulness for her, by affection, by kindness, thou wilt be able to lay her at thy feet. For there is nothing more powerful to sway than these bonds, and especially for husband and wife. A servant, indeed, one will be able, perhaps, to bind down by fear; nay not even him, for he will soon start away and be gone. But the partner of one's life, the mother of one's children, the foundation of one's every joy, one ought never to chain down by fear and menaces, but with love and good temper. For what sort of union is that, where the wife trembles at her husband? And what sort of pleasure will the husband himself enjoy, if he dwells with his wife as with a slave, and not as with a free-woman? Yea, though thou shouldest suffer anything on her account, do not upbraid her; for neither did Christ do this.[80]

So that no stone is left unturned and no husband may plausibly claim ignorance about the dictates of Ephesians 5 in regard to the parameters of the Christian husband, Chrysostom specifically admonishes against certain dysfunctional and despotic husbandly behaviors:

Neither, however, let the husband, when he hears these things, on the score of his having the supreme authority, betake himself to revilings and to blows; but let him exhort, let him admonish her, as being less perfect, let him persuade her with arguments. Let him never once lift his hand—far be this from a noble spirit—no, nor give expression to insults, or taunts, or revilings; but let him regulate and direct her as being wanting in wisdom. Yet how shall this be done? If she is instructed in the true riches, in the heavenly philosophy, she will make no complaints like these. Let him teach her then, that poverty is no evil. Let him teach her, not by what he says only, but also by what he does. Let him teach her to despise glory; and then his wife will speak of nothing, and will desire nothing of the kind. Let him, as if he had an image given into his hands to mould, let him, from that very evening on which he first receives her into the bridal chamber, teach her temperance, gentleness, and how to live, casting

[80] Ibid., loc. 120430–120441.

down the love of money at once from the outset, and from the very threshold.[81]

On this same passage in Scripture, St. Thomas highlights the fact that husbands bear the duty of loving their wives chastely and exclusively. On this matter, too, the Christian standard proves to be uniquely high, compared against other religions:

> [St. Paul] states: "husbands, love your wives." For certainly it is from the love he has for his wife that he will live more chastely and both of them will enjoy a peaceful relationship. If he should love another more than his own wife, he exposes both himself and his wife to division. Husbands, love your wives and be not bitter towards them (Col. 3:19).[82]

St. Paul, after giving wives a strong exhortation toward domesticity in Titus 2:6–7 (which we discussed earlier), goes on to say the following to husbands: "Likewise urge the younger men to control themselves. Show yourself in all respects a model of good deeds, and in your teaching show integrity, gravity."

Clearly, the Christian faith has been far better for the plight of women worldwide than any feminist movement. No other world religion, monotheistic or polytheistic, gives the robust argument against spousal abuse that Christianity does. According to it, wife beating is as absurd as masochism—flesh beating flesh of the same body—and morally more repugnant than beating a servant (which St. Paul also forbids). Contrast the ancient teachings of Chrysostom against the baseless assertions of twentieth-century

---

[81] Ibid., loc. 120684–120697.

[82] Thomas Aquinas, *Commentary on the Letters to the Galatians*, 319.

feminists, who assumed that ancient Christians mimicked barbaric practices against their wives:

> And I say not this for a wife to be beaten; far from it: for this is the extremest affront, not to her that is beaten, but to him who beateth. But even if by some misfortune thou have such a yokefellow allotted thee, take it not ill, O woman, considering the reward which is laid up for such things and their praise too in this present life. And to you husbands also this I say: make it a rule that there can be no such offence as to bring you under the necessity of striking a wife. And why say I a wife? since not even upon his handmaiden could a free man endure to inflict blows and lay violent hands. But if the shame be great for a man to beat a maidservant, much more to stretch forth the right hand against her that is free.[83]

In short, Christian husbands are enjoined to participate in the highest and best treatment of wives in the history of the world. The observant Christian husband, in conformity with his non-egalitarian household taxonomy, outdoes each of the worldviews in human history, which includes the radical egalitarianism of feminism. The Christian patriarch proves the most self-sacrificial, lordly, charitable lover of his wife and engineer of her ultimate good.

Christian Marriage: Foundation of the Patriarchy

While recapitulating some of the main precepts of the needfulness of the patriarchy, Colossians 3:18–21 insinuates an indispensable attribute of Christian marriage that has gone unsung, to

---

[83] *Complete Works of Saint John Chrysostom*, loc. 67936–67942.

this point: the harmony of well-ordered matrimony: "Wives, be subject to your husbands, as is fitting in the Lord. Husbands, love your wives, and do not be harsh with them. Children, obey your parents in everything, for this pleases the Lord. Fathers, do not provoke your children, lest they become discouraged."

When these categories are summarily satisfied, Christian marriage is the most beautiful conceivable human friendship. The few observant marital couples you've ever met are accordingly the only true best friends you've ever actually met. Consider also what John Chrysostom writes about Ephesians 5 (with my emphasis):

A certain wise man, setting down a number of things in the rank of blessings, set down this also in the rank of a blessing, "A wife agreeing with her husband." (Ecclus. xxv. 1.) And elsewhere again he sets it down among blessings, that a woman should dwell in harmony with her husband. (Ecclus. xl. 23.) And indeed from the beginning, God appears to have made special provision for this union; and discoursing of the twain as one, He said thus, "Male and female created He them" (Gen. i. 27); and again, "There is neither male nor female." (Gal. iii. 28.) *For there is no relationship between man and man so close as that between man and wife, if they be joined together as they should be.* And therefore a certain blessed man too, when he would express surpassing love, and was mourning for one that was dear to him, and of one soul with him, did not mention father, nor mother, nor child, nor brother, nor friend, but what? "Thy love to me was wonderful,' saith he, 'passing the love of women." (2 Sam. i. 26.) For indeed, in very deed, this love is more despotic than any despotism: for others indeed may be strong, but this passion is not only strong, but unfading. For there is a certain love deeply seated in our nature, which imperceptibly to ourselves knits together these bodies of ours. Thus even from the very beginning woman sprang from man, and afterwards from man and woman sprang both man and woman.[84]

You won't hear this outside of Christianity—and not even frequently enough there: if man and wife are not best friends, then they're not practicing the religion correctly. I regularly tell my adult theology students that, if you are married but consider your best friend to be anyone but your spouse, you're doing Christianity wrong. Here is the key idea in Chrysostom's treatment of Ephesians 5: "For there is no relationship between man and man so close as that between man and wife, if they be joined together as they should be."

Other religions, worldviews, and philosophies neglect this truth, or reject it altogether. Indeed, many such worldviews fail the basic monogamy standard set by Christianity.[85]

---

[84] Homily XX, in *Complete Works of Saint John Chrysostom*, loc. 120365–120377.

[85] Leo XIII wrote the following of polygamy in *Arcanum*: "Moreover, plurality of wives and husbands, as well as divorce, caused the nuptial bond to be relaxed exceedingly. Hence, too, sprang up the greatest confusion as to the mutual rights and duties of husbands and wives, inasmuch as a man assumed right of dominion over his wife, ordering her to go about her business, often without any just cause; while he was himself at liberty 'to run headlong with impunity into lust, unbridled and unrestrained, in houses of ill-fame and amongst his female slaves, as if the dignity of the persons sinned with, and not the will of the sinner, made the guilt.' When the licentiousness of a husband thus showed itself, nothing could be more piteous than the wife, sunk so low as to be all but reckoned as a means for the gratification of passion, or for the

In another location, Chrysostom makes a crucial connection between wifely submission and the loveliness and superlative intimacy of Christian marriage. He writes:

For there is nothing which so welds our life together as the love of man and wife. For this many will lay aside

---

production of offspring. Without any feeling of shame, marriageable girls were bought and sold, like so much merchandise, and power was sometimes given to the father and to the husband to inflict capital punishment on the wife. Of necessity, the offspring of such marriages as these were either reckoned among the stock in trade of the common-wealth or held to be the property of the father of the family; and the law permitted him to make and unmake the marriages of his children at his mere will, and even to exercise against them the monstrous power of life and death. So manifold being the vices and so great the ignominies with which marriage was defiled, an alleviation and a remedy were at length bestowed from on high. Jesus Christ, who restored our human dignity and who perfected the Mosaic law, applied early in His ministry no little solicitude to the question of marriage. He ennobled the marriage in Cana of Galilee by His presence, and made it memorable by the first of the miracles which He wrought; and for this reason, even from that day forth, it seemed as if the beginning of new holiness had been conferred on human marriages. Later on He brought back matrimony to the nobility of its primeval origin by condemning the customs of the Jews in their abuse of the plurality of wives and of the power of giving bills of divorce; and still more by commanding most strictly that no one should dare to dissolve that union which God Himself had sanctioned by a bond perpetual. Hence, having set aside the difficulties which were adduced from the law of Moses, He, in character of supreme Lawgiver, decreed as follows concerning husbands and wives, 'I say to you, that whosoever shall put away his wife, except it be for fornication, and shall marry another, committeth adultery; and he that shall marry her that is put away committeth adultery'" (nos. 7–8).

even their arms, for this they will give up life itself. And Paul would never without a reason and without an object have spent so many pains on this subject, as when he says here, "Wives, be in subjection unto your own husbands, as unto the Lord." And why so? Because when they are in harmony, the children are well brought up, and the domestics are in good order, and neighbors, and friends, and relations enjoy the fragrance.[86]

Note Chrysostom's emphasis on St. Paul's Herculean "pains on this subject" and the reason for such pains: the critical, indispensable importance of wifely submission to all other interactions in well-functioning society. Wifely submission does not detract from spousal harmony; it enhances spousal harmony! Contrast St. Paul's great pains to broach the subject with the modern Church's great pains to avoid it.

Moreover, notice in the following commentary on 1 Corinthians 11 St. Thomas's poignant language referring to the needfulness of the man for the woman and vice versa. Nowhere outside the Christian tradition is such a strong conception of male-female complementarity adumbrated:

Neither is the man without the woman ... in the Lord, namely, in the grace of our Lord Jesus Christ, nor the woman without the man, because both are saved by God's grace: for as many of you as were baptized have put on Christ (Gal 3:27), and then he adds: there is neither male nor female, namely, differing in the grace of Christ.[87]

---

[86] *Complete Works of Saint John Chrysostom*, loc. 120391–120396.

[87] Thomas Aquinas, *Commentary on the Letters to the Corinthians*, 230–231.

Consider Chrysostom's florid praise, in his commentary on Titus 2:2–5, for the efficient, well-ordered loving Christian household, headed by a strong patriarch. It is offset by harmony and fellow feeling by all members of the family:

This is the chief point of all that is good in a household, "A man and his wife that agree together." (Ecclus. xxv. 1.) For where this exists, there will be nothing that is unpleasant. For where the head is in harmony with the body, and there is no disagreement between them, how shall not all the other members be at peace? For when the rulers are at peace, who is there to divide and break up concord? as on the other hand, where these are ill disposed to each other, there will be no good order in the house. This then is a point of the highest importance, and of more consequence than wealth, or rank, or power, or aught else. Nor has he said merely to be at peace, but "to love their husbands." For where love is, no discord will find admittance, far from it, other advantages too spring up.[88]

On the same passage in Titus 2, St. Thomas expounds upon Chrysostom's remarks about familial harmony. Thomas even brings the desideratum of household harmony — which follows upon wifely submission (which gives to a husband what he is "due") and husbandly charity — into the context of civic fellow feeling and what we might today refer to as subsidiarity:

In regard to the first St. Paul says, "to love their husbands." For love is a husband's due: "a good wife is the crown of her husband" (Prov 12:4); "my soul takes pleasure in three

---

[88] *Complete Works of Saint John Chrysostom*, loc. 126546–126555.

things, and they are beautiful in the sight of the Lord and of men: agreement between brothers, friendship between neighbors, and a wife and husband who live in harmony" (Sir 25:1).[89]

This important social and theological connection flows naturally from the Christian teaching on marriage alone. It simply cannot be found in religions or philosophies wherein the marital relation is not viewed sacramentally and vocationally. A husband and a wife — non-equals, according to Christian teaching — "get each other to Heaven" insofar as the leadership of the husband and the submission of the wife comprises a life's worth of work toward complementarity. That which is sacramental, vocational, and non-egalitarian flow together.

For his own part, St. Augustine waxes on beautifully about marriage even and especially in its aged, less physically beautiful state:

And this seems not to me to be merely on account of the begetting of children, but also on account of the natural society itself in a difference of sex. Otherwise it would not any longer be called marriage in the case of old persons, especially if either they had lost sons, or had given birth to none. But now in good, although aged, marriage, albeit there has withered away the glow of full age between male and female, yet there lives in full vigor the order of charity between husband and wife: because, the better they are, the earlier they have begun by mutual consent to contain from sexual intercourse with each other: not that it should

---

[89] Thomas Aquinas, *Commentary on the Letters to the Philippians*, 437.

be matter of necessity afterwards not to have power to do what they would, but that it should be matter of praise to have been unwilling at the first, to do what they had power to do. If therefore there be kept good faith of honor, and of services mutually due from either sex, although the members of either be languishing and almost corpse-like, yet of souls duly joined together, the chastity continues, the purer by how much it is the more proved, the safer, by how much it is the calmer.[90]

There exists another category—which ought to furnish especial interest from "Christian feminists"—for separating patriarchal Catholic marriage from all previous world teachings on it: the extra niceties and dignities associated with the Church's sacramental elevation of marriage.[91]

For instance, Catholicism uniquely empowers young adults who fall in love with the capacity of becoming spouses. This

---

[90] Augustine, *Of the Good of Marriage*.

[91] In the truest sense of the term, Christian matrimony under a system of patriarchy enhanced non-fabricated, non-imagined female rights to their pinnacle. Consider what Pope Leo XIII says on the matter: "A law of marriage just to all, and the same for all, was enacted by the abolition of the old distinction between slaves and free-born men and women; 'and thus the rights of husbands and wives were made equal:' for, as St. Jerome says, 'with us that which is unlawful for women is unlawful for men also, and the same restraint is imposed on equal conditions.' The self-same rights also were firmly established for reciprocal affection and for the interchange of duties; the dignity of the woman was asserted and assured; and it was forbidden to the man to inflict capital punishment for adultery, or lustfully and shamelessly to violate his plighted faith." Leo XIII, *Arcanum*, no. 14.

much should be carried out, even to the point of disempowering fathers of would-be brides and would-be grooms. Pope Leo XIII writes: "It is also a great blessing that the Church has limited, so far as is needful, the power of fathers of families, so that sons and daughters, wishing to marry, are not in any way deprived of their rightful freedom."[92]

This argument proves especially potent when placed in the context of the arranged and semi-arranged marriages associated with other religions, both polytheistic and monotheistic. Christianity uniquely requires that young women choose their husbands (as forcefully as it requires the same of young men with regard to their wives). Failing this, in fact, a wedding is not sacramentally valid. This sacramental dignity of Christian marriage was a change in the fabric of female lifestyle quality in world history!

Conclusion

It is undeniable: the patriarchy is the Christian teaching on marriage. As the reader has by now seen, the literality of male headship over households was taught as explicitly in the first Christian century as it was in the twentieth.

The patriarchy is a mandatory—not a permissive—condition of running a Christian household. Moral and social catastrophe—such as the universal sexual and familial dysfunctions of our own era presciently described by the earliest Church Fathers—promise to follow upon a denial of the Christian teaching of household as patriarchal monarchy. Christian teaching requires the wife to be almost ever-present in the home, as its beating heart, and the patriarchal standard for wifely treatment by husbands is much higher than any other worldview. As these

---

[92] Leo XIII, *Arcanum*, no. 15.

conditions come together, a well-ordered Christian household that honors such requirements provides the most possible happiness for all its inhabitants here on earth.

So, why did feminists mount such a violent attack? What animated their self-destructive color revolution? The next chapter will provide the entire historiography of the feminists, beginning with Eve's diabolical dalliance in the Garden of Eden.

3

Feminism's Origins

Everything expressed in the foregoing chapters summarizes the cultural juggernaut, feminism. More carefully put, chapter 1 proffered a list of feminism's *symptoms*. The origin of these symptoms needs explaining. To the reader, feminism appears to be the grey ghost, seen virtually everywhere but detected practically nowhere in post-Christian society today. Like any doctor presented with a sweeping catalogue of a patient's symptoms, the opponent of feminism must proceed to an examination of the hidden first causes of the problem. Doctors call this an "etiology." This chapter will tend to an etiology of feminism.

As the reader will see, feminism must be defined in all its phases as the attempted overthrow of the patriarchy. Such an attempt by the feminist conspirators belongs no more to one phase of feminism than any other.

Our examination of feminism's causes will not begin with the typical hagiography regarding its "three waves." You can get that anywhere else, from any women's-studies seminar or any program on late-morning television. While this chapter will indeed reexamine feminism's three waves and conclude about them in a revisionist way, our reexamination will only follow upon a neglected preliminary look at the ancient conditions that enabled and shaped them.

Indeed, both halves of Western civilization's pseudo-intellectual class (the academy, alongside entertainment and news media) are enthusiastically and explicitly feminist. Everybody knows. Both halves portray feminism's birth as a part-accidental, part-inevitable one-off, like Athena springing from Zeus's head. And both halves are always deucedly assuming that feminism can be mixed with any other worldview, however unlikely: for example, conservatism, Christianity, the pro-life movement, and so on. It cannot. Examining feminism's ancient prefigurements, together with a proper view of its three modern waves, one will easily see *why* it cannot.

The usual account of the three historical generations of feminism goes back as far as the middle of the nineteenth century, and no further. In *The Encyclopedia of Feminism*, Lisa Tuttle explains that "first wave feminism" begins around the year 1860.[93] In another place, she recapitulates about feminism's birthday, stating, "The beginning is usually considered to have been the Seneca Falls Convention of 1848."[94] At any rate, feminism's champions never endeavor to explain what philosophy and theology underlie those nineteenth- and twentieth-century "waves" of the phenomenon in the first place. Why would they? To do so, after all, is to militate against the good name of feminism.

We, however, will not allow the neglect to continue. So, we will do just what feminism's yes-men have not: we will start at the beginning.

---

[93] Lisa Tuttle, *The Encyclopedia of Feminism* (New York: Facts on File Publications, 1986), 114.

[94] Ibid., 368.

To this end, the present chapter will show historically and philosophically that feminism is an ancient diabolical attack on the family, making just a few, limited appearances until early-modern devolutions of Christian philosophy allowed feminism to emerge in three or four barely distinguishable "waves." Our historical treatment centers upon the recent, widespread, Christian consumption of the idea, which happened by and through radical modernism inside and outside Christianity and which mischaracterized the first of those waves as innocuous and salutary.[95] It is neither of these.

The frontal attack on males seen today meant first a focused barrage on both *masculinity* and *femininity*. But before even the possibility of that, feminism required the foothold of a certain few errors in Christian philosophy and theology, as mentioned above. Feminism proves to be simply the next (perhaps the final) stage of the modernist attack on Christendom, which is another name for "the patriarchy."

A History of "Christian" Feminism?

As the reader surveys feminism's chronological development, this book will ask over and over: Why are conservatives and Christians so sharply inclined toward locating a Christian version of feminism rather than rejecting in a *carte blanche* manner the possibility of such a blasphemous hybrid? Common sense admonishes the latter. In this brief section, it is asked only as a sidebar to our history of feminism, but later in the book it will be asked more directly. What secret force has ensured the universal

---

[95] This chapter's etiology of feminism will cover both the supply (where it came from) and the demand (why surprising parties consumed its premises) of the movement.

preclusion of published, outright rejections of feminism, even from corners of the ideological landscape that claim to oppose it?

No matter how harshly a Christian or conservative book entering the scene initially promises to vituperate feminism, that book's author invariably winds up articulating at least once that his critique doesn't involve the endorsement of women "being a doormat,"[96] or "going back" to such a historical status. Such commentators will usually utter something cautionary culminating in the expression "barefoot and pregnant," without spending any time demonstrating that barefoot, pregnant women are thereby harmed or unhappy. Already, then, the premise is bought and the ship is sunk. (In fact, during the warm months of the year, my wife spends most of her time around the house barefoot — often pregnant! She loves her life.)

Only a feminist should embrace the idiotic precept that in bygone, more Christian ages of human history, women were ever "doormats."

Even secular conservative authors should universally acknowledge the beneficence of society's return to authentically Christian teachings in faith and morals. As far as the treatment of women is concerned, Christianity got things right all along, with no "developments" needed. While the issue of women's fundamental rights certainly proves to pose a challenge for, say, Islam (relevant in both the past and the present), it never did for Christianity. Christianity led the world to the most crucial historical step for women's dignity: a view of matrimony that required the independent consent of women to the marital bond, without which the

---

[96] Carrie Gress, *The Anti-Mary Exposed* (Charlotte, NC: TAN Books, 2019), *passim*.

sacrament cannot in any case occur.[97] Moreover, such a require-ment was imposed by Christian theology from the very beginning, even *previous to* the recognition of marriage as a sacrament.

None of this, of course, represents an instance of "Christian feminism," but rather of Christian dignity consistently applied to females. Feminism cannot take credit for the teachings of Christ and His Church.

Anyway, what sort of Christian conservative who self-consciously dreams of reclaiming a more beautiful erstwhile Christian era makes room for even a single self-contradicting reservation like Christian feminism? The answer is, most of them. And it is a shame. Consider recent examples of such schizophrenia.

In *The Anti-Mary Exposed*, Catholic author Dr. Carrie Gress raises many excellent points against "radical feminism"[98] but surgically restricts her criticism to the radical form of the move-ment that arose in the 1960s. Whenever she characterizes the common woman, Gress usually extols her as a kind of (non-radical) leader — as "the soil of culture"[99] — much as moderate feminism would do. Gress also errantly suggests that "women correspond with ends, whereas men correspond with means,"[100] lending to another justification of moderate feminism. Her point seems to contradict the Christian notion that prudence — the

---

[97] Archbishop John C. Nienstedt, "The Four Pillars of Sacramental Marriage," The Catholic Spirit, July 3, 2013, https://thecatholic-spirit.com/only-jesus/the-four-pillars-of-sacramental-marriage/.

[98] Gress, *The Anti-Mary Exposed*, cover flap.

[99] Carrie Gress, "120: Toxic Feminism and Its Antidote — Dr. Carrie Gress (Free Version)," interview by Patrick Coffin, *The Patrick Coffin Show* (podcast), March 19, 2019, https://www.patrickcoffin.media/toxic-femininity-and-its-antidote/.

[100] Ibid.

ruler's virtue — corresponds more intimately with the leading role of men.

Moreover, it remains tactically unclear to the reader whether Gress aims to equate Catholic Magisterial teaching regarding the "due subjection of wife to husband"[101] and wives' "submitting to their husbands in all things" (see Ephesians 5:24, NIV) with her admonition against women "being a doormat."[102] One scratches his head pondering the conceptual connection at work in Gress's insinuations, in frequent writings, speeches, and interviews. While neither her reader nor her listener can be entirely sure, it certainly sounds as if she conceives of wifely submission as being a doormat.

Or consider the eminent Harvey C. Mansfield's book *Manliness*. He writes: "This book is about manliness. What is that? It's best to start from examples we know: our sports heroes, too many to name; Margaret Thatcher, the British prime minister who is the mightiest woman of our time (What! a woman, manly?); Harry S. Truman, who said 'the buck stops here.'"[103] Why include a woman among examples of manliness, and why *begin* that list with a woman?! He's not merely being cheeky. In *Manliness*'s opening salvo, Mansfield justifies the oxymoron: "Today the very word manliness seems quaint and obsolete. We are in the process of making the English language gender-neutral, and manliness, the quality of one gender, or rather, or one sex, seems to describe the essence of the enemy we are attacking, the evil we are eradicating."[104] Mansfield then

---

[101] Pope Pius XI, encyclical *Casti Connubii* (December 31, 1930), no. 72.

[102] Gress, "Toxic Feminism and Its Antidote."

[103] Harvey C. Mansfield, *Manliness* (New Haven: Yale University Press, 2007), ix.

[104] Ibid., 1.

proceeds to an embarrassed half-defense of the employment of the word to designate just one sex — after, of course, designating a woman with it!

Also consider this Ben Shapiro tweet, from January 2019: "My wife (who it is rumored, is a doctor) stayed up all night with my five-year-old because my girl has a brutal cough due to flu (tonight is my turn). My wife then got up and went to work to care for her patients. That's feminism. Not murdering babies outside the womb."[105] Shapiro is correct — that *is* feminism: a mother not intending evil but leaving her ailing child in order to care instead for the children of strangers, for money. Sadly, the very gifted and otherwise conservative Shapiro — together with at least sixty-nine thousand conservative fans who "liked" his tweet — appears to be embracing it without understanding its evils. In this way, feminism seems to be a real dividing line between the small number of conservatives who understand its full implications and everyone else (including many good conservatives like Shapiro).

Also, in May of 2019, good conservative news sites and journals like Breitbart unselfconsciously celebrated the fact that "unemployment rate for women falls to lowest since 1953."[106]

These instances of conservative dithering on feminism, compared against all the many examples produced in chapter 1, are mere reminders. The common theme of conservative- or

---

[105] Ben Shapiro (@benshapiro), Twitter post, January 30, 2019, 10:20 a.m., https://twitter.com/benshapiro/status/109067616192 1744896?s=12

[106] John Carney, "Unemployment Rate for Women Falls to Lowest Since 1953," Breitbart, May 3, 2019, https://www.breitbart. com/economy/2019/05/03/unemployment-rate-for-women-falls -to-lowest-since-1953/.

Christian-feminist schizophrenia will be treated much more squarely in later chapters, but in this one, the bare fact that such a paradox exists should be borne in mind as a point of departure in the development of historical feminism. Notwithstanding Christendom's proud history of chivalry, by the time of the middle-nineteenth century—and the generations immediately following it—conservatives were (and still are!) willing to "go soft" on first-wave feminism. What follows is a historical attempt to explain why.

Eve and Lilith: The First Feminists?

Even though we don't celebrate it, all believing Jews and Christians have a reasonable case for calling Adam and Eve the first feminist couple in the history of the West. In other words, Adam and Eve show that although feminism is anything but natural, it constitutes an easy pitfall for human beings. For one thing, the occasion for the Original Sin constitutes the first instance of "gender bending" ever. For another, the role played by the serpent in the debacle shows that feminism was the centerpiece of history's first diabolical plot against the flourishing of the human family. Accordingly, we must begin our treatment of the root causes of feminism in Genesis 2, quite a bit further back than its usual treatment, which begins in the nineteenth century.

A plain reading of Genesis chapters 2 and 3 establishes the following facts: God "planted a garden and placed there the man whom he had formed." This man, Adam, was charged by God with "cultivating and caring for" the garden. Adam is then placed in charge of naming the animals, before Eve is created. God, seeing Adam's need for an intimate helper, puts Adam into a deep sleep and creates Eve from his rib. Adam then names Eve, saying "for out of man has this [woman] been taken." Adam and

Eve then are described as "one body," showing the functional complementarity of men and women. Then the serpent appears and interrogates Eve rather than Adam. Eve finds herself tempted by the fruit as "desirable for gaining wisdom." In a reversal of roles, Eve leads Adam, "who was with her, and he ate it" (Genesis 2:8–3:6).

In other words, buried within the abrupt narrative voice of Genesis, we discover Adam standing next to his wife, passively watching and allowing human history to go off the rails. He was not off hunting or building a shelter in another part of the garden, as one might assume from his inactivity. Instead, he watched idly nearby as Eve traded her birthright to the Deceiver. This foolish role reversal by Adam and Eve would eventually require a New Man and a New Woman in order to remediate the human situation. St. Jerome summarized this primordial catastrophe thus: "death through Eve, life through Mary."[107]

Eve certainly did her part in the fall of mankind from grace: the first sin was hers. But special shame should be reserved for Adam, the very first derelict head of household in a long line of such men through human history. Instead of lovingly protecting his wife from the fulsome dangers of the garden, he allowed her exposure, dialogue, and collusion against God. What's more, he allowed a gender-bending encroachment by Eve on his God-given role as leader, protector, and household spokesman (much as most modern husbands do!).

This is no biased characterization. In fact, the feminists themselves usually give scriptural Adam and Eve a more honest interpretation than modern Christians themselves. Whereas Christians today are eager to bring all parties within the fold and

[107] St. Jerome, *Epist.* 22, 21; *PL* 22, 408.

palliate them, feminists have eagerly agreed that Eve's rebellion and Adam's dereliction comprised something like proto-feminism (applauding it, of course, rather than lamenting it). This facilitates the task at hand—showing why the later attempt at "Christian feminism" went irredeemably and necessarily awry.

According to Katie Scott-Marshall at the *Dangerous Women Project*, Eve's shameful historical characterization within Christendom was unfair yet undeniable: "Eve became known as the source of Original Sin, responsible for the fall of mankind, and she became a blueprint figure for all subsequent women; the reason for their menstrual suffering, their pains during labour, and a cautionary tale as to why they should submit to their husbands."[108] Scott-Marshall continues, exhorting that "the prevalence of Judeo-Christian discourse in western culture has meant that the story of Adam and Eve has been enduring."[109]

Indeed, the feminist fixation with Eve has also been enduring. Her role proves uncomfortable yet fascinating for the feminists.

Like most feminists, Scott-Marshall imagines that this warrants a full frontal assault on perennial Christian teaching regarding sexual relations: "The Bible declares that Eve was made from the rib of Adam, to be his 'helper,' and so she is often cited by traditionalists as evidence of God's intentions for gender complementarianism, rather than full gender equality in terms of shared tasks and responsibilities."

Scott-Marshall seems to understand the definition of Christian sexual complementarity only too well, characterizing more

---

[108] Katie Scott-Marshall, "The Enduring Legacy of the Original Dangerous Woman," *Dangerous Woman Project*, October 9, 2016, https://dangerouswomenproject.org/2016/10/09/eve-dangerous -woman/.

[109] Ibid.

accurately than many Christian apologists the unequal appor-
tionment of authority it invokes. She rightly understands that
complementarity poses a direct fundamental threat to the feminist
project: "complementarianism, the idea that men and women
were created 'equal but different,' and intended to take on different roles has been hotly disputed by feminists, theologians and
scholars alike." Complementarity, Scott-Marshall understands, is
the opposite of egalitarianism because it expresses sexual equality
only *in dignity* and nothing else.

As her article's title clearly indicates, Scott-Marshall applauds
Eve's defiance of her husband and her rejection of God. Like a
rebellious teen, she laments not Eve's disobedience but, rather,
her punishment. Scott-Marshall and the feminists bemoan only
the fact that Eve *got caught.*

In fact, like many feminists, Scott-Marshall goes further and
prefers not Eve but Adam's apocryphal first wife, "Lilith," who
commits the crime without doing the time:

> In the Jewish book *The Alphabet of Ben-Sira,* an anony-
> mous medieval text, Eve is Adam's second wife, and his
> first is a woman named Lilith. Lilith refuses to sleep with
> or to submit to Adam, and when he attempts to coerce her
> into an inferior position, she voluntarily leaves Eden and
> engages in sexual relations with demons. God sends angels
> to her, who threaten to kill her new demonic offspring un-
> less she returns to Adam. She refuses, and so God makes
> a second wife for Adam, Eve. Although this version is
> not commonly known, it is fascinating in its depiction
> of Lilith, a fictional female figure who not only defies
> patriarchal order but also manages to evade the same pun-
> ishment as Eve. Lilith's rejection of complementarianism

and Eve's sentencing to a life of being "ruled over" by her husband are still struggles that carry enormous relevance for modern day women, where women still take up the majority of caring roles and are often assumed to be primarily responsible for child-rearing.

As this passage amply shows, feminism enthusiastically applauds the anti-patriarchal (even demonic) defiance by Lilith. According to the explicit articulation of the feminist account, Lilith defies not only Adam but, more importantly, the order of nature and God. What's still more laudable to feminists, Lilith does so while escaping punishment, unlike Eve. Scott-Marshall concedes that "it might seem somewhat strange to be appreciative or even in admiration of Eve [or Lilith], given that patriarchal religious traditions so often cite [Eve] as the sole cause of all women's woes and encourage us to blame her for them." But admiration is a badly kept secret. Moreover, Scott-Marshall barely tries.

Eve's semi-defiance and Lilith's open rebellion were too important to feminism to be condemned, according to Scott-Marshall: "Eve, and perhaps even more so the figure of the lesser-known Lilith, are hugely significant in the patriarchy's configuration of women as a threat in the first place. These are not women who submitted to their husband, or even to God. The enduring legacy of Eve is not that of original sin as we would be led to believe, but of the original dangerous woman."

Tempting as it may be to trivialize the mostly apocryphal nature of the story of Lilith, Christians should not relegate it to total obscurity. Lilith, sometimes called Lamia, makes an unexplained appearance in the book of Isaiah, if nowhere else in the Christian Bible. Moreover, it would be silly to assume on the basis of Lilith's near-extraneity with regard to the Christian tradition that the popular culture has not taken notice of her, especially feminism.

Indeed it has. Think of Sarah McLachlan's annual feminist Lilith Fair music festival. In the 1990s, McLachlan started the tour, knowingly deriving its name from the "biblical Jewish lore that Lilith was Adam's first wife."[110] Also, consider the Lilith Fund, which "supports the right of all Texans to make their own reproductive choices regardless of income."[111] Also, recall Frasier Crane's defiant, feminist, man-hating ex-wife Lilith, on two of the most popular sitcoms of all time, *Cheers* and *Frasier*. The name and the concept of Lilith have scarcely escaped the notice of Hollywood writers.

If the reader still doubts the importance to feminists of the inhabitants of Eden, consider the recent Netflix serialization of the children's books *A Series of Unfortunate Events*, which, like the majority of other entertainment media, is fraught with specifically anti-Christian feminism. Feminism (and genderism) is conceptualized by the series as the antithesis of the Christian worldview, once again packaged as a celebration of Original Sin: the resolution to the three-season series involves a "brave" serpent who gives a life-saving apple to Violet, the young feminist leader of the siblings, who then offers it to her brother, Klaus.[112]

---

[110] "Lilith Fair," Wikipedia, lasted edited June 8, 2021, https://en.m.wikipedia.org/wiki/Lilith_Fair.

[111] Lilith Fund website, Lilithfund.org.

[112] Mark Hudis and Barry Sonnenfeld, *A Series of Unfortunate Events*, season 3, episode 7, "The End," January 1, 2019. The final episode, naturally, lionizes gays and transgenders and even expresses the following brainwash to its children-centered audience: "All decent people acknowledge" the validity of the LGBT movement.

The Case for Patriarchy

Until very recently, almost all feminists casually observed the fact of the adversarial relation between feminism and the Christian interpretation of Genesis. In an infamous op-ed for the *Washington Post*, writer Pamela Milne wrote: "The story of Eve in the book of Genesis has had a more profoundly negative impact on women throughout history than any other Biblical story. For at least 2,000 years it has been interpreted in patriarchal and even misogynist ways by male Biblical scholars and theologians."[113]

Considering that the apostolic tradition requires fundamental alignment between modern and original scriptural interpretation, Pamela Milne acknowledges that what is to feminism "patriarchal" or "misogynist" is but a nonnegotiable axiom for Christians—which, in a sense, it is.

But Milne understands that Genesis and its first Christian interpreters would never dream of applauding Eve's defiance: "Early Christian writers depicted Eve as subordinate and inferior to Adam—because she was created after and from him—and as weak, seductive and evil, the cause of Adam's disobedience," she writes. "Not only was Eve regarded as 'the mother of all living things'," but "she was also held up as the paradigm for the evil inherent in all women."

"These concepts formed the basis for later deprecatory patriarchal Christian theologies of woman," Milne concludes.

For most feminists, the *brand* of Christianity at issue failed to matter. Christian "misogyny" was not just a Catholic thing, after all. Protestantism initially brought no more feminist-friendly interpretations of the Bible than Catholicism. Milne makes this

[113] Pamela Milne, "Genesis from Eve's Point of View," *Washington Post*, March 26, 1989.

clear: "The themes of [female] inferiority, evil and seductiveness continued to be emphasized in the writings of Luther, Calvin and Knox, and remain disturbingly prominent in the 20th century in places as diverse as papal encyclicals and TV fundamentalist preaching." (Aside from her choice of adjectives, Milne is exactly correct.) All this forces her to conclude about Christianity that its "consequences for women of our day can be devastating."

Consider this key paragraph in Milne's op-ed regarding the compatibility of biblical teaching and feminist belief, which nearly proves the entire thesis of this book single-handedly:

> Until quite recently the traditional interpretation of Genesis 2–3 went virtually unchallenged. But now many women find such patriarchal and misogynist views unacceptable. Some choose to reject both the interpretations and the biblical account itself. Others believe that the Eve story can be recovered from patriarchy through feminist analysis and interpretation. Theirs has been a long — and so far generally unsuccessful — effort.[114]

Tell that to the Christian feminists of our day, please, Ms. Milne!

In every other sense, however, Milne is wrong. The point here is simultaneously to highlight the *recentness* of any attempt at outright "Christian feminism" and the *ancientness* of Genesis's potential for feminist perversion in this direction. Disregard whether feminism is fundamentally incompatible with Christianity, or merely incommensurate with nineteen centuries of pre-feminist Christian teachings (which appears to be a distinction without a difference). The point — ceded by feminists such as Milne — remains that Genesis 2 and 3 preclude all but the most desperate

[114] Ibid.

attempts (first witnessed after nineteen Christian centuries) to reconcile Genesis with feminist principles. [115]

The takeaway principle can hardly be missed: feminists' readings of Genesis 2 have almost always agreed with us as to the incompatibility of Scripture and feminism. They've also almost always agreed that Eve had some of the revolutionary qualities of a pre-feminist. Even when feminists venture to disagree with the affirmative characterization of Adam and Eve's pre-Fall complementarity, it has usually only been in order to suggest, laughably, that Eve didn't go *far enough* in her subversion—as Lilith did—or, more insanely, that the Bible itself was holding out Eve's behavior as exemplary. As far as anyone except the "Christian feminist" is concerned, both of these claims may be dismissed out of hand.

The Enlightenment's Elimination of Categories

Millennia after Genesis was written but centuries before "male" and "female" could be completely eliminated in the popular mind, natural categories such as "masculine" and "feminine" needed to be expunged. Only then could feminism thrive.

Before a woman could fool society's many dupes into thinking that she should sometimes *act like* or even *be* a man—mimicking and exaggerating the inchoate role swapping of Adam and Eve—it had to be widely believed that the characteristics pertaining to nature's categories such as *masculinity* and *femininity* were fungible. This would be inaugurated by a degradation of Catholic philosophy in the late Middle Ages, leading to the

---

[115] This is evident within the tendentious writings of feminists treating of Christianity, such as Elizabeth Cady Stanton and Phyllis Trible.

time period known as the early Enlightenment during the early modern period. Insofar as it repudiates the categories of things God inscribed into creation, this set of errors belies not only feminism but all the recent strains of ideological subversion: relativism, voluntarism, fideism, secularism, modernism, Marxism, and so on.

In this section, we will very briefly describe this group of errors, collectively here called nominalism.[116] Shortly, we will explore how nominalism provided feminism a faulty but convincing basis for vilifying those who maintain that it is natural for a man to act *manly* or a woman to act *womanly*. But first, let's examine a few examples of the symptomatic depth of feminism's repudiation of categories, which proves both counterintuitive and counterfactual when measured against commonsense conclusions taken from several of the sciences.

Feminism, of course, rejects human history's unmistakable teaching that femininity and masculinity involve natural calls to differing virtues (which I will examine in chapter 4). Currently, feminists and transgenderists effectuate this rejection through the mechanism of "virtue signaling," as well as its inverse, "sex shaming," which together serve to ostracize and condemn all who maintain the natural oppositeness of male and female properties.[117]

---

[116] Nominalism is a complex philosophy in its own right. To do the worldview justice, it would require lengthy tomes on its inception alone (which have been written!). It is here treated only as one of the undeniable headwaters of feminism. Thus, we describe merely its most basic aspects, especially those relevant to feminism.

[117] All this produces a muddled feminist point of view on transgenderism, since feminists bemoan the appropriation by transsexuals

The Case for Patriarchy

Consider the *Encyclopedia of Feminism*, wherein Lisa Tuttle condemns femininity as "the socially determined expression of what are considered to be innately female attributes, virtues and deficiencies, as displayed through costume, speech, posture, behavior, bodily adornments and attitude."[118] In other words, she expresses the feminist absurdity that feminine qualities are just a synthetic and not a natural article of female self-expression. Tuttle continues by presuming what she sets out to prove, writing that "although it is presumed to have a biological basis, the fact that femininity is imposed rather than natural is obvious by the way that young women must be taught how to behave, and are punished if they fail to appear properly feminine."[119]

To an astute reader, this does not turn out to be so "obvious" at all. In fact, it is absurd.

Every indication in the field of neuroscience suggests that the difference between the human sexes accrues to nature in the first place, not to nurture. Even fetal brain researchers such as Dr. Leonard Sax — card-carrying members of the medical

of properties of females, but draw upon the same nominalism that transsexuals do in order to defend their position. Tuttle (a feminist!) writes on page 325–326 of *The Encyclopedia of Feminism*: "Transsexualism has also been called 'gender dysphoria.' Most transsexuals would describe their problem in terms similar to 'a female mind trapped in a male body.' Because it detaches gender from biology yet reinforces the importance of sexual stereotypes, the concept of transsexualism is a contradiction which raises and disturbs many of the questions feminists have been asking about differences between the sexes and what they mean. It is a subject which makes most feminists uneasy." In short, we see a feminist schizophrenia regarding transgenderism, especially today.

[118] Tuttle, *Encyclopedia of Feminism*, 106.
[119] Ibid.

establishment, which has often capitulated to the feminist lobby—have confirmed that before babies even "enter" a given culture, they already bear strong neurobiological inclinations based exclusively on their sex:

> Individual genes are transcribed in the human brain from the prenatal period through infancy, childhood, adolescence, and throughout adulthood. They found that the biggest female/male difference in gene transcription in the human brain, for many genes, is in the prenatal period.... Again, I have not yet found an advocate of the Butler/Fine school [feminist view of cultural heteronormativity] who is even aware of this research, let alone responded to it. If the Butler/Fine theory was correct—if gendered differences in brain and behavior are primarily a social construct, and not hardwired—then we ought to see zero differences between the female brain and the male brain in the prenatal period, but large differences between adults, who after all have had the misfortune of living all their lives in a heteronormative patriarchy. But the reality is just the opposite: Female/male differences are generally largest in the prenatal period, and those differences diminish with age, often dwindling to zero among adults.[120]

In other words, prenatal neurobiology shows the precise *opposite* of the feminist claims about the effects of heteronormative culture. It shows that the culturally conditioned brain in our day

---

[120] Leonard Sax, M.D., Ph.D., "A New Study Blows Up Old Ideas about Girls and Boys" *Psychology Today*, March 27, 2019, https://www.psychologytoday.com/ca/blog/sax-sex/201903/new-study-blows-old-ideas-about-girls-and-boys.

inclines toward androgyny rather than male- or female-governed behaviorism. Dr. Sax points out another, even more convincing neurological study, to the same effect:

> Now we have another, even more striking study of the human brain prior to birth. In this study, American researchers managed to do MRI scans of pregnant mothers in the second and third trimesters, with sufficient resolution to image the brains of the babies inside the uterus. They found dramatic differences between female and male fetuses. For example, female fetuses demonstrated significant changes in connectivity between subcortical and cortical structures in the brain, as a function of gestational age. This pattern "was almost completely non-existent in male fetuses." They note that others have found, for example, that female infants have significantly greater brain volume in the prefrontal cortex compared with males. They conclude that "It seems likely that these volumetric differences [found after birth] are mirrored by [the] differences observed in the present study.[121]

Outside of neuroscience and back in the realm of social science, even the waffling Harvey C. Mansfield counters feminism's rejection of objective categories in the domain of male and female behavior:

> The evidence the social scientists compile on the differences between the sexes is useful for refuting those [like Tuttle!] who deny sex differences or regard them as easily changed, and there is fascination in being shown small but

---

[121] Ibid.

significant differences in the ways that men and women do the same things in daily life. These differences are observable by anyone who cares to look and available in the stereotypes of common sense, but it is reassuring to see science catch up with truth and confirm in interesting ways what we already know.[122]

Well said, Mr. Mansfield! As shown by the Harvard professor, Tuttle's nominalistic criticism of the rearing of young females abjectly fails to capture and describe human nature. Together, the natural and social sciences decry this failure in feminism's reasoning.

Most importantly, the ethical science also confirms the failure of feminists to support their claim that heteronormativity accrues to nurture rather than nature. Aristotle taught over two millennia ago that human predispositions toward virtue operate hand in hand with virtue-instruction, not against it. This is an article of common sense, anyway. Nature goes together with nurture, a basic fact of human life which turns out to be the animating principle behind all forms of education (not just education in how to be manly or womanly).

Aristotle teaches that nature confers upon humanity the capacity for virtue, but that any given virtue must be developed by both instruction and habit.[123] In other words, the *potential* for virtue comes from nature, while the *actualization* of that virtue comes from good instruction and good habit; most people think of these latter as the two components of education.

So, in the *Encyclopedia of Feminism*, Tuttle rejects not only "gender roles" but the possibility of all virtue — indeed, all

---

[122] Mansfield, *Manliness*, x.
[123] Aristotle, *Nicomachean Ethics* 2.

pedagogy—because she suspects that human nature cannot simultaneously be predisposed and coached in a certain action. Piano lessons, for example, violate her nominalistic credo—and feminism's. If they are internally consistent, then feminists must suspect that human beings are not naturally "musical" since piano teachers impose regimens of strict formation on the musical habits of piano students. The rigorous program of instruction such teachers impose render it "obvious," as misconceived by Tuttle, that imposed habit-formation within students is nonnatural. "If you have to teach it, then the student should never bother knowing it," she seems to reason.

By the same token, Tuttle also must then deny that certain students are more gifted than others (and accordingly that piano skill comes more naturally to those who are more gifted). Ask any piano teacher: this is an absurd view of instruction.

So more clearly now, the reader sees why we must examine the basis by which all natural categories—up to and including masculinity and femininity—began to be doubted in the modern world: nominalism. According to the *Catholic Encyclopedia*, nominalism "denies the existence of abstract and universal concepts, and refuses to admit that the intellect has the power of engendering them."[124] For the nominalists, "what are called general ideas are [at most] only names, mere verbal designations, serving as labels for a collection of things or a series of particular events."[125]

---

[124] Maurice de Wulf, "Nominalism, Realism, Conceptualism," *Catholic Encyclopedia*, vol. 2 (New York: Robert Appleton Company, 1911), NewAdvent, http://www.newadvent.org/cathen/11090c.htm.

[125] Ibid. When the movement was brand new in the late medieval period, its earliest adherents were Catholics William of Ockham

At most, the nominalists see a category as a made-up designation in the human mind, with little or no objective connection to nature. History's leading nominalist, William of Ockham, wrote: "I maintain that a universal is not something real that exists in a subject ... but that it has a being only as a thought-object in the mind."[126] Peter Abelard attempted a moderate form of nominalism called "conceptualism," which "admits the existence within us of abstract and universal concepts, but it holds that we do not know whether or not the mental objects have any foundation outside our minds."

Within a couple of centuries, Martin Luther would take Ockham's razor to an even more extreme level with the Protestant Reformation. Luther's loyal devotee Melanchthon wrote that Luther "applied closely to the writings of Ockham, the acumen of which author, he preferred to Thomas and Scotus."[127] From 1501 until 1511, Luther studied and worked at the University of Erfurt, a hub of nominalist professors which he considered his "spiritual home."[128] Accordingly, strong traces of nominalism may

---

and Peter Abelard, who, to varying degrees, rejected all categories not logically necessary for explanations involving natural phenomena. In other words, with nominalism the world came to doubt that when we observe plants and animals in nature, the categories "plant" and "animal" designated by our words for them actually exist *out there*.

[126] James M. Ziccardi, *Medieval Philosophy: A Practical Guide to William of Ockham* (Bloomington, IN: Booktango Publishers, 2013).

[127] Philip Melanchthon, *The Life and Acts of Martin Luther* (Malone, TX: Repristination Press, 1997).

[128] "Herzlich willkommen in der Blumenstadt Erfurt!," accessed January 6, 2020, Erfurt, https://www.erfurt-tourismus.de/all-about-erfurt/main-topics/luther-and-the-reformation/?=1.

be found in all his foremost theological teachings, such as *sola fide*, *sola scriptura*, and the bondage of the human will.

Applied to the will of God and to the order of creation, nominalism led directly to the Protestant view of a creation whose categories could not be intelligible to mankind: *nature nor God discloses such categories for human beings to discern.* (It is also why, for Protestants, Scripture really was the only instrument at human disposal that affords an intelligible view of the world.)

In sum, what all this means is that, even more than it was an attack on the Church, Luther's Reformation comprised an even sharper uptick in the rigor of Europe's popular abandonment of the belief of natural categories. Of course, in the sixteenth century, the elimination of categories was primarily directed against the Church. But this emphasis would change in the seventeenth and eighteenth centuries, bringing the tip of the spear closer to the culture of feminism. Since the concept had already been popularized that nature discloses no categories whatsoever, the false notion had potently armed the subsequent "first wave" feminists who wanted to fundamentally alter humanity's view of the two sexes.

After nominalism grew into mainstream philosophy, virtually all modernist thinkers dismissed Thomas Aquinas's "moderate realism," which accurately posited that concepts and words bore some objective relation to the real world. At that point in late medieval history, on the basis of nominalism, the relationship between faith and reason came to be viewed as antithetical. This was the beginning of formal modernism, and all categories' objective existence began to be doubted.

Nominalism, when applied to Christianity in the sixteenth century, destroyed the popular connection between faith and reason (in the form of Protestantism). When applied to moral categories in the eighteenth century, nominalism destroyed the popular belief in objectivity (and thereby created early relativism). When applied to the categories of "male" and "female" in the nineteenth century—combining as it did with long-standing preternatural human flaws such as those of Eve and Lilith—nominalism created first-wave feminism. Feminism picked up speed quickly from there.

Fast-forward to 2021. Everywhere, on commercials, on billboards, and in magazines, we hear or read the nominalistic platitude "Fight like a girl." Consider the fact that this expression preexisted the false supposition that fighting like a girl is somehow a positive thing. In fact, the analogy always meant the precise opposite: obviously, girls are generally very bad at fighting, and so to fight like a girl means to fight badly.

But, contra nature, colluding sloganeers in large companies began in the last decade to use the expression to designate the proposition that, somehow, girls are now good at fighting.

How in the world did this happen? The answer is, of course, this errant view that nature discloses no absolutely true categories for human beings to discern. If the public can be fooled into believing that nature discloses no unchanging categories, after all, then any political lobby can simply outwait previous worldviews more in line with nature's otherwise unyielding scientific demands.

In reality, the biological fact of human female diminutiveness is as unchangeable as that of the anti-aerodynamic interaction of a rock's mass and gravity. But in the middle 1800s, nominalism coalesced with something now termed "first-wave feminism" which would enable that expression surreptitiously to reverse meaning roughly 160 years later.

First-Wave Feminism

As we enter into treatment of the historical waves of feminism, a brief explanatory interlude is due. We should observe here the modicum of momentum that the anti-feminism movement has, by now, gained in response to the many catastrophes of late-twentieth-century feminism. Good but unambitious books against it have been written. With the crucial caveat that feminism infiltrated the popular culture and then expunged the term, it remains true that many American[129] and European[130] women have recoiled from the term "feminism" itself: fewer and fewer women seem to identify as feminists, on these accounts. In some conservative quarters, it has even grown almost politically correct to criticize the murderous excesses and furious bacchanals of second- and third-wave feminism.

Yet the insidious, pro-first-wave-feminism narrative obtains, even and especially among right-wingers desperate not to appear reactionary. Plain and simple, conservatives usually laud first-wave feminism. While more of this sort have rejected second-wave feminism in our day than in the seventies and the eighties, still precious few conservatives are willing to reject first-wave feminism, which is tantamount to rejecting the feminist movement writ large. Even one of the foremost "good books" against feminism referred to above proudly dons the cover blurb "A

---

[129] Megan Keller, "Poll: Less Than Half of Female Millennials Identify as Feminist," *Hill*, August 14, 2018, https://thehill.com/business-a-lobbying/401804-poll-less-than-half-of-female-millennials-identify-as-feminists.

[130] Dr. Christina Scharff, "Why So Many Young Women Don't Call Themselves Feminist," BBC News, February 6, 2019, https://www.bbc.com/news/uk-politics-47006912.

powerful prescription for a truly liberating Catholic feminism."[131] (I shall further refer to and borrow from that book below.)

This right-wing support of first-wave feminism is a fatal problem for the elimination of the overall malady, which has clearly infiltrated deep by now.

Support in such unexpected quarters seems to be premised upon the altogether unfounded notion—laboriously generated and popularized by feminists—that first-wave feminism was inarguably and ineluctably salutary: "It gave women the right to vote. That's all," an inquirer will be scolded churlishly. These devil's advocates on the right wing will draw a distinction of kind—a wall of separation—between feminism's first and second waves. Again, this is not a natural presumption but rather the product of an arduous brainwashing campaign by the feminist academy and entertainment media.

The second wave, they insist, is a totally different *kind* of ideology than the first. They insist it is not a more developed or aggressive version of the same movement. The reader should bear this in mind as we examine first-wave feminism.

If it can be demonstrated that first-wave feminism was itself pernicious, germinating all or most of the incipient ideas associated with later feminism—if in nascent form only—then the implication would clearly be that none of feminism's waves were good. And if so, then there is quite a case for the view *no Christian feminism and no good feminism*.

My research on first-wave feminism turned up just such a conclusion. As stated in the *Encyclopedia of Feminism*, feminism's earliest iteration appeared in 1848 at the Seneca Falls

---

[131] Gress, *The Anti-Mary Exposed*, back-cover blurb by George Weigel.

Convention in New York. The work product of this meeting of the world's first declared feminists was the *Declaration of Sentiments and Resolutions*, written by Elizabeth Cady Stanton. When one brackets all the *Declaration*'s bullet points associated with women's enfranchisement and focuses only upon the document's other action items, he comes to see in bold colors the many midnightly purposes of first-wave feminism.

When considering Stanton's five points below, also consider that, during the mid-late first wave, in 1932, William Z. Foster—head of the American Communist Party—made most of the exact connections between first- and second-wave feminism that I do here (and that Stanton did). While my argument situates feminism within a longer timeline than that which begins with socialism, Soviet communists and American socialists certainly did their part to fast-forward feminism's advance. Foster quotes a feminist Soviet socialist named Anna Razamova in his thematic connections:

> All these institutions for child welfare mean a great deal in the life of the working woman. They free her from the necessity of spending all her time at home, cleaning, cooking, and mending. While she is at work she can be sure that her child is being well taken care of, and that it is supervised by trained nurses and teachers, and gets wholesome food at regular hours.[132]

Then he adds that "the free Russian woman is the trailblazer for the toiling women of the world. She is beating out a path which,

---

[132] William Z. Foster, *Toward Soviet America* (New York: Coward-McCann, 1932), 309.

ere long, her American sister will begin to follow."[133] One sees, between 1848 and 1932, an inchoate but well-defined preview of second-wave feminism. At many times, the themes we associate with second-wave feminism even shine through unsubtly and robustly in the *Declaration*.

The *Declaration* by Elizabeth Cady Stanton bears five points of recognizable overlap with today's feminism; I refer to them below as "points of concern."

The first point of concern for any conservative defender of first-wave feminism is the *Declaration*'s following line item: "The history of mankind is a history of repeated injuries and usurpations on the part of man toward woman, having in direct object the establishment of an absolute tyranny over her."[134] Immediately, one notes the unrestrained nature of the document's criticism

---

[133] On the previous page, Foster writes that "in freeing the woman, socialism liquidates the drudgery of housework. So important do Communists consider this question that the Communist International deals with it in its world program. In the Soviet Union the attack upon housework slavery is delivered from every possible angle. Great factory kitchens are being set up to prepare hot, well-balanced meals for home consumption by the millions; communal kitchens in apartment houses are organized widespread. Every device to simplify and reduce housework is spread among the masses with all possible dispatch. To free the woman from the enslavement of the perpetual care of her children is also a major object of socialism. To this end in the Soviet Union there is being developed the most elaborate system of kindergartens and playgrounds in the world—in the cities and villages, in the neighborhoods and around the factories." Note how important these socialist "developments" prove to be for both first- and second-wave feminism.

[134] Elizabeth Cady Stanton, *A Declaration of Sentiments and Resolutions* (Nashville: American Roots, 2015).

of men, Western civilization, and by implication, Christianity. This is the sweeping, nonspecific language of violent revolution. Because, *inter alia*, the language leading up to this paragraph self-consciously mimics the style and substance of the Declaration of Independence, one clearly infers the revolutionary mien of this passage. But its anti-Christian vitriol conjures images of the French and Russian revolutions rather than the American one. Declarations of this sort, by their character, enumerate injustices worked on victims by tyrants and then eliminate such injustices. The revolutionary document's upshot is that the Christian "patriarchy"—established by the Church as part of her social teachings and her Magisterial history—has much to atone for. And this simply is impossible from a properly Christian position.

What ought to be the second point of concern in *Declaration of Sentiments and Resolutions*, for Christians evaluating first-wave feminism, reads: "In the covenant of marriage, she is compelled to promise obedience to her husband, he becoming, to all intents and purposes, her master—the law giving him power to deprive her of her liberty, and to administer chastisement."[135] Almost as suddenly as the women's franchise seemed to be the document's topic, now Holy Matrimony itself falls under first-wave feminism's knife. The *Declaration* imputes the "power to deprive her of her liberty" specifically to the common law. But clearly much more is hereby insinuated by first-wave feminism's critique, since American law or jurisprudence never enforced wifely obedience, after all. Only the Christian law of Scripture and Tradition does that. Thus, the male householder—the role of man within the complementarian, Christian sacrament of

[135] Ibid.

marriage—must, in these terms, be seen as the culprit and the target of even early feminism.

The concerning third point of the 1848 *Declaration* continues the steep escalation in Stanton's unrestrained revolutionary tone. It complains that man "has monopolized nearly all the profitable employments, and from those [woman] is permitted to follow, she is permitted but a scanty remuneration. He closes against her all the avenues to wealth and distinction which he considers most honorable to himself."[136] So, now, in addition to anticipating subsequent feminism's designs on the eradication of family roles, first-wave feminism also sets male-breadwinning, single-income households in its crosshairs.

Just in case a conservative devil's advocate dismissed the concern in the previous paragraph as a "fluke" in the document of some sort, the current one establishes first-wave feminism's *means* in order to accomplish the eradication of the family: women must be in the workplace. (Someone please explain how this first, nascent iteration of feminism can be distinguished by degree *or* kind from second-wave feminism! Indeed, they barely appear to be distinguishable at all.)

The *Declaration*'s fourth point of concern reads more like an item from third-wave feminism than second, which demonstrates what a narrow spectrum feminism appears to be, when viewed chronologically. It says that man "allows [woman] in Church, as well as state, but a subordinate position, claiming apostolic authority for her exclusion from the ministry, and with some exceptions, from any public participation in the affairs of the Church."[137]

[136] Ibid.
[137] Ibid.

The *Declaration's* word "claiming" betrays entirely the spurious notion of a feminist Christianity. What sort of authentic Christian mocks the authority of the apostles? Moreover, putting forward a female ministry (or a female-headed household or a female-breadwinner household) requires an *in toto* expulsion of the disciplinary norms of traditional Christianity from feminist ranks. Feminism, then, chooses an aggressively and nakedly anti-Christian posture as far back as 1848, with basically all parties acknowledging it—except, of course, those "Christian feminists."

Finally, the fifth point of concern in the *Declaration* most explicitly squints at second-wave feminism's moral and sexual emphasis: Man "has created a false public sentiment by giving to the world a different code of morals for men and women, by which moral delinquencies which exclude women from society, are not only tolerated, but deemed of little account in man."[138]

And there it is: even as far back as 1848, the moral and sexual concupiscence of males is enshrined and made exemplary for females. Never let anyone—neither conservatives like Gress nor liberals like Milne—tell you that first-wave feminism wasn't about increasing female sexual vice. As will be discussed later in this book, there exists a complex balance of divergence and convergence between male virtue and female virtue that becomes a system of "patriarchal virtue." Those patriarchal virtues are artlessly handled here in the 1848 *Declaration*. At any rate, the mainstream narrative—upheld by conservatives and liberals alike—regarding the supposedly benign and even admirable aims of first-wave feminism are hereby left in a smoldering ruin.

More importantly, the document's connection to second-wave feminism has been firmly established by the mere enumeration of

---

[138] Ibid.

the non-franchise-related clauses of 1848's *Declaration of Sentiments and Resolutions*. As promised above, my analysis sidestepped all the usual hagiographic trappings of first-wave feminism scholarship, a veritable echo chamber of false talking points and details that prove unnecessary in view of the *Declaration*, which leads quite linearly to second-wave feminism.

Second-Wave Feminism

According to most popular accounts,[139] the "women's liberation movement" or second-wave feminism[140] of the late 1960s centered presumptively new women's aims upon more than just voting. Yet, seen above, in five specific points of concern, first-wave feminism was *already about more than just enfranchisement*—much more. In this section, I will evidence my claim that second-wave feminism literally added nothing new to the first wave.

In order to show the connection between first- and second-wave feminism, I begin my analysis of the latter by recounting a passage appearing within one of those good but incomplete books written by conservative scholars critiquing the "toxic femininity"[141] of so-called *radical* feminism (but self-consciously

---

[139] Tuttle, *The Encyclopedia of Feminism*, 359.

[140] Martha Weinman Lear, "The Second Feminist Wave," *New York Times*, March 10, 1968, https://www.nytimes.com/1968/03/10/archives/the-second-feminist-wave.html. Lear is here credited as having coined the term.

[141] Gress, *The Anti-Mary Exposed*, 10. Gress efficiently dismantles much about second-wave feminism, but at times puzzles the reader by tacitly endorsing its greatest prize, equality (as she does further down on the same page): "Women have always desired equality … but our current culture isn't seeking it through the grace of Mary." She lists respect as the other desideratum women should seek through Mary, which is appropriate. But Mary did not seek

excluding almost all critical mention of feminism before the second wave).[142] In Dr. Carrie Gress's introductory chapter to *The Anti-Mary Exposed*, she recounts the following dialogue, furnished by ex-feminist Mallory Millett (which we've already once referenced, *supra*) from a feminist roundtable meeting in New York City in the early 1970s:[143]

"Why are we here today?" the chairwoman asked.

"To make revolution," they answered.

"What kind of revolution?" she replied.

"The cultural revolution," they chanted.

"And how do we make cultural revolution?" she demanded.

"By destroying the American family!" they answered.

"How do we destroy the family?" she came back.

"By destroying the American Patriarch," they cried exuberantly.

---

political equality with her husband, Joseph, except in the sense of dignity alone. One detects no small amount of ambivalence in Gress's approach to women's virtues. It is fitting that on the same page, when listing these, Gress leaves out the crucial female virtue "humble obedience" from her list, even though she complained earlier on the same page that second-wave feminists "would rage against the idea of anything resembling humble obedience."

[142] To be fair, Gress writes that "the 1950's were no idyllic Camelot; they were simply the initial consequences of the great wars and the radical social upheaval and destruction they caused. This incubator of radical feminism is hardly a time to be coveted" (page 67). But Gress drastically underemphasizes the role of first-wave feminism.

[143] Mallory Millett, "Marxist Feminism's Ruined Lives," *FrontPage Mag*, September 1, 2014, https://archives.frontpagemag.com/fpm/marxist-feminisms-ruined-lives-mallory-millett/.

"And how do we destroy the American Patriarch?"
she probed.

"By taking away his power!"

"How do we do that?"

"By destroying monogamy!" they shouted.

"To make revolution": Firstly, the second wave's (New York City, 1970s) goal of "making revolution" squares directly with the first wave's (Seneca Falls, 1848) goal of forcibly eliminating the "repeated injuries and usurpations" constituting "absolute tyranny" by men over women. It is the language of top-down Jacobin-styled French Revolution, rather than the highly restrained American Revolution, whose language it borrowed.

"The cultural revolution": Secondly, the idea of a "cultural revolution" (New York City, 1970s) clearly involves the diminution and subversion of traditional family roles. Family is the seat of genuine culture. The women in the New York City boardroom clearly intended to perform that subversion. Back in 1848, upstate New York at Seneca Falls, it had been articulated by the feminists that working such a change in the social fabric of the West would require the dissolving of the "promise [of wifely] obedience to her husband." If obedience were to go, then the family itself would have to be altered or abolished, requiring the elimination of the family hierarchy.

"Destroying the American family": Outside of countries operating under forcibly socialist regimes — which are admittedly more convenient for the anti-religious tyrannies of feminism — the female citizens are not usually so ready to meet revolutionary muster by betraying their husbands. And so, in free societies such as ours, if feminism is to thrive, then women must be economically incentivized to disobey, to remain out of the home,

away from their children, and to make independent fortunes for themselves off the abandonment of rearing of their children. This is best accomplished by enticing women into the workforce—as the Seneca Falls feminists knew as early as 1848.

"Destroying the American Patriarch": Interestingly, the fourth moment of the 1970s uprising involves hailing the destruction of the patriarchy, a term that includes not only the extirpation of the household husband and father—the priest of the domestic church—but, by implication, the dominion of parish priests as well. As interestingly, the reader is no longer surprised to find this theme more explicitly developed in the first wave of 1848 and the second wave of the 1970s. Indeed, this contradicts everything we've ever been told about the relation borne between first- and second-wave feminism. With the words, "by destroying the American Patriarch," the concept of feminist anti-religiosity becomes fixed.

"Destroying monogamy": Finally, this fifth moment of second-wave feminism most aptly characterizes the primary part of the popular conception of the women's liberation movement. The destruction of monogamy stands as the most visible aspect of feminism's second wave. Feminists of this era prescribed the destruction of sexual virtue as the best means of "equalizing" whatever disparity they observed in the male and female sexual predispositions. But like each of the previous moments of second-wave feminism, this final one was anything but unprecedented. It was prefigured. In Elizabeth Cady Stanton's *Declaration* from 1848, she clearly anticipates the selfsame solution to the ethical disparity caused by a "different code of morals for men and women, by which moral delinquencies" were supposedly condemned in women but overlooked in men. This feminist "solution" (a term here to be used sparingly) to the alleged ethical

disparity had not changed much between 1848 and the early 1970s.

All in all, one finds a striking similarity—approaching perfect identity—between the first and second waves of feminism. It is high time that critics of feminism begin telling this truth about the connection between the first and second waves, which almost single-handedly proves the thesis that there is no salutary feminism.

Third- and Fourth-Wave Feminism and the Moon-Beesly Complex

Some popular anti-feminist memes have summarized feminism's historical developments thus: *First-wave: we want to be equal to men. Second-wave: we don't need men. Third-wave: we are men.* The problem with this pithy characterization is a mathematical one: being "equal to" a man and "being" a man are the same thing. The meme's language camouflages its hidden, unrealized assertion: aside from the three waves' respective degrees of popular success, almost no substantive development in the waves has occurred at all!

At any rate, nobody seems quite sure how to characterize third-wave feminism, aside from the affirmative trait that it occurred later in time than the second wave.

We've seen how the popular account of feminism purposely mischaracterized the close connection between the first and second waves as discontinuous. Progressives view these first two waves as inchoate, underdeveloped feminism. "Conservative feminists," meanwhile, see the first wave as a nobler and purer form of feminism that bears no obvious relationship with the second and third waves. Both are wrong.

Feminists regularly advertise that "third-wave feminism began in the early 1990s, responding to perceived failures of the second wave."[144] It's a distinction of degree, which is really all the concept of *waves* insinuates in the first place.[145] Of this distinction, feminists usually can be heard saying incredibly banal, self-evident things like: "the third wave ... refers to a continuation of, and a reaction to, second-wave feminism."[146]

Other times you'll hear that third-wave feminism develops the second wave by enhancing the emphasis on race and socioeconomics — specifically through the narrative form now in vogue.

Clearly, the real shift between the second and third wave seems to be a tonal one, not one of substance. As toxic as the rhetoric of the second wave seemed to be, the flavor that trickled down to popular representations of it turned out rather tongue-in-cheek, if obnoxious and sexually licentious: *anything you can do, I can do better*. One may consider this cheeky, but not quite a satisfaction of the promise of an open declaration of war on men by women. By contrast, the third wave openly encourages more acrimony between wives and their husbands. The third wave seems, for lack of a better term, the most bitter.

Here's a vastly more interesting and informative way to characterize the third wave. I call it the "Daphne Moon–Pam Beesly Complex." Daphne and Pam are the female lead characters on

---

[144] Sally Ann Drucker, "Betty Friedan: The Three Waves of Feminism," Ohio Humanities, April 27, 2018, http://www.ohiohumanities.org/betty-friedan-the-three-waves-of-feminism/.

[145] Linda Nicholson, "Feminism in Waves: Useful Idea or Not?" *New Politics* 12, no. 4 (Winter 2010), https://newpol.org/issue_post/feminism-waves-useful-metaphor-or-not/. The "waves" of feminism have been helpful in one area: obscuring the general idea of the attack on the patriarchy, and its origin in the 1848 Declaration.

[146] Ibid.

two of the most successful sitcoms in television history: *Frasier* and *The Office*, respectively. The Moon-Beesly Complex seems to "take the pulse" of cultural third-wave feminism accurately and historically, especially because Daphne's inception on *Frasier* dates to the very year in which some claim the third-wave began, 1993.

Consider the striking likenesses between the "personal narratives" of Daphne and Pam, likenesses that remain strong through three distinct phases of each character's life: pre-courtship, courtship, and marriage. The arc of each series shows a feminist devolution in the respective character's personality; the devolution is a temperamental one whereby Daphne and Pam become markedly less effeminate and clearly more combative.

Pre-courtship: Both characters, while single, work menial indoor jobs traditionally reserved for unmarried women: Daphne is a glorified live-in housemaid (for twenty daily minutes she acts as a physical therapist), and Pam is a receptionist. While single, both Daphne and Pam have demure, amicable, unassuming, classically effeminate personalities. While single, both Daphne and Pam habitually defer to the judgment of their eventual husbands, Niles and Jim (who are merely close friends of the women at that stage); they do so willingly, in good cheer, and in good faith. Both characters have fiancés other than their eventual husbands with whom they eventually sever ties in order to be courted by those eventual husbands.

Notwithstanding the feminist setting of the workplace wherein both romances slowly bloom, Daphne's and Pam's romantic friendships with Niles and Jim are premised upon a generally classical Christian conception of man and woman. As such, they are difficult not to cheer for. While single, both Daphne and Pam are usually smiling—especially in the presence of their eventual husbands, who clearly make them happy.

The Case for Patriarchy

After all, even Hollywood's third-wave feminist writers (in the 1990s and early 2000s) were not immune to the cinematic allure of true romance. As such, true romance necessarily involves complementarity, a natural power differential favoring the man, female dependence and protectedness, male leadership and protection, and so on. For as long as each lasted, the romantic, seasons-long development of the Daphne-Niles and Pam-Jim romances captivated the audiences of both series as the primary feature of each show. But after both fictional couples finally came together, the writers of each series seemed to have felt they exhausted their capacity — or the audience's patience — for pre-modern man-woman complementarity. In other words, both shows benefitted from the classical qualities of romance during the pre-courtship period of flirtation.

Then, after the real courtship had begun, Daphne and Pam's temperaments begin notably to change for the worse. The speed and duration of the change varies with each character, but the phenomenon is unmistakable.

Courtship: By the time of their engagement, Daphne and Pam have each mandated professional promotions, or at least enhancements in their employment status that are nakedly motivated by cinematic "equality" with their new boyfriends/fiancés. For a time, Pam even becomes a salesman like Jim, while Daphne's housemaid role is deliberately underemphasized once Niles begins courting her. Her role as a "health-care worker" (which was marginal in the earlier seasons, and almost a gag in itself) is played up. Both series embraced romantic traditionalism in the realm of male-female inequality before a courtship began, but not after.

The "mood" of each couple also changes drastically sometime during the beginning of the courtship. Feminism requires this change. By the time of their engagement, both Daphne and Pam have offered to shack up with Niles and Jim, another fixture of feminism. Pam conditions cohabitation upon a marriage proposal; Daphne offers to cohabitate but backs out for an incidental reason.

The writers of both series also express feminist ambivalence about the concept of male-provided housing. In *The Office*, this ambivalence appears especially stark: Pam initially celebrates enthusiastically after Jim buys her a home, but in later seasons, she chides him for having elected a unilateral financial decision. In *Frasier*, Daphne temporarily backs out of her promised cohabitation with Niles, not because it is immoral but, rather, because she feels it would expose her to undue woman-shaming from her mother (whom Niles exclusively supports and houses, strangely enough). The long and short of it is that Daphne and Pam have each, by the brief term of their engagement, inculcated a novel yet distinct anti-gratefulness clearly related to the sexual dynamics circumscribed by breadwinning.

Marriage: In marriage, the burgeoning ungratefulness of Daphne and Pam turns quickly to voluble resentment. The most common facial expression worn by both female leads is, by this point in the series, a grimace — especially when in the presence of their husbands, Niles and Jim, who each clearly make them unhappy most of the time. Both female characters also rule their husbands with an iron fist, while the men cower from their wives in most episodes. Both married couples present an uncomfortable, querulous milieu.

Virtually any *Frasier* or *Office* episode centering on the married couple (which is rare at this late point in each series, as the show's producers seem to assume no one wants to view a show on marriage) is a narrative in the cycle formed by husbandly idiocy followed by a groveling apology. Jim and Niles, once attractive, professionally proficient, witty, and urbane in the eyes of their eventual wives, have become doddering, incompetent, dishonest, sneaky eunuchs in marriage. Daphne and Pam were once diminutive, prudent, docile, pretty, heedful, and sweet; both of them close their respective series menacingly, frowningly, hardened, shrill, and bitter. It's an utter shame.

In conclusion, what's unexpected in this "Moon-Beesly" portrait of third-wave feminism is the counterintuitive *recession* — in chronological relation to second-wave feminism — in aggression by females against men who aren't their spouse or fiancé. (According to the "Moon-Beesly" iteration of third-wave feminism, single women should still be pretty nice to new men they're interested in.) While wives' attitudes regarding husbands certainly worsens and becomes more bellicose, third-wave feminism's single women seem warmly and amicably to regard single men they come to like, in an almost traditional way. That is, in the third wave, prospective boyfriends seem to be treated quite well, even by feminists: apparently, feminists are not immune to the natural human drive to romance, which depends on complementarity and traditional roles.

The increased acrimony of third-wave feminism seems mostly restricted to the marital domain. At any rate, third-wave feminism differs from second-wave insofar as its female operatives (whether wives or all women) more openly express disdain for a chosen class of men (whether husbands or all men), compared with the subtler rebellion insinuated by the second wave.

Just as few have accurately characterized third-wave feminism, the fourth wave is even murkier, although its adherents claim that it furthers the "intersectionality"[147] of the previous wave, usually through digital means.

---

[147] Kristen Sollee, "6 Things to Know about 4th Wave Feminism," *Bustle*, October 30, 2015, https://www.bustle.com/articles/119524 -6-things-to-know-about-4th-wave-feminism.

Conclusion

So, the three waves of feminism establish some of history's starkest "distinction without a difference." As promised in the introductory section to this chapter, the fabrication by feminists of those false distinctions involved three preconditions: a pre-feminist, post-Edenic, gender-bending inclination toward the devil's *non serviam* stemming from Eve's defiant role in Original Sin; an errant Catholic philosophy, nominalism, which proved terribly effective across male-female categories; and sufficient ill will during the rise of mid-nineteenth-century modernism for applying the first two elements in order to attack the family in a tripartite feminist way.

Since first-wave feminism germinated all the deadly properties seen later in the second and third waves, we cannot afford to speak of it as the "original, good feminism." Such a thing does not exist. All feminism attempts to overthrow the patriarchy. In the next chapter, we will see more specifically why this translates to the proposition that there is no "Christian feminism."

Because it might have confused our careful treatment of the pedigree of feminism, we deliberately neglected a single, conspicuous element in the historical development of the neurotoxin: the admonition against Soviet feminism insinuated in Our Lady's cautions against "the errors of Russia" in 1917 at Fatima. In closing, that element is now worth noting.

The "second secret" of Fatima includes the following Marian prescription:

> I shall come to ask for the consecration of Russia to my Immaculate Heart, and the Communion of Reparation on the First Saturdays. If my requests are heeded, Russia will be converted, and there will be peace; if not, *she will spread her errors throughout the world*, causing wars and

persecutions of the Church. The good will be martyred, the Holy Father will have much to suffer, various nations will be annihilated.[148]

In regard to Soviet Russia, the spreader of global error, a word of caution is due. The years of the most aggressive Soviet feminism, from 1917 until 1926, after which time "Stalin initiated a move away from the sexual revolution,"[149] fall in between the typical emplacement of feminism's first and second waves. Should this chapter's treatment have listed within its feminism genealogy the Marxist-Leninist advance of the sexual revolution (which was "first introduced into mass circulation by Grigory Batkis, director of the Moscow Institute for Sexual Hygiene, via his pamphlet *The Sexual Revolution in Russia*"[150]), it might have muddled the conclusion that feminism's waves were not much disparate. Indeed, they are not.

Nonetheless, what took place in popular sexuality in the United States in the 1960s was prefigured in Soviet Russia in the decade beginning in 1917. Accordingly, the sexually charged nature of Soviet feminism seems to be a nonnegligible part of the Fatima message. Starting the same year that Mary appeared at Fatima, "Bureaus of Free Love were established in many Russian towns; *Komsomols* (Communist youth) were placed in [Russian] communes where everyone lived and had sex together; in June

[148] Donna-Marie Copper O'Boyle, "Three Secrets of Fatima Revealed," *Catholic Exchange*, May 11, 2017, https://catholicexchange.com/three-secrets-fatima-revealed.

[149] Grzegorz Gorney and Janusz Rosikon, *Fatima Mysteries* (Warsaw: Rosikon Press, 2016), 152–153.

[150] Ibid., 153.

1918 there was a nudist demonstration in St. Petersburg."[151] This means that, to the extent it is partly differentiable from other waves, a prominent feature of the second wave of feminism can reasonably be seen as one of the foremost "errors of Russia" to which the message of Fatima referred.

When the Virgin warned that Marxism would spread throughout the world, and especially throughout the West, feminism is no doubt what she had in mind. The fact that Soviet feminism sexualized the masses decades prior to the feminist-sexualization of its American adherents only serves to prove that the three "waves" of feminism present a distinction without a real difference: the diabolical spirit of the feminine *non serviam* operates in slightly modified ways at different times and places. Yet its goal is unified.

Although not all feminists are Marxists, and although there exists a substantial share of accidental ideological overlap that accrues to "convergent evolution," it is undeniable that (what is called) Russian second-wave feminism anticipated the American rendition by half a century. And the eventual American iteration took shape in startling ways. The Communists account for this.

This point seems all the more inescapable, considering that Marx and Engels published the *Communist Manifesto* in 1848, the exact same year that Elizabeth Cady Stanton published *A Declaration of Sentiments and Resolutions* in upstate New York. What remains beyond doubt is the fact that the primordial (that is, diabolical), philosophical (that is, nominalist), and accidental (that is, demographically opportunist) forces that produced feminism also coalesced in Marxism, and around the same time. Whether primordial, philosophical, or accidental, these forces

---

[151] Ibid.

came together to wage a highly adaptative attack on the perennial teachings of Christianity about the patriarchy. Now that we have addressed the constitution of the attack, we may proceed to the constitution of the Christian defense: patriarchal virtue.

4

The Patriarchal Virtues

Thus far, I have articulated an overarching cultural annulment, one seeking to undo the unnatural and peculiar claims made by feminism. My chapters to this point have motivated a list of the things that woman *is not, yet is popularly claimed to be*. I've recurred to theology, philosophy, culture, and history in order to substantiate that list. In other places, I have offered mini-histories of the mendacities of feminism in order to refer my readers to the provenance of its midnightly motives.

Anticipating the hypothetical reply by feminists — specifically the "Christian" type — proves difficult and unfruitful. It also proves unnecessary. After all, there is precious little ground, if any, upon which the matter of a "Christian feminism" or even a "natural law feminism" may reasonably be premised. So all defenses of the self-contradictory notion will, by their very nature, be flailing, premised exclusively upon manufactured definitions.

As seen in the previous chapter, the definition of womanhood in our era has been hopelessly (and deliberately) corrupted, with the result that our expectations of women have waxed both tragic and comedic. At the very same historical moment as they have been most defiled and debased, females have been fashioned into an untouchable, sacred class. The simultaneity of these two opposite changes in the popular view of women betrays something diabolical — or at least something with a desperately destructive will.

Even moderates and nonradical liberals have taken notice. Comedian Bill Burr recently joked on a late-night talk show: "Women [have become] overrated; we went from one extreme to the other."[152] While beautiful, true femininity could never possibly be overrated, feminist anti-femininity proffers nothing salutary.

As seen in the first chapters, feminism has popularized the lie that women are good at everything — or, at least, everything masculine. Shortly before our era, even atheists took notice: "The worst, to be sure, is the female coquetting with male mannerisms, with the manners of ill-bred boys,"[153] as Nietzsche once wrote. As the first chapters of this book demonstrated, sometime during the nineteenth century, self-loathing feminists, socialists, and cultural engineers grew bored with the female virtues and began encouraging widespread female aspiration to the male virtues. To the chagrin of Western civilization, they "fixed what wasn't broken" and thereby created a monstrosity.

Moreover, this phenomenon presents the very portrait of *ressentiment*, the French idea of slavishly celebrating a weak thing or concept based upon its vices, then rebranding them in delusion as virtues.[154] Above all else, *ressentiment* fears and envies

---

[152] Bill Burr, interview by Conan O'Brien, *Conan*, TBS, August 23, 2018.

[153] Friedrich Nietzsche, *Twilight of the Idols* (Cambridge, MA: Hackett Publishing, 1997), 81. Even a broken (anti-Christian) clock is right twice daily in the case of Friedrich Nietzsche on the feminists.

[154] Nietzsche, *Twilight of the Idols*, 79: Nietzsche describes female *ressentiment* as "full of petty sullen wrath against all masculine

strength and hierarchical paternalism. Alexis de Tocqueville writes the following of the anti-hierarchical phenomenon in American society:

> It has been supposed that the secret instinct which leads the lower orders to remove their superiors as much as possible from the direction of public affairs is peculiar to France. This is an error, however; the instinct to which I allude is not French, it is democratic; it may have been heightened by peculiar political circumstances, but it owes its origin to a higher cause. In the United States the people do not hate the higher classes of society, but are not favorably inclined towards them and carefully exclude them from the exercise of authority. They do not fear distinguished talents, but are rarely fond of them.[155]

This much can be applied to everything pertaining to the masculine, by the nineteenth- and twentieth-century feminists. *Ressentiment* describes a common feature in all of the postmodern, secular-humanist, "democratic"[156] ideologies like those universally

---

spirit ... plebian in the lowest instincts and related to Rousseau's *ressentiment*: consequently a romantic — for beneath all *romantisme* there grunts and thirsts Rousseau's instinct for revenge." This seems to be an apt description of feminism.

[155] Alexis Tocqueville, *Democracy in America* (Chicago: University of Chicago Press, 2002), 209.

[156] Ibid., 208. For example: "It cannot be denied that democratic institutions strongly tend to promote the feeling of envy in the human heart; not so much because they afford to everyone the means of rising to the same level with others as because those means perpetually disappoint the persons who employ them. Democratic institutions awaken and foster a passion for equality which they can never entirely satisfy. This complete equality

insinuated in the post-Enlightenment West, but it captures feminism most aptly of all. The feminists have by now cultivated a world-dominating "slave morality,"[157] fathomed as an impossible admixture of beauty and strength, accomplishing neither and seeking to subdue all the stultified world before a new androgynous femininity rebranded as might.

Before launching into an explanatory list of the patriarchal virtues, one important caveat bears mention: in this chapter, we will see that the classical virtues discussed by ancient Greeks and early Christians were technically neuter but designated male subjects far more aptly than females. For the classical and medieval ethical treatises were oriented at the acquisition and cultivation of moral leadership: "public-spiritedness," improving the *polis*, and cultivating political excellence. Rightly, these were associated with men.

I will begin my investigation with the lodestar of male virtue, *leadership*, in mind. Leadership is the virtue that orients all the others toward household mastery. Following Aristotle,

---

eludes the grasp of the people at the very moment when they think they have grasped it, and 'flies,' as Pascal says, 'with an eternal flight'; the people are excited in the pursuit of an advantage, which is more precious because it is not sufficiently remote to be unknown or sufficiently near to be enjoyed. The lower orders are agitated by the chance of success, they are irritated by its uncertainty; and they pass from the enthusiasm of pursuit to the exhaustion of ill success, and lastly to the acrimony of disappointment. Whatever transcends their own limitations appears to be an obstacle to their desires, and there is no superiority, however legitimate it may be, which is not irksome in their sight."

[157] Friedrich Nietzsche, *On the Genealogy of Morality* (New York: Penguin Classics, 2014).

the *Catechism of the Catholic Church* defines the purpose of the home as "education in the virtues" (2223). Not surprisingly, virtue and family bear a mutually constitutive rapport: virtue engenders strong familial bonds, which themselves, in turn, strengthen virtue. In this chapter, I will discuss the makings of male leadership and what its cultivation requires of men and women, both individually and collectively. They are the virtues cherished by a Christian society—a society that is, in its essence, patriarchal.

Happiness, Habit, and Unity of Virtue

In our day, we hear the platitude that women are "holistic" and that men are not. This is a half-truth. Women are holistic in residual vestiges of their approach to their natural calling. Men, too, are holistic but have so abandoned their manhoods that male holism rarely shines through. In short, men act most comprehensively with regard to the cultivation and exercise of leadership, the primary male virtue. Their happiness, habits, and attainment of all the major virtues are exercised together when they head their families rightly. So when, in this section, we discuss the exercise of the major virtues together, note that this always indicates the activity of family leadership for a man.

In Christianity's first millennium and a half, virtually all Christians embraced the ancient Greek view of ethics, which centers on the development of good habit (that is, virtue) as the key to creating happiness. Roman Catholics still embrace it. As a matter of fact, the classical Greek "words for habit and character are essentially identical."[158] As used in the Christian sense, which

---

[158] Brewer Eberly and Brian Mesimer, "Reforming Virtue Ethics," *Mere Orthodoxy*, December 4, 2018, https://mereorthodoxy.com/

was derived from the ablest of those Greeks—Aristotle—the word "happiness" designates not pleasure but, rather, the "good life": full, moral, human flourishing in accordance with mankind's godly final end. The ancient word for this concept of the supreme good was *Eudaimonia*.

The concept, however, is not restricted to antiquity; it still governs our discussion of patriarchal virtue in the present day. Aristotle got things right, even if he has been ignored lately.

During those first Christian fifteen hundred years, this commonsense philosophical model centering on the habituated acquisition of virtue was the *only* one fully endorsed by Christendom. Only after the sixteenth century's Reformation was there such a thing as a brand-new sort of Christian—a Protestant—who did *not* subscribe to this general system of "virtue ethics."[159] With most of the Reformers following Martin Luther's lead, which rejected the full possibility of free will, virtue, and the Aristotelian version of the natural law, "Luther [became] well-known for rejecting root and branch the ethical heritage of

---

reforming-virtue-ethics/. This source also includes the wisdom that "virtue ethics arose in a pagan Greek milieu and was propagated most clearly by Aristotle, a non-Christian philosopher. Even so, virtue ethics enjoys a robust history of Christian appropriation and integration with orthodox theology and philosophy. Boethius was one of the first to attempt a synthesis, while Thomas Aquinas offered a systematic Christian interpretation of virtue ethics through the integration of Aristotelian ethics with Augustinian theology. (Aristotle, Aquinas, and Augustine are clearly a formidable team.)"

[159] Aristotle's virtue ethics was anathema to Protestantism's view of man's unfree will and lack of liberty, his wicked and confused intellect, his total depravity of character, and Creation's moral inscrutability.

the classical world, famously deriding Aristotle as a 'damnable, arrogant, pagan rascal.'"[160]

For the Christian West, the best of these moral treatises came from Plato and especially Aristotle, interpreted by and through St. Augustine and especially St. Thomas, respectively. Both Plato and Aristotle imagined that virtue ethics was inseparably connected to politics, pairing the concepts of human liberty, good habits, private virtue, the natural law, and public virtue[161] (or public-spiritedness). Again, this public emphasis of ethics constitutes the male-centered thrust of the cardinal virtues to be discussed below, although applicable in variant ways to both sexes — that is, to all members of the patriarchy. As I've said, wives should participate actively as vested helpmates in the public goals of their husbands.

Plato and Aristotle also agreed that *Eudaimonia* equals the "good life in general" referred to by political science, which therefore contains all the other many goods of human life.

It must be emphasized that the Aristotelian term "happiness" stands in stark contrast to today's errant secular definition, which is best interpreted as "pleasure." Happiness, under the classical and Catholic tradition, equals the total expression of human blessedness, simultaneously rational, moral, and practical. All

---

[160] Thomas Albert Howard, "Philipp Melanchthon and the American Evangelical," *Pro Ecclesia* 18, no. 2 (2009): 170.

[161] Public virtue — widespread among an active, vigilant, moral citizenry — is made possible only by the aggregation of private virtue, shared in by the majority of any republic. Therefore, Thomas Jefferson and the American Founders were correct in citing Aristotle as one of the four most important influences on the American republic. In fact, almost every American founder shared the view that "without virtue in the people ..."

the virtues are geared toward this supreme good of happiness, described by the science called ethics. Aristotle writes of this science: "Will not then a knowledge of this Supreme Good be also of great practical importance for the conduct of life ... like archers, having a target to aim at?"[162]

The key to the moral life and the happy life — very nearly identical in Aristotle's work — inheres in what Aristotelians call the "function argument": a given thing must actualize its potency specific to the kind of thing it is. Fulfilling this function determines whether the thing constitutes a quality rendition of whatever it is. In sentient beings, the self-conscious actualization of potency reduces to what we call happiness. Simply, it is knowing that you are accomplishing what you were made for.

In non-sentient beings, we simply refer to their proper functioning as "adequateness": when we describe whether a wrench serves its function effectively or not, we are taking into consideration whether or not we would fairly call it a "good" or "adequate" wrench, even though a wrench cannot be happy. Wrenches, like all things, have a unique *telos* (goal) and *ergon* (intelligible functionality), the two criteria that dictate whether an item fulfills its reason for being. If someone attempted to use a hammer — with its own disparate *telos* and *ergon* — as a wrench, it may prove feasible, inefficiently and temporarily. But a hammer does not make a useful, naturally identifiable, or efficient wrench for very long. This is because the functions and goals of different things are not fungible.

But in the realm of manufactured objects, the harm of misuse usually reaches not the object itself but only the user's goal for his implementation of the object. And the harm here is at

---

[162] Aristotle, *Nicomachean Ethics* 1, 2, 2.

worst mere inefficiency: hammers used as wrenches will waste the craftsman's time and obscure his project but will not harm him.

On the other hand, the function argument applies to human beings in a far graver way. If we misspend our opportunities to be happy, we risk catastrophe. Moral experimentation has never resulted in anything but human ruin, as we will see below in the realm of sexual ethics and sexual identity. With regard to human *Eudaimonia*, Aristotle's function argument describes the very fate of the individual in question. Thus, the interplay between happiness and the function argument becomes central to the entire field of Christian ethics, excepting Luther and the Protestants.

Although happiness applies only to humans, the fulfillment of natural functions may be described among the entire span of living things, in Aristotle's philosophy: from "plant souls,"[163] which grow and take in nutrients; to "animal souls,"[164] which do the above and additionally locomote and perceive; to "human souls," which do the above and additionally act rationally and morally. Only the last two qualities, unique to human ability, constitute the ingredients for happiness. In other words, man's capacity for reason and morality, properly disposed, combine to yield *Eudaimonia*.

When Aristotle considers the soul (the will and intellect together) of human beings, the *telos* he associates with it is mankind's uniquely rational moral purpose. Humans were created in order to make good, right, and true actions. We are smart in order to be good. The uniquely intelligent animals called human beings preclude their own ability to thrive when they fail to actualize this rational moral purpose. As such, immoral humans—almost

---

[163] Aristotle, *De Anima* (New York: Penguin Classics, 1987), 2, 1.
[164] Ibid., 2, 2.

always through avenues that substitute pleasure for true happiness[165]—will certainly be miserable, no matter how rich or famous they become.

Consider the regular front-page inhabitants of popular tabloid magazines. Also, interrogate the common yet stupid assumption by most readers of tabloid magazines that, on the basis of wealth and pleasure alone, happy lives are being enjoyed by the sleazy celebrities at issue. Aristotle writes that "common [nonvirtuous] men equate the Good with pleasure, and accordingly are content with the life of enjoyment."[166] In other places, he refers to this as a life fitting only for beasts of burden, not humans.[167]

In summary, human beings ensure their own misery by violating their rational-moral goal and function. Conversely, they can all but ensure their happiness through rational, moral action (although Aristotle, a shrewd realist, admits that profoundly bad luck or hard circumstances will interfere with the happiness of a moral man). And what is the means by which moral happiness is won?

Happiness for Plato and Aristotle was defined in relation to the habituation of virtue. A virtue is not acquired until habit has made it a man's "second nature," or something akin to this. Citing Aristotle, Abp. Fulton J. Sheen says that "character resides in man's will, not in his intellect."[168] This is because, as

---

[165] Pleasure cannot be *Eudaimonia*, because it involves only physical sensation and no virtue; since man was created to be virtuous, he cannot achieve happiness without actualizing his moral potency. Remember, this is Aristotle's function argument: man will not be happy unless he becomes what he was created to be.

[166] Aristotle, *Nicomachean Ethics* 3.

[167] Ibid.

[168] Fulton J. Sheen, *Life Is Worth Living* (Dumont Television Network, 1952).

Aristotle teaches, having good character involves moral excellence, which "is not an act but a habit."[169] Moral virtue is produced by character-molding repetition. Nature does not *force* us to be moral, although it *does* give us the intellectual capacity to receive virtue.[170] Deliberately chosen habit brings that capacity to maturity. An example should clarify.

Imagine that it is the week after Christmas. Like most Americans, you probably overate holiday foods during the run-up to Christmas. Also like most of our countrymen, returning to a healthy diet and exercise informs all or part of your New Year's resolution. If you're especially out of shape, then the component of your resolution devoted to exercise—a daily jog, for instance—will prove especially difficult. The moment in which the need for exercise became clear in your head was the precise moment (after the holidays) when you looked down at the bathroom scale: thereafter, you *know* you've gained weight and need to alter something, even and especially if you don't want to follow through with action.

In order to reorient yourself toward a new virtue—fitness—which is to say, a new habit, you need to know (a) the existence of the virtue of fitness and (b) your recent failures in that domain. You have to know it before you can do it, as the Aristotelian maxim goes. Armed with prospective virtue in your intellect but not yet in your will, you wake up early on January 2 to do your first jog. You go through with it, hating every moment. Your will revolts. Your body is sore all day. The only motivation prompting you to wake up on January 3 and jog all over again is your intellect.

---

[169] Aristotle, *Nicomachean Ethics* 3.
[170] Ibid., 2. "Nature gives us the capacity" for virtue.

Suffice to say that you have not yet acquired the virtue of fitness. The litmus test for this distinction is pleasure, which is a mark of your will rather than your intellect: you still loathe your runs over the next weeks. That's how you know that the virtue of fitness is not yet in your character, even though you're sticking with the daily jogs.

But your intellectual knowledge about fitness is sufficiently strong such as to hold you to your course. By March 1, assuming that you've held fast, the story has slowly changed. Now you enjoy your runs somewhat. Your will is giving way to your intellect! After another month's passage—by April 1, say—the virtue of fitness has fully transferred from your intellect to your will: this is signified by the fact that if you fall ill and miss one of your daily runs (which are no longer imposed coercively by your intellect), you are actually *pained* by the loss of the run. You miss your "runner's high." You've created a good habit of fitness, and only at this point—the point at which you gladly do the run for its own sake, without even thinking about it—have you mastered the virtue.

Aristotle spelled all this out more specifically than his teacher Plato did. But it is presumed that the two greatest ancient philosophers agreed more or less about the basic way that habit functions on the path to *Eudaimonia*.

Where Aristotle sharply disagreed with his teacher Plato was upon the ground of a so-called universal good, also known as a "unity of the virtues." This proves relevant for our investigation, since we will discuss how men can recapture the various excellences required to defeat feminism. Plato imagined that there existed a kind of super-virtue that helped a man to acquire all the others, like the One Ring of Power, which brings all the lesser rings. For both logical and moral reasons, Aristotle rejected this possibility out of hand, saying he must "review the difficulties of a universal good."[171] He writes further that "good cannot be a universal general notion; if so it would not be predicable in all the categories."[172]

As one considers the relation between male leadership and each of the cardinal virtues mentioned below, it may be tempting to view these four as something like unifying virtues. (The word "cardinal" means "hinge," after all.) There exists an undoubtable connection between them. But in actuality, the relationality between the four does not imply that they can all be gotten at once. The means of receiving all these virtues—habituation beginning with recognition—is always the same. This indicates that the process of habituation must be applied afresh to each new sort of moral excellence. Some of the cardinal virtues even facilitate the acquisition of the others, so they are *partly* mutually constitutive. But again, they have to be pursued one at a time because they are separate excellences.

Famously enough, women are attracted to confident leadership in men. This means that happy sexual identity in men requires the acquisition of the confidence and leadership requisite to win and maintain admiration from women. But as a prior condition, this requires the cardinal and supernatural virtues—the desiderata that confer such a warrant for confidence and leadership.

Without committing Plato's error of assuming that the four virtues might be acquired all at once, it is safe to say that leadership equates to a manly *exposition* of all four well-seasoned virtues, presumably acquired one by one sometime during youth. Obviously, most virtuous men will continue to fine-tune the balanced

[171] Ibid.
[172] Ibid.

implementation of all these interplaying virtues during and after the attraction of a mate. As we will see below, understanding the centrality of the prime male virtue, leadership (that is, chastened leadership), to the full enactment of the cardinal virtues requires a modicum of conceptual overlap in the virtues' definitions, although as I explained above, the acquisition of one does not guarantee the acquisition of any of the others.

The Cardinal Virtues

As is written in the Wisdom of Solomon: "If anyone loves righteousness, her labors are virtues; for she teaches *temperance* and *prudence, justice* and *fortitude*; nothing in life is more profitable for mortals than these" (Wisd. 8:7, NIV, emphasis added). These four cardinal virtues comprise the short list of male desiderata that, if attained, will restore to society a benevolent patriarchy — and many good things pursuant to that. Gentile Athens (and even pagan Rome) gave assent to religious Jerusalem in the invocation of these four primary natural excellences. From two radically different cultural perspectives, the ancient Greeks and the ancient Jews agreed that these four cardinal virtues together govern all the other natural virtues.

Of all these pagans and Gentiles, it was Aristotle whose ethical writings prove the most granular and accurate, which is why Thomas Aquinas adhered to them so closely. But pagans like Plato and Cicero and early Christians like Ambrose and Augustine prove to be worthwhile ethics instructors as well. As such, our examination of the cardinal virtues will be primarily guided by Aristotle and, by implication, Thomas, with nonnegligible tidbits from the other four ancient ethicists.

The four cardinal virtues, labeled as such by St. Ambrose, prove indispensable to the reclamation of male leadership, whereas the exercise of leadership itself, or what we could call the chastened self-possession by males, is needed to direct or manage the acquisition and exercise of the cardinal virtues. This "catch-22" makes the acquisition of manly virtue the challenge of a lifetime.

Manly Prudence

Prudence, or *phronesis*, involves the practical, real-time decision-making associated with mastery over each random situation in life. Randomness is the watchword, and prudent men are exquisite at "rolling with the punches," making fluid decisions on the fly. Prudence especially means knowing when to apply a given virtue and to table another: when to be brave instead of charming, or vice versa. Regardless of the disagreement between Plato and Aristotle concerning the *means* of acquiring the many virtues, no one can doubt that the eventual possessor of multiple virtues needs a "governor" virtue that suggests the one among many virtues to be selected extemporaneously for any given situation. This one is prudence.

All individuals need prudence, but *leaders* (in order to be good leaders) need it most of all and are evidently best at acquiring it.

The prudent man is able to deliberate well about "what is advantageous as a means to the good life in general."[173] Aristotle designates prudence as the virtue for people with charge over others. Citing Aristotle, Thomas Aquinas adds something about kingly rule that applies perfectly to the realm of family rule:

> In *Politics* 3 the Philosopher says, "Prudence is the proper virtue of a ruler." Therefore, kingly prudence must be a special kind of prudence. I respond: As is clear from what

[173] Aristotle, *Nicomachean Ethics* 6, 5, 1.

was said above (q. 47, aa. 8–12), it belongs to prudence to rule and to give commands. And where one finds a special type of rule and command within human acts, there one also finds a special type of prudence. Now it is clear that in the case of someone who has to rule not only himself but the complete community of a city or kingdom, one finds a special and perfect type of rule.[174]

What matters is that more than anyone, men, the rulers of family and culture, need the leadership-applied prudence described by Aristotle and Thomas, even if these men are not all kings.

Some of the other natural law thinkers add bold contour to our examination of Aristotelian and Thomistic prudence.

Cicero mostly accepts Aristotle's definition of prudence, adding to it a Stoic spin and three sub-parts that prove quite helpful for our examination of male virtue: *memory*, *understanding*, and *foresight*.[175] Young men training to be husbands and fathers must cultivate the kind of memory that serves their families to gain the morally upward path in the future; their understanding of the circumstances of life must be extemporaneous and deft. Their prudent view of the past and present must combine to yield a sort of nonsupernatural prescience in service of the moral and spiritual health of their families.

Augustine adds the perspective that "prudence is the knowledge of what to seek and what to avoid,"[176] pointing household

---

[174] Thomas Aquinas, *Summa Theologiae* II-II, q. 50 (the subjective parts of prudence).

[175] Cicero, *De Inventione* 2, 160. Cicero here offers a base definition of prudence: "Knowledge of things that are good or bad or neither."

[176] Quoted in Thomas Aquinas, *Summa Theologiae* II-II, q. 47, art. 1.

fathers to the Decalogue-like proposition of governance that positive and negative commands should be meaningfully distinguished. Teaching children what to *seek* versus what to *avoid* involves differing prudential pitfalls. Also, ever mindful of the highest virtue of *caritas*, Augustine sharpens prudence's reference thereto: "Prudence is love distinguishing with sagacity between what hinders it and what helps it."[177]

This becomes especially relevant when we consider, in the supernatural virtues below, the father's unique capacity for parsing rule-enforcement from rule-dispensation. For Augustine, the prudential distinction rests entirely upon what generates the most love for the obedient wife or child. Plato lends his voice in agreement with Aristotle (and later, Thomas) to the effect that, for all the reasons listed above, prudence pertains in its highest form to rulers and fathers,[178] to whom the enforcement of norms falls.

In the specific context of chastened male leadership, prudence requires a dispassionate command by the intellect over the appetites, especially over the sexual appetite, which is most known for obscuring righteous male judgment. In this sense, prudence branches into another cardinal virtue, temperance, which will be discussed below. Since prudence involves real-time decision-making, it requires freedom from the most distracting passion, the very one whose overindulgence constitutes the easiest pitfall in the life of a male. It is safe to say that a prudent man will always ably apply his practical reason in interactions with females, largely because the subject of the householder's leadership — his

---

[177] Augustine, *De Moribus Eccl.* 15.

[178] Plato, *The Republic* (Cambridge, MA: Hackett Publishing, 2004), 427e.

wife—looms large on his mind *in abstracto*, well before he has even met her.

Fatherly prudence also applies in a special way to the application of *exceptions to household rules*. Whether to follow the rule or grant an exception: this question practically forms its own subvirtue. Prudent men thrive in deciding when to enforce a given rule or, conversely, when to observe an extenuating circumstance that warrants an exception. Prudential exceptions distinguish the activism entailed by male leadership—carving out distinctions requires energy "above and beyond" mere rule following—from the faithful yet servile passivity and observance entailed by categorical female submission to rules of thumb.

Suffice to say, a man owes his wife (and children) his prudent judgments in real time: these "snap decisions" that our lives summarily comprise are what keep the family out of danger, happy, healthy, and functional. Prudence is the ruler's intellectual virtue (whereas justice is the ruler's moral virtue). During and after his shrewd decision-making, prudence benefits all the subjects of the ruler's rule—for instance, the family. Furthermore, as we will see below in the realm of the supernatural virtues, prudence governs the related application of *mercy*, which ends up being a prominent part of the ruler's virtue.

Manly Justice

Alongside prudence, justice is the cardinal virtue most directly associated with kingly leadership—especially when the two virtues combine. Justice measures a man's commutative and distributive restraint in the administration of power. The former measures how fairly a leader punishes and rewards his people, while the latter measures how evenly a leader honors the property and contracts between and among his people.

In his section on justice, Aristotle writes that "office will show a man: for in office one is brought into relation with others and becomes a member of a community."[179] In other words, as our opening section insinuated, the leadership a chastened man exercises over his home is the best way to test a man's mettle. As the great writers such as Shakespeare and looming statesmen such as Lincoln inquired: *What will a man do with a little power?* Even if he heads only his household, rather than an entire city or state, the measure of a man's justice is his ultimate test.

Aristotle uses the term "justice" in two primary ways, whose mutual confusion, he warns, provides an easy pitfall. He writes that "it appears that the terms justice and injustice are used in several senses, but as their equivocal uses are closely connected, the equivocation is [often] not detected."[180] The virtue of *general justice*, on the one hand, concerns the willing submission to moral, well-made laws, meaning that Aristotle considers "justice in this sense [to be] perfect virtue,"[181] citing the proverb "in justice is all virtue found in sum."[182] Having read this, one must be very careful not to make Plato's mistake of presuming that all virtue can be acquired together.[183] Aristotle merely seems to mean that general justice should be received as a descriptive term for a man who has already acquired them all one by one.

More important is Aristotle's treatment of the virtue of *particular justice*, the characteristic of fairness in a just man who

---

[179] Aristotle, *Nicomachean Ethics* 5, 1, 16.

[180] Ibid., 5, 1, 7.

[181] Ibid., 5, 1, 15.

[182] Ibid.

[183] "Plato's Shorter Ethical Works," *Stanford Encyclopedia of Philosophy*, July 6, 2005, https://plato.stanford.edu/entries/plato-ethics-shorter/#7.

rejects blanket equality. More precisely, justice constitutes the habit of giving to each his due. The just employer who owes Employee A $50 and Employee B $100 does not "split the difference" by giving $75 to each, which would be equal but unfair. Instead, the just employer gives to each his due — $50 and $100, respectively — which proves fair but unequal.

As Aristotle teaches, the unjust man will take more of the good — for himself or his friends — and less of the bad, than is due. Unjust, egalitarian rulers might even take from certain strangers to give to other strangers. Either way, whether abstractly or concretely, Thomas channels Aristotle by articulating that the unjust executive or legislator would abolish justice altogether by equalizing outcomes:

> Further, nature does not fail in necessities, as I said above, and therefore neither does the art of civil government, but this would happen if possessions were equalized among families, because citizens would die of penury, which would lead to the corruption of the polity. It also follows that the equalization of possessions is unsuitable from a consideration of the gradation of personages, as well as from human nature. There is a difference between citizens just as there is between members of a body, to which I compared a polity above: moreover, the virtue and function of different members is different. It is well known that someone who is noble must make greater expenditures than one who is not noble — it is for this reason, for example, that the virtue of liberality is called magnificence in a ruler on account of the great cost involved. This could not happen where possessions were equal.[184]

---

[184] Thomas Aquinas, *De Regimine Principum* 4, 9, 76.

For Aristotle and Thomas, the father must be the ultimate champion and guardian of familial justice, just as the ruler must vigilantly guard against injustice in the state. (In our investigation below of the supernatural virtues, we will see justice and prudence combine in a perfect way.) The other natural law thinkers lend further insight to our Aristotelian, Thomistic interrogation of fatherly justice.

Cicero, for instance, considers justice "the habit of mind that preserves the common utility while also giving to each what is his due,"[185] which emphasizes not only the objective definition but also its subjective groundwork in the mind of the ruler. The objective distinction is practically worthless in the life of the family unless it is well understood by its administrator, the father. Cicero here, too, qualifies six helpful natural law subparts invoked by justice, invaluably instructive for the household father: religion, piety, consideration, retribution, honor, and truth.[186]

Most importantly among these subparts, we must recall that as the priest of the household, the father is the only one who can compellingly proffer his sons a path to religion and piety; accordingly, households without religious fathers secularize fast! Note the correlation between the subpart Cicero calls truth and what was said above about the unwavering objective commitment by fathers to fairness over equality.

Augustine returns our analysis to his perennial emphasis on fatherly love, referring all lesser virtues back to it: "Justice is love

---

[185] Cicero, *De Inv.* 2, 160.

[186] These six subparts pertain to the natural law and are adopted and developed by Thomas Aquinas, along with one of Cicero's three subparts belonging to the law of custom: equity. We will discuss the principle of equity in the section on caritas below.

serving only the loved object, and therefore ruling rightly."[187] The household father must love and serve the Father in Heaven, the source and summit of his love for his family, and from which all justice stems. Accordingly, the father who does not pray and worship sacramentally cannot love properly and thus rule his family properly. Plato identifies justice above and beyond the social classes of his republic because it governs the proper relationship between those classes.[188] This means that, in the Christian era, justice becomes the objective standard to which fatherly prudence aspires.

In our own doomed post-Christian era, coextensive with the feminist proposition of female power, the unjust type of equality described above has achieved a manic popularity. This new effeminate assumption regarding justice is basically the default position of mothers who run households in lieu of their husbands: that giving to each their due is somehow cruel or heartless. But this view has not preponderated through "bad optics" such as the appearance of self-seeking or self-interest. Instead, it has done so through a kind of maternal appeal that elevates some chimera of "mercy" over justice. In almost every case where the popular viewpoint prevails, the moral exception will swallow the merit-based rule — so much so that the exception has *become* the rule. This is the telltale sign of our harrowing, post-justice life in a feminist-socialist era.

In sane homes, the head of the household insists upon justice, partly through his insistence upon prudence. He acknowledges that his good wife and the heart of the household might, left to her own devices, unintentionally debilitate fairness by

---

[187] Augustine, *De Moribus Eccl.* 15.
[188] Plato, *The Republic* 427e.

recourse to an overabundance in equality and "mercy." Accordingly, male headship artfully sidesteps too much input from or deference to the wife, in this particular arena. Feminist Western society is awash in false justifications for the lionization of egalitarianism and injustice: for example, rightly paying Employee A less than Employee B has too often been maligned as "unmerciful," "pharisaical," or even "overemphatic of justice" (which is impossible!).

Under the spurious assumption that mercy competes with justice—another easy pitfall for society's nonleaders forced to act as leaders—a false dichotomy has been erected between the two. This is a symptom of widespread weak leadership. On the other hand, we will see below in the section on the three supernatural virtues how the kingly disposal of the two natural virtues prudence and justice are synthesized and perfected through supernatural *caritas*.

Manly Fortitude

Fortitude turns out to be the cardinal virtue most popularly and best understood. Its relation to manly leadership is self-evident. Aristotle teaches that fortitude does not mean a lack of fear of evil, since many evils should rightly be feared. Instead, it requires the manly fearing and then braving of the right things at the right time and in the right way.[189] Every honorable man heading a household does well to manage his own self-expectations by remembering this.

More precisely, Aristotle defines courage thus: "Courage is the observance of the mean between fear and confidence."[190] What

[189] Aristotle, *Nicomachean Ethics* 3, 6, 2.
[190] Ibid.

he means is that only a rash man rushes in to fight ten opposing soldiers at once (an excess of fortitude), while only a cowardly man refuses to stand and fight one-on-one in battle (a deficiency of fortitude). The man of fortitude will stand and brave the sort of evil[191] — death in combat — that might reasonably result from any battle. He will do so not because of his strength in battle alone, but in the first place because

> the courageous man in the proper sense of the term will be he who fearlessly confronts a noble death, or some sudden peril that threatens death; and the perils of war answer this description most fully. Not that the courageous man is not also fearless in a storm at sea (as also in illness), though not in the same way as sailors are fearless, for he thinks there is no hope of safety, and to die by drowning is revolting to him, whereas sailors keep up heart because of their experience. Also, courage is shown in dangers where a man can defend himself by valour or die nobly, but neither is possible in disasters like a shipwreck.[192]

To put it a slightly different way, as J.R.R. Tolkien's manly exemplar Aragorn prognosticates: "A time may come soon," said he, "when none may return. Then there will be need of valour without renown, for none shall remember the deeds that are done in the last defence of your homes. Yet the deeds will not be less valiant because they are unpraised." (Ironically, Aragorn admonishes a woman in this passage, Éowyn, who would be the first defender of Rohan's women and children if the country's soldiers were all to be slaughtered.)

[191] Ibid., 3, 7, 7.
[192] Ibid., 3, 6, 10.

Citing Aristotle, Thomas Aquinas adds important detail to the definition of fortitude, especially in defense of the proposition that fortitude indeed falls within virtuous categories:

> The virtue of the soul is perfected, not in the infirmity of the soul, but in the infirmity of the body, of which the Apostle was speaking. Now it belongs to fortitude of the mind to bear bravely with infirmities of the flesh, and this belongs to the virtue of patience or fortitude, as also to acknowledge one's own infirmity, and this belongs to the perfection that is called humility.[193]

Compared with the other cardinal virtues, fortitude is uniquely well understood in men. Yet, as our example shows, fortitude is needed in others besides chastened, manly leaders. Like each of the other cardinal virtues, it is no stretch to say that a sort of fortitude pertains specifically to good wives following the lead of good husbands, who (as just and brave men) often wind up exposed to accumulated dangers that cowardly men have obviated. Like all virtue, fortitude is applicable to all people who bother to habituate it, not exclusively to men.

But it should appear decidedly different in a courageous woman. For instance, a woman under attack from foreign forces should not be expected to exercise fortitude in the same way as her husband or his brothers-at-arms. As in the case of Tolkien's Éowyn, courageous combat would be at most a last resort. Yet today's feminism has fashioned the formerly derisive term "fight like a girl" into aspirational language. It has used *ressentiment* to make a vice into a virtue.

Primarily, the courageous wife under siege should stoically and efficiently discharge her preparatory duties as required by her

---

[193] Thomas Aquinas, *Summa Theologiae* II-II, q. 123.

husband, or by the community of men arranged for her family's defense: rationing food, acting as triage nurse, cooking, packing, cleaning, mending, organizing—all of which are *truly* difficult to do under the sudden threat of death.

But having stipulated all that, fortitude involves, in the fullest sense, the chastened heads of household, since they alone find themselves responsible for artfully avoiding or effectively confronting the evils that threaten to befall their households. Civil society's husbands are the ones who must at a moment's notice rush headlong into the pack of orcs to fight to the death. In its very purest form, fortitude is not *a* manly virtue, but *the* manly virtue. As we will see in more granular detail below, and as was prefigured above, the very purest enactment of fortitude is not even mortal combat but rather the priestly act of self-sacrifice (which is possible only under the supernatural virtue of faith).

Even given fortitude's uncommonly accurate reputation among the virtues, the natural law tradition adds some hidden insight to the topic. Cicero equates fortitude with "the considered undertaking of dangers and endurance of hardships,"[194] explicating the virtue's subparts as *magnanimity, confidence, patience,* and *perseverance.* The first two constitute the "sexy" parts of manly fortitude—perhaps those first sought by females during courtship—while the latter two constitute its unsung necessities that slow-bloom with especial potency during fatherhood.[195] Consider the following paradigm instance of the magnanimous subpart of the moral excellence in the film *Braveheart: "Ego nunquam*

---

[194] Cicero, *De Inv.* 2, 163.

[195] Thomas Aquinas, in the fortitude paragraph quoted shortly above, clearly drew from Cicero with regard to the equation of fortitude and patience.

pronunciari mendacium! Sed ego sum homo indomitus": I never lie, but I am a savage!

Regarding confidence, consider the implications of the popular 2021 beta male's emphasis on *appearing* confident to women instead of *having the grounds* for true confidence. As always, Augustine ties the cardinal virtue fortitude to love: "Fortitude is love readily bearing all things for the sake of the loved object."[196] Modeled after the love of our Heavenly Father for His Son and of His Son for us, the love-inspired forbearance of fear and agony modifies fatherhood quintessentially. Augustine reminds us that phenomenal bravery with no direct object in mind proves to be a myth. It is inhuman, as Augustine points out. Finally, Plato naturally places fortitude in the social class of warriors, which, within the logic of the household, falls to the father, who is not only king in the modern sense, but also warrior-king[197] in the ancient and medieval senses.

Manly Temperance

Temperance concerns the observance of the mean in regard to bodily pleasures, the vices of which are called *profligacy*, on the side of excess, and *insensibility*, on the side of deficiency. Because "men of this [latter] type scarcely occur, we have no special name for them"[198] and will instead discuss the soft men who forfeit their households through profligacy.

But temperance is more than just balance in food or sex; it constitutes a balanced approach to all of life. A manly leader must be temperate because a balanced milieu is required in his

---

[196] Augustine, *De Moribus Eccl.* 15.

[197] Plato, *Republic* 427e.

[198] Aristotle, *Nicomachean Ethics* 3, 6, 8.

household—ranging from lighthearted joy to solemn worship, from frivolity to suffering. Too much of any single mood can flood a household with differing sorts of dangers. Temperance comprises manly leadership that strives after a familial balance of the tempers. It calls men to be not only morally good but smart and strong and funny and chaste as well. In other words, temperance turns out yet another virtue that Platonists might be readily willing to mistake for a unity of the virtues.[199]

The natural law tradition offers household fathers a few additional angles by which to approach the acquisition of temperance. Thomas Aquinas offers a possible reason for the easy Platonic mistake of temperance as a medium for the other virtues: "Human virtue is that which inclines man to something in accordance with reason. Now temperance evidently inclines man to this, since its very name implies moderation, which reason causes. Therefore temperance is a virtue."[200] If Aristotelian virtue centers on the "golden mean," then temperance seems to seek and locate with especial acuity the necessary household mien of moderation. In a similar vein, Cicero defines "temperance" as "the domination of reason over desire and over other incorrect inclinations of mind, domination that is firm, attaining the norm,"[201] the latter of which is the mean between vicious extremes. He lists the subparts of temperance as *continence*, *clemency*, and *modesty*.

By implication, then, Cicero describes a temperate husband "like a rock," as Bob Seger sang—a man of fatherly, Petrine equanimity. Augustine adds to manly dependability the nuance of

---

[199] Examples of Plato's view of a unity of the virtues comes from *Laws* 693b–c, 692d–693b. See also the *Charmides* (at 161b–163d) and the *Protagoras* (at 330d–333b).

[200] Thomas Aquinas, *Summa Theologiae* II-II, q. 141.

[201] Cicero, *De Inv.* 2, 164.

sacrificial totality. For Augustine, the idea of temperance is "love giving itself entirely to that which is loved."[202] One immediately thinks of the father as the priest, who sacrifices himself if necessary. In addition to the standard elements of the definition of the virtue, Plato writes that temperance is "a kind of orderliness,"[203] associating it with the producing classes—farmers and craftsmen—although Plato also admitted that temperance proves necessary in the acquisition of the higher virtues associated with higher classes.[204]

We already saw how the domain of the prudent man overlaps with that of the temperate man, insofar as he virtuously avoids indulgence in the bodily pleasures, with the goal of keeping his prudential judgments corporeally unencumbered. After all, when such pleasures are resorted to superabundantly, they slowly begin to enslave the man's will and eventually his intellect, disrupting the right governance of his prudence.

Naturally, temperance interacts with the other cardinal virtues as well.[205] Habitual intemperance, for example, will diminish a given man's fortitude, unduly softening him, since exposure exclusively to pleasure will condition that man to cowardly avoid all dangers. Danger proves distasteful to all men but especially to good-time seekers. Also, the intemperate man who cultivates

---

[202] Augustine, *De Moribus Eccl.* 15.

[203] Plato, *Republic* 435e.

[204] Ibid., 427e, 425b.

[205] Recalling how all of the cardinal virtues overlap, we must do our best to bear in mind that each virtue should be pursued on its own merits, notwithstanding its indefinite connection to the others. Even in cases where imprudence, injustice, and cowardliness do not apparently underlie an act of intemperance, the manly need for its amendment and future avoidance proves self-evident.

a pleasure-addled household will eventually come to care little for the virtue of fairness in the realms of commutative and distributive justice, both of which call a just father to frequent acts of self-denial.

Simply put: manly fixation with bodily pleasure makes its own ruin. A householder can never be self-possessed without temperance. In fact, Aristotle distinguishes between the obsession with bodily pleasures (which is vicious) and mental pleasures (which is not vicious) precisely because one poses immediate dangers to the will and the other does not. Examples of mental pleasures, including worldly ambition or obsession with learning, do not involve the same softening of the will as does the indulgence of the body. Overambition represents a vice, to be sure, but it is a different one from that of profligacy.

Explaining that no man ever lost his temperance by sniffing too many roses,[206] Aristotle — the master of distinctions within distinctions — narrows still further the *sort* of bodily pleasures to which the profligate is attracted: "those which man shares with the lower animals, and which consequently appear slavish and bestial."[207] Because man shares the five senses with beasts, his overstimulation in them may result in the forgetful neglect of his own intellect, which the beasts — a kind of exemplar for profligates — altogether lack. In real-world terms, this results in the forfeiture of manly household leadership.

But not all five of the senses were created the same. The two primary senses that wind up being the easy pitfalls of the

---

[206] "Hounds do not take pleasure in scenting hares, but in eating them; the scent merely made them aware of the hare." Aristotle, *Nicomachean Ethics* 3, 10, 7.

[207] Ibid., 3, 5, 8.

Aristotelian profligate are "touch and taste."[208] To return our analysis to the masculine context of leadership, this means that men forfeit the leadership of their households through overindulgence in food and sex. While the overabundance (or underabundance) of emphasis on marital sexuality suggests self-evident problems in the realm of male-female household relations, our analysis benefits from including treatment of the dangers of indulgence in food.

Think of the sort of self-possession conjured by the Great Depression image of Jim Braddock, the "Cinderella Man," giving up his breakfast to his hungry daughter so that she might eat double rations. His act of extreme temperance — portion forfeiture — is also one of the starkest acts of servant-leadership. Not only does he, the father, have more duties than his daughter to perform throughout his long day, but he has a bigger body as well. In this sense, temperance goes far beyond the demands of distributive justice: the fairness principle of proportionalism dictates that Jim's bigger body naturally and rightfully requires more food than his daughter's. But Jim, a suffering servant, joyfully makes do with less. And temperate self-denial represents something that a profligate eater simply could not perform, for love or money, even if he wanted to.

Ironically, a profligate actually turns out a kind of impotent, even though we've been brainwashed so as to think of sexually intemperate men as hyper-potent. Overexposure to food (or sex) renders a man unable to do without it. This is the sheer opposite of the presumed effect of the stockpiling of a given resource. Only temperate men can do without for periods of time. One thinks of the words of Augustine: "A good man is free, even if he is a

---

[208] Ibid.

slave; a wicked man is a slave, even if he is king."[209] So let it be said that temperance is the cardinal virtue that most directly invites household husbands and fathers to be liberated within the most adverse conditions—balanced, multifaceted, and even creative in their approach to leadership's challenges.

The Supernatural Male Virtues

All human beings share naturally in the possibility of acquiring the cardinal virtues. Men share with one another the possibility of sharpening those cardinal virtues into the spearhead of leadership. But without three supernatural gifts from Jesus—and three Christ-transformed offices from the Old Testament that prefigured His new gifts—a home's manly leadership will be inchoate at best.

Through Baptism, all Christians (children, women, and men) share in the vivacity of Christ's offices: priest, prophet, and king. Christians alone will pursue the highest virtues, faith, hope, and love, whereas even virtuous pagans will, through the course of God's graciously created nature, pursue and capture the cardinal virtues described above.

But unlike Christian women and children, laymen (as husbands and fathers) must come to participate directly in the three simultaneous offices of Christ. Men must be priest, prophet, and king within their households. By studying and emulating Christ's manly relation to His Bride, the Church, householders reproduce in the microcosm of the home an anagogical priesthood, prophethood, and kingship. Ordained priests actually fill one of these offices (in a special ordained way), but not the other two. This literal participation in priesthood ensures the higher honor of

[209] Augustine, *The City of God* 4, 3.

the ordained vocation than the lay. Yet the quotidian challenge of the marital vocation dictates that husband-fathers participate in all three roles at once.

Interrogate the fact that a household father cannot consecrate a host in the way that an ordained father can, although he must "consecrate" his entire household to the "source and summit of the faith." So doing requires three distinct, simultaneous approaches to sacrifice and three concomitant supernatural virtues. Given the manifold challenges of being a husband and father, we will examine why a man cannot be priest of the household without also becoming a willing prophet and a good king. The watchword in the householder's domain is *balance*, requiring a father to be, in a fallen way, "all things to all"[210] in his family.

All around us, we are beset by the degeneration of the moral fabric of households. Properly disposed householder leadership cannot manage for a single day without active kingliness, priestliness, and prophetliness within fathers.[211]

Of course, women share a Christian Baptism with their husbands, which predisposes them toward undeniable female iterations of the three supernatural virtues. Women are called to faith, hope, and love as well—but from their own perspective of fundamental obedience. Faith, hope, and love "present" differently

---

[210] 1 Corinthians 9:19 (NIV): "For though I am free from all men, I have made myself a servant to all, that I might win the more." This passage is relevant to the office of king, where the man's victory is emphasized, and to that of priest, where the man's self-denying service is emphasized.

[211] Peter Kreeft, "Christian Themes in *Lord of the Rings*," Biola University talk, January 7, 2014; Tolkien's fiction brings out the colors of priest, prophet, and king most boldly because it uniquely employs a three-protagonist format.

when they are oriented, on the one hand, at leadership, or on the other, at obedience.

But the natural and sacramental roles of the man's priesthood of the *ecclesiola* specifically insinuate a uniquely male Christological application.[212] The part of the passage from St. Paul referenced above reads: "For though I am free from all men, I have made myself a servant to all, that I might win the more." This passage proves relevant both to the office of king, where victory and vindication are emphasized, and to that of priest, where self-immolation and self-sacrifice are indispensable. Very shortly, we will examine these in greater detail.

A functional incompleteness within fatherhood should be supposed whenever a household father eagerly fills one role but not the other two: these offices invoke three distinct, yet overlapping forms of manly leadership exampled by Christ. In the emulation of the single true example of these three offices —Christ's—the hopelessly flawed head of household ultimately requires the supernatural virtues to sharpen his four natural virtues. Happily, Scripture furnishes us with a hierarchical arrangement of these Heavenly excellences: *fides*, *spes*, and *caritas*. St. Paul writes:

> When I was a child, I spoke as a child, I understood as a child, I thought as a child; but when I became a man, I put away childish things. For now we see in a mirror, dimly, but face to face. Now I know in part, but then I shall know just as I also am known. And now abide faith,

---

[212] Patrick Morley, "Exploring a Husband's Role as a Prophet, Priest and King," *Charisma*, January 6, 2020, https://www.charismamag. com/life/men/18610-exploring-a-husband-s-role-as-a-prophet-priest-and-king.

hope, love, these three; but the greatest of these is love.
(1 Corinthians 13:11–13)

Whereas, in the previous section, man gained and maintained his
naturally appointed headship through four natural virtues—prudence, justice, fortitude, and temperance—presently we will see
how three supernatural virtues "perfect" the ostensible contradictions or tensions of priority existing between these four natural,
cardinal ones.[213] Working downward from the highest virtue,
we will examine how these supernatural excellences correspond
meaningfully with the roles of king, prophet, and priest.

Caritas: The Kingly Virtue

A householder's participation in the highest office of Christ,
king, represents the supernatural virtue *caritas* (his *love, charity*).
Righteous men leading their households must be kingly in their
distillation and presentation of paternal love. As St. Augustine
constantly reminds us, this is the highest and the greatest virtue
for a man to attain.

In the domain of manly leadership, *caritas* entails the patriarchal care exercised over disciples and subordinates that unfailingly serves their best interests. Kingly love is not for the faint of
heart. The concept of kingly service should not be perverted into
a subordinate, effeminate capacity: unlike the corresponding Marian office pointed at by devoted womanly *caritas*, the office of king
equals the ultimate position of earthly leadership. Often, *caritas*

---

[213] When each supernatural virtue is paired with a natural virtue
(or virtues), the portion of the overlap being designated in these
pages is that which corresponds with the reclamation of manly
leadership. Thus, "inter alia" will appear in the description
showing the overlap.

should "feel" like affection. Other times, it will "feel" tough. This is because *caritas* is the perfected, supernatural exercise of two natural virtues—justice and merciful prudence—at once. Recall how Aristotle and Thomas consider prudence to be the ruler's virtue, in one sense, and justice in another.

If those two parallel lines could be bent to meet somewhere in eternity, their nexus would be called kingly *caritas*. And it has existed on earth exclusively in the person of Jesus Christ. In this sense, the king's role is a perfectly charitable mediation of justice and prudence—the perfect admixture of prophetic admonition and priestly mercy. So, the householder's kingly *caritas* is the equivalent of justice-mercy, or just-prudence—two natural virtues in their supernatural, plenary, grace-infused form.

In terms of the ensured victory of good over evil, the kingly role of household fathers provides but an approximate glimpse of the present and future Social Kingship of Christ, the King of kings. Notwithstanding the redemptive value of suffering and defeat exampled by priests, household fathers need to win certain battles. There is a time for winning. For instance, we must not regard as dispensable the ultimate triumph in the spiritual combat exampled by a father's proper moral instruction to his household. Rather, he must triumph over the devil in gaining Heaven for his family. The stakes are too high for defeat.

Among these instances of his office, the king's simultaneous "justice-mercy"—being gentle and tough at once—arises from the supernatural virtue *caritas* associated with him. This kingly virtue mixes strengths of both the prophet and the priest. It is superlatively instructive for husbands and fathers. Prudence and justice culminate naturally in higher, supernatural *caritas*. All good men strive to lead their households in this fashion.

Consider Aragorn's sometimes surprising disposition of justice and mercy with regard to various opponents in *Lord of the Rings*. His decisions might strike as capricious an observer untutored in justice, prudence, and *caritas*. But, like the decisions of the wise household father, they prove anything but arbitrary. Aragorn shocks viewers by ruthlessly dispatching many foes with extreme prejudice, after laboriously and deliberately preventing the traitorous Grima Wormtongue's beheading by King Theoden of Rohan. What is one to make of this? Aragorn's logic is not inscrutable, as the incautious viewer may receive it to be. On the contrary, his logic is kingly, a frangible admixture of justice, prudence, and mercy. A manly leader must administer over his household precisely such a Christ-imitating sort of just, prudent *caritas*. So doing requires skill and strength, statecraft and subtlety.

Neither strong justice nor mild mercy are sufficient without the other. Things are not nearly as simple as the denizens of the twenty-first century have been spuriously led to believe.

Spes: The Prophet's Virtue

A householder's participation in the second office of Christ, prophet, amounts to the measure of his supernatural virtue of *spes*, or hope. The prophet is God's representative to man. Righteous men must, from time to time, chasten their families through prophetic admonition, an unpleasant yet indispensable role of household fathers. The leader must correct and punish in order to ingrain good habits in his followers. Accordingly, the prophet is marked by his never-ending hope in the receptivity of his people, his family, to the message of God. The dictates of Heaven require that he must never give up on his people.

While the Old Testament prophets appeared dauntless and bold, "voices crying out in the wilderness" (Isaiah 40:3, NIV), they lived somewhat apart from the people of Israel rather than with them. The Old Testament prophets would periodically re-connect with the people by venturing among them and then chastening them harshly. But because the prophets could, like John the Baptist, recede to their own living space, they did not depend upon such a careful or artful expression of the prophetic message as the household father does. It's difficult to share a home with those whom one chides; in this sense, perhaps the biblical prophets had an *easier* time of things than fathers do.

Given human nature, the ancient prophets' remoteness from the people of Israel enhanced their audacity. By contrast, modern men administering Christian households face the additional prophetic task of being, at times, the bearer of ill news or harsh punishment from within the same household as the people they chasten. Ac-cordingly, a householder needs extra efficacy from the natural virtue of temperance, as perfected by the supernatural virtue of *spes*. While the prophet remains ever hopeful for the conversion of the hard hearts of his people, he must (to some extent) disconnect himself emotionally so as to deliver dispassionately the true message of God. Such a disconnection would contradict the maternal nature of household mothers. "Tough love" must be fatherly.

Let's put this into its proper context. The king wins by win-ning; as we will see below, the priest wins by losing; the prophet, unique with regard to both of these, wins by divorcing his message from the terms of triumph or defeat altogether. For the prophet, the message is the thing. Think of Tolkien's prophet in *Lord of the Rings*, Gandalf the Grey. Not only are his actions deeply informed by his office, but by analogy, they are prophetically instructive to household fathers.

Throughout the arc of the events of *Lord of the Rings*, Gandalf makes limited yet accurate prognostications. While householders enjoy no supernatural capacity for prescience, they are charged with the task of making the best decisions for their families' future, with only complicated and fallible information at hand.

Secondly, Gandalf proves to be a pilgrim who never quite stays put. In the religious sense, the prophet-father, like the miniature "pilgrim Church" he oversees, must be a perennial wanderer, cleaving to his wife and kids and following the path at his feet (to wherever it is holiest for them). Moreover, in the natural sense, the householder migrates according to the exigencies of his breadwinning.

Thirdly, Gandalf acts as both moral *and* practical guardian of Middle Earth's people of good will, a prophetic admixture of the properties of priest and king. As we discussed at the beginning of this chapter, the connection between moral and practical male guardianship is *bodily* — men are big and strong and contemplative for a reason. Fathers must never second-guess their own design.

Fourthly, Gandalf plays *consigliere* to heads of state. The householder stands as emissary and diplomat to other family heads, needfully trading news and advice between and among the houses. Gandalf often ventures apart and away from those he heads as their itinerant prophet, returning to them from time to time "with tidings and counsel"; similarly, householders must offer news and tips from abroad to their own people.

Last but not least, Gandalf sometimes yells at the company upon returning from his travels, disappointed with their performance in his absence. This friction with his disciples includes instances when we see Gandalf solemnly, if infrequently, butt heads with his chief lieutenant Thorin Oakenshield and, later, Aragorn. (In some sense, the prophet is in charge of even the king.) Consider the identical way that good household fathers must occasionally chasten their chief lieutenants, household mothers, in order to correct the course on the family's way.

As mentioned above, the household prophet's supernatural hope corresponds with his natural virtue of temperance. Unlike the king and the priest, the prophet thrives without rhetoric of kingly triumph and priestly defeat. Both the former and the latter fail abjectly in defining the prophet's dearest end: the cultivation of his people's love for God. In such cases, the householder finds his mission defined by *hope*. The good household husband and father ceaselessly and supernaturally hopes that his *ecclesiola*—wife and children—will follow his holy example and his temperate corrections, with neither reservation nor resentment. The prophetic hope is a never-ending yearning for the good of his troubled people, through thick and thin—not unlike Gandalf. Greater tact is required of a household prophet than was needed of the prophets of Israel, who could afford to chasten intemperately, from a remote location. When living in the same household as those being scolded, the father must moderate his tone and sharpen his hope, on his family's behalf. Doing this without completely watering down the message is the defining feature of the manly office of prophet.

Fides: The Priestly Virtue

A householder's participation in the third office of Christ, priest, amounts to the measure of his supernatural virtue of *fides* (his faith). The priest is man's representative to God. We should not expect to see householders, in their priestly capacity, "winning" like the king but, rather, dying to themselves. The mark of the priest is to win by losing.

On behalf of his friends, the priest must turn his back on his friends—facing God instead—and make sacrifices on their behalf. The priest's sacrifices range from the small to the large. Through Christ's example, we now know that priestly faith may even be tested through the ultimate sacrifice: the sacrifice of one's very life.

In order to do the impossible and die willingly for his people, the priest must center his household ministry upon the supernatural virtue of *believing without seeing*. Whereas ordinary priestly sacrifice requires daily faith, extraordinary priestly self-sacrifice requires extraordinary faith. Contrast the "red martyrdom" in a priest's willing one-time self-sacrifice, with "white martyrdom," a priestly kind of daily dying to oneself. Once again, in *Lord of the Rings*, we see both types of martyrdom in Frodo. He suffers daily on the road to Mordor and eventually his aggregated bodily wounds culminate in his exceptional passage to the Undying Lands.

Fides should be conceived as a supernatural perfection of the natural virtue of fortitude. Whereas the triumphant, ruling, domestic king elevates the natural virtues of justice and prudence to *caritas*, the Christlike self-sacrifice of a domestic priest demands of him the purest fortitude and thus the highest faith. St. Paul meant precisely this when he wrote that a man must lay down his life for his wife and family.

Throughout the events of *Lord of the Rings*, the chief of priestly sacrifice, Frodo, suffers injuries on behalf of his friends: he gets stabbed first on Weathertop, then again in the Mines of Moria, and is stung by Shelob. A household father, as moral and practical guardian of the home, must expect no less. The continual wounding of Frodo represents the worldly fact that not all battles can be won by even the best priestly men.

In this regard, a household father should not inculcate only the triumphalism of the king. Indeed, there exists a time for noble defeat: the shadow of the Cross of Christ should loom large on the landscape of the man who heads a wife and children. Life is a serious affair. As Christ carried His Cross onto Golgotha, Frodo carried the One Ring onto Mount Doom—a task for which he volunteered when no one else would. In addition to the joyful task of teaching his son how to win, this final priestly lesson of noble defeat may be the trickiest assignment of the household father. He must learn not only to win for Christ, but also how to lose.

Summer is the season of plenty, of long days and family time. But winter looms around the corner; the inevitable loss and death during winter should not be raged against. And the priestly father must teach his wife and children the difference between the seasons: one must make profitable, holy usage of the long days of summer, fighting to survive and thrive; but in winter one must retreat and accept the defeat of the warmth, until the new life of the Parousia.

In summary, the household father must deftly balance the sacred triumphalism of a king and the holy fatalism of a priest. He must, at other times, disregard consequences in favor of principles, like a prophet. He must tune his household to the notes of both suffering and joy. He must bring the strengths of each of the Old Testament offices to bear in their proper time and in the prudent manner. The household father must "be all things to all men"—priest, prophet, and king—by imitating Jesus within his own home.

Conclusion: The Unlearning of Feminism

A brief biographical note is in order. I have ten years' experience teaching students aged from middle school through college. My pedagogical experience brought about many surprise "revelations," to be sure. But just as certainly, one revelation stands out among the many: this one truly shocked me.

Even in a politically and culturally conservative region, I was surprised to find that the most "dangerous" lesson I ever gave our students was female and male virtue-instruction oriented at opposite, complementarian goals. Even the most conservative parents of this era were threatened by the educating of young men and women about the sexually disparate purposes of their education itself.

Indeed, a male education must differ at least partly from a female education, insofar as schooling is instruction in the moral and intellectual virtues that vary between the sexes. Evidently, a large number of parents take offense at the Christian institutions of young and fruitful matrimony, male leadership with female fealty, households by single breadwinners, and sex-specific training in accordance with the latter.

Whereas Catholic teachers in politically liberal areas habitually contend with parents about homosexuality, abortion, contraception, and other so-called hot topics, none of these ever gave rise to a single confrontation with a parent in my experience. Instead, it was the senior-year Philosophy of Man course—which, of course, also deals with women and the binary lay vocations—that really got students thinking (and some parents fuming).

As my former students proceeded on to college and confronted the cost of feminism firsthand, they usually returned home at Thanksgiving, at Christmas, and in the summer reporting a renewed dedication to the sexual anthropology they had been taught in their senior year. They had seen firsthand the "human cost" of feminism at university. Its toll is undeniable.

Yet, curiously, it was usually in this phase of the development of my former students' anti-feminist resolve that their conflicts with their parents began in earnest. Liberal, moderate, and conservative parents began to object only after their college kids took full, personal ownership of the Christian anthropology of sex. When theology lessons in Catholic school remained abstract (if compelling), parents of the older generation overlooked the retrograde sympathies of their offspring; but when those offspring combined their Catholic lessons with the subsequent reaffirmation of cautionary illustrations from real life, that resolve on behalf of Christian sex roles was deemed "too much" to be tolerated. In our conservative area—where no complaint had ever been tendered about classroom lessons against homosexuality or contraception—parental complaints rolled in.

Sex-specific education in the virtues proves to be a frightening threat to the existing order of militant secularism. Using only synonyms for the cardinal and supernatural virtues and offices of Christ examined above, we may fairly say that a Christian layman must be shrewd, brave, fair, and balanced. He must be God's representative to the family, his family's representative to God. He must, quite simply, be the best and most heroic man in his wife's and children's view. Only these seven qualities taken together will make a leader out of him—leadership for which he was born—even if these strengths appeared only in inchoate form during the courtship of his eventual wife.

The man who, with holy fear and trembling, works out those seven virtues will doubtlessly acquire the primary male virtue, the eighth: leadership. Many good Christian householders today have earned all but the last, lacking only the fortitude to assert their leadership. After all, feminism working through the popular culture, has aggressively and narrowly targeted the patriarchy of the home. Many good men have constructed unled but otherwise decent homes simply because they lacked the fortitude to contradict the popular culture by justly demanding godly obedience of their wives. Instead, they crack pusillanimous, fatalistic jokes about wifely disobedience, which trivialize and even justify the ideology's fatal toxins: "Ask my boss." "Happy wife, happy life." "I just live here." "I just do what I'm told." "It's taxation without representation—I pay the bills, I but have no say."

Happily, a fraction of these disempowered men eventually come to inquire how they can turn the tables on their wives' habitual disobedience. The answer is simple: stop joking fecklessly about wifely disobedience and explain to your wife the spiritual deadliness of the subversion of Christ's relation to His Church! Explain to your wife clearly the vocational first principle that disobedience of a husband equates to a wifely lack of love for Jesus, just as failing to lead and defend is a husbandly lack of love for Christ.

It's that simple. When St. Paul gave his famous scriptural "instruction for Christian households," his primary goal was to apply Christology to the Christian home: "Wives, submit yourselves to your own husbands as you do to the Lord. For the husband is the head of the wife as Christ is the head of the Church, his body, of which he is the Savior. Now as the Church submits to Christ, so also wives should submit to their husbands in everything" (Ephesians 5:22–24, NIV).

Although "Christian feminists" have popularized a tempest-in-a-teapot debate about this straightforward scriptural passage, the mention of "submission" in our concluding treatment is merely secondary. St. Paul's intent in the passage was clearly to mark a Christological distinction between husband and wife: man acts as Christ to the miniature Church—his wife and kids. Christ offered to and through his Church a path to Heaven. Vocation, whether ordained or married, simply determines what an individual's specific path to Heaven is. When a wife refuses to obey her husband, she abandons her own primary means of loving and obeying Christ (as when any member of the Church refuses to obey one of His commands). Similarly, when a husband refuses to lead his wife, he abandons his primary means of salvation through Christ.

Speaking of which, humility is the foremost virtue of Christian confusion. Perhaps this is the note to close on. In the household, humility means a sort of priestly (male) forfeiture of one's life or a wifely (female) submission of the will in all things. But contrary to popular opinion, humility does not negate a fighting spirit in the cultural combat. In fact, humility even *requires* men to fight in winnable skirmishes, when the survival of justice or the common good depends on triumph. Accordingly, self-mortification—which weds a man's kingly triumphalism and his priestly fatalism—belongs to the spiritual realm, ensuring that a victorious culture warrior does not become brash or cocky, but instead remains pious and meek in prayer. In his masterpiece *The Way*, St. Josemaría Escrivá writes that without self-mortification a man can never become prayerful. For many timid men, entering the fray is precisely the mortification they need.

In the private home or in the public arena, most men today must reclaim their office of leadership by humbly accepting a more confrontational role. Privately, they must simply insist with their wives upon their leadership. Publicly, they must begin announcing this private truth loudly. Only in this way can public virtue begin to be restored.

5

How to Take Back Western
Culture from the Feminists

Each of the previous chapters of this book prompts the reader in a single, clear direction: away from feminism. The reader is now armed with knowledge about the symptoms and signposts of feminism, the Church's longstanding teaching on the household patriarchy and against feminism, the tricky history of feminism, and the anti-feminist patriarchal virtues.

The primary remaining question is this: What anti-feminist *action* is insinuated by all this knowledge? What should actually be *done* about feminism?

The response must take hold of society one family — one married couple — at a time. This chapter will detail how to effect this change.

Recalling that feminism is, in the main, an attack on chastity, the primary counteraction by the anti-feminist layman should be *weaponized chastity*. Bear in mind that chastity is not necessarily the categorical equivalent of celibacy. Celibacy would mean avoiding intercourse altogether. Rather, I mean the "virtuous refraining from that sexual intercourse which is regarded as contrary to morality or religion."[214] It invokes abstinence before marriage and chaste sexual relations thereafter.

Whereas the feminist popular culture has sexualized premarital life and desexualized marital life, weaponized chastity involves the precise opposite: desexualizing premarital life and resexualizing marital life.

Think of the popular conduit of the great lie, feminist popular media, which has by now bedeviled most everyone in society. For generations, one instance of popular media, Nora Ephron's screenplay *When Harry Met Sally*, was the oracular dating guidebook for those young adults who were weighing marriage "on the scene." Here is a sample of the film's slander against the institution of marriage:

> When Joe and I first started seeing each other, we wanted exactly the same thing. We wanted to live together, but we didn't want to get married because anytime anyone we knew got married, it ruined their relationship. They practically never had sex again. It's true, it's one of the secrets no one ever tells you. I would sit around with my girlfriends who have kids—well, my one girlfriend who has kids, Alice—and she would complain about how she and Gary never did it anymore. She didn't even complain about it now that I think about it. She just said it matter-of-factly. She said they were up all night, they were both exhausted, the kids just took every sexual impulse out of them.[215]

---

[214] *Collins English Dictionary*, s.v. "chaste," https://www.dictionary.com/browse/chaste.

[215] *When Harry Met Sally*, directed by Rob Reiner, performed by Billy Crystal, Carrie Fisher, Meg Ryan, and Bruno Kirby (Castle Rock Entertainment and Nelson Entertainment, 1989).

Consequentially speaking, this proves to be feminism's most diabolical lie, glamourizing premarital life and denigrating marital life, by spurious reference to the selfsame criterion: sex. The great lie efficiently reversed how the cultural mainstream "feels" about the two epochs in the life of laymen: before and after marriage.

In a rightly ordered society, naturally and supernaturally well-suited to weaponized chastity, the term "sexy" would (literally and figuratively) be exclusively applied to marriage. After all, matrimony is the sole institution or station in life whose essential act—the marital act—is sexual intercourse, a holy thrill long awaited throughout the premarital life. Contrary to the popular contraceptive frame of mind, Catholic teaching renders marriage the only *naturally sexual* status for a human being. (This holds true even among married couples in the secular world, since even among pagans the natural law dictates that only married couples actively attempt to conceive children.) Sacramentally speaking, of course, the prospect of a highly sexualized marital life doubles as also being a *supernaturally* true Catholic proposition.

If the married reader finds these notions idealistic or inaccurate, then he is doing matrimony all wrong. If your marriage is not sexy, then change it immediately. Do things the Catholic way. This chapter will explain how to turn it all around, since the turnaround requires a few daring yet delicate intra-couple conversations, within the confines of the sacrament.

The cultivation of male leadership begins with a chaste courtship. Make no mistake: there can be no restoration of patriarchy in Western society until men and women embrace the patriarchal values in their own lives. We cannot restore the Social Kingship of Christ until we enthrone Him in our own hearts, embracing Him as our Lord and serving Him as our Master.

Chaste Male Assertiveness and the
Failures of the Beta Male

According to both the natural law and the supernatural law, Aristotle's view and the *Catechism*'s, family begins with the pairing of a virtuous male with a virtuous female. But how are these two to find one another and thereby grow together in virtue? How might a young man—the initiator of the entire cycle of courtship based upon mutual virtue-attraction—come by the admirable qualities necessary for attracting a virtuous female?

One must begin with this question, examining the primary virtue that males must possess *before* approaching females for courtship. (Remember: courtship bears the direct purpose of household creation). Without proper grounding, the whole setup might look like a catch-22. This primary male virtue of initiation must be named male leadership, without which neither men nor women in the laity can achieve happiness.

As we observed last chapter, the first word in manly virtue must be *leadership*, which is wrought from male chastity. Accordingly, we must examine the nearly inestimable value of chastity in the making of the manly leader. Chastity frees up a single young man's will and intellect for self-possession and the eventual possession (or repossession) of his own family. We might take an analytical end run when considering the role of male chastity in eliminating the chthonic depravities of feminism: recall from chapter 3 that even the first-wave feminists sought to enslave men sexually, trading opportunely on the untamed lust of men. In other words, the feminists weaponized sexuality. What follows clarifies how chastity might and must be counter-weaponized in the twenty-first century.

The unchastened male intellect operates at half-speed compared with the chastened version, and with more frequent errors.

The will of the unchaste male pursues practically nothing besides sex, even when the man in question naively believes he is pursuing some nobler quarry. Sadly, a man can master neither his environment, his family, his opponents, nor his own salvation until he first masters his own sexuality. If leadership is the first male virtue, then any comprehensive list of the other male virtues must include the corresponding excellence most prominent in the domain of premarital male rapport with females: chastity (and its fruits).

Right off the bat, interrogate the degree to which our own day lacks both male leadership and male chastity. The matching deficiencies turn out to be conspicuously related.

The strict observance of sexual ethics proves to be closely linked with salutary patriarchal activism (that is, leadership). On the other side of the coin, chaste male leadership cultivates and encourages the corresponding female virtues of fealty, receptivity, and docility (which, too, are lacking today). Because chastity has been subverted, perversity rules; it does so under a would-be "matriarchy" attempted by feminists in the 1960s, yet custom-designed roughly one century prior to that.

Today's cultural scene can best be described as nature turned upside down. We see *manufactured* male passivity and female activism in basically every corner of the West: at home, in the academy, at the workplace, in civics, on the playground—even in sports. Men and women first swapped ethical and, thereafter, practical roles.

Over thousands of years of human history, the role of moral leadership was man's to forfeit. On a close inspection, modern man's sexual indiscretions seem to have inaugurated his disempowerment.

To pitch it from the opposite perspective, promiscuity can never constitute or cultivate true manhood. The *telos* of human sexual intercourse is a signpost informing us that, unlike animal sexuality, human sexual activity must, by its nature, be reserved for building and strengthening matrimonial family, the "original cell" of civil society (CCC 2207). Human flourishing involves sexual and procreative dignity, while animal (and plant) flourishing do not.

In the early Christian Church, the Platonic scholar and Catholic martyr Boethius wrote: "Man towers above the rest of creation as long as he realizes his own nature, and when he forgets it, he sinks lower than the beasts. For other things to be ignorant of themselves is natural; for man it is a defect."[216] In the context of sexual relations, Boethius's wisdom would typify human promiscuity as unnatural, and animal "promiscuity" (if such a thing existed) as natural. For a man to impregnate many women proves utterly inconsistent with human nature; for a bull to impregnate many cows turns out to be perfectly consistent with animal nature. The proof is in the pudding: animal unrestraint in regard to human sex has proven the key feature in the ruin of mankind.

First, let's examine how the premeditated, popular, century-long[217] cultivation of sexual vice led to a widespread male shrinking from presumptive leadership—namely, widespread cultural failures in chastity in the 1960s resulted in the perverted role swapping of the sexes.

---

[216] Boethius, *The Consolation of Philosophy*, rev. ed. (London: Penguin Books, 1999), 2, 5.

[217] Recall from chapter 3 that the first-wave feminists, such as Elizabeth Cady Stanton, began scheming to popularize sexual promiscuity (toward the end of female domination) as far back as 1848 at the Seneca Falls Convention. Thus, here we refer to cultural failures in chastity as a "consequence" rather than a "cause."

While some have been tempted to characterize the demands of Christian sexuality as a more onerous imposition upon males than females, accruing to natural differences between the two sexes, chastity proves equally important in the two. This moral fact is undeniable. Yet, for the purposes at hand, we will focus on how chastity proves indispensable for the reclamation of male leadership.

The fact of male leadership, until very recently, has never been doubted. Leaving aside the obvious anatomical biology which insinuates it—strength, agility, speed, "dating" brain science[218]—one must simply consult thousands of years of human culture in the domain of courtship. Given Christian complementarity and the marital becoming of one flesh, the ways that the two sexes view one another proves determinative in how each sex views itself. Every man's self-esteem is largely constituted by his wife's esteem, and vice versa (to be discussed in later sections of this chapter). This rapport begins with the very first date.

After all, the male has always borne responsibility for the proper construction of his romantic relationship from the ground up and from the very moment courtship begins. The approach of the female and the "initiation of the conversation" fall on his shoulders, as do the *actual* and *opportunity* costs of the first date, not to mention the moral and practical caretaking of the female during the date. And if the date goes well, the purview of male responsibility only expands rapidly. In the prospective domain of

---

[218] Emory University Health Sciences Center, "Study Finds Male and Female Brains Respond Differently to Visual Stimuli," *ScienceDaily*, March 16, 2004, www.sciencedaily.com/releases/2004/03/040316072953.htm. The amygdala has been shown by these findings to be activated in the dating male brain but not in the female counterpart.

the family the couple seeks to build together, these instances of male initiative on the first date are culture- and nature-derived signposts. They put us on notice that human societies do not ubiquitously produce male-led courtship arbitrarily. Those men who have accepted the "meaninglessness" of male-initiated conversation, "beta males," have broken the mold and created a new, truly ruinous one.

Leadership in Courtship

In addition to being a meaningful signpost, male-initiated courtship proves a decisive first step in the formation of chaste, male-led relationships.

The rule's indispensability is proven by its own breaches. If, for example, a man refuses from the outset to discharge his duty of chaste leadership over his prospective household—specifically by courting a woman with the subverted formal object of having sex with her before marriage—a negative twofold effect follows in every instance. First, the power roles are reversed as the male becomes the passively supplicating petitioner, the disempowered one begging permission for his sexual advances. Then, the proper moral and sexual roles are subverted and inverted, as the woman assumes the mantle of moral guarantor on behalf of the couple. She is "goalie" from that point onward. From the point of view of both dynamics and morality, the authority has come to be the woman's to lose. This is why the feminists encourage promiscuity!

Either way, the nonvirtuous male, having forfeited his leadership through his breach of chastity, will end up emasculated. This is the case whether the female renders a virtuous or vicious decision regarding the male's premarital sexual advances. If, on the one hand, she rebuffs his sexual advances, she keeps her honor and henceforth owns the practical and moral headship in the way that nature intended *him* to do. If, on the other hand, she submits to his sexual overtures, then both parties will remain forever cognizant that he forfeited his nature-intended mantle of authority—only, in this case, neither the submitting female nor the predatory male courting her retains that moral authority.

Without an intervening religious conversion sometime in the couple's future (which proves difficult yet possible), this initial forfeiture of male leadership will come to typify the entire relationship. A promiscuous man—or, rather, half a man—cannot fully give himself to his eventual bride. Knowledge of his sexual indiscretions, with her or others, plagues and embitters her, if subconsciously. The forfeiture of the moral headship will continually emasculate the man and debase the woman with a shrill, spurious sense of usurpation.

This is happening all around us in the popular culture, which is why men are so woefully emasculated. The totality of this cultural phenomenon in the West today appears utterly without precedent. Accordingly, the primary male virtue should be conceived of as a couplet: chastity and activism—that is, righteous assertion of leadership.

On the other side of the aisle, each of society's variant factions seeks to divorce chastity from the proposition of male leadership, each for its own reason. The feminists and radicals do so to retain their commandeered power, while secular or tepid Christian conservatives seek to continue their divorce of practical from religious ideas so as to negate the most compelling motive for returning to society's most spurned virtue: chastity.

The upshot is that our neo-pagan popular culture will embrace a boxer's sexual abstinence but never a saint's. If temporary abstinence appears to be connected to an imminent victory in a sport or contest, as in boxing, society will bend the knee to it.

The Case for Patriarchy

Recall Mick telling Rocky to "lay off the pet shop dame" while training for his title bout with Apollo Creed. Rocky fans gladly accept Mick's admonition. But that affirmative response by the popular culture quickly reverses if the abstinence being invoked is indefinite in duration, or if it's invoked in the name of Christian virtue instead of victory in a sport.

In the interest of repairing today's degenerate Western culture, one must work with and improve upon whatever raw material he's set before. Thus, this chapter and this book seek to accept the boxer's imperfect chastity but to enlarge upon its moral and temporal scope. A properly conceived boxer's mentality, if popularized, would single-handedly win the day and restore male leadership to society. A true leader must be coarse but not crass, tough but not rough, and in the world but not of the world. Only the Christian man—the one true "fighter" in the right-minded sense of the term—can accomplish all this at once.

By implication, the many flavors of the 2020 beta male—the "macho" type, the "intellectual" type, the "artistic" type, etc.—are *made from* unimproved sexual promiscuity. Counterintuitive at first, this insight may be proven by recourse to a simple cataloguing of all one's grown-up male friends. Think of them. Of all the ex-jocks and all the ex-nerds you ever knew, odds are that only the anomalous Christian alpha retains an easy, charming, winsome leadership over his household. Not unrelatedly, only his household functions as it should.

Either way, all the ex-jocks and ex-nerds you ever hung out with scratch a meager, amoral, get-away-with-what-you-can living, consisting in "asking permission" from their ill-tempered "boss" at every turn. The fatal malady is plainly observable in society, which suffers from its ongoing throes. Men and women everywhere are miserable.

Such universal gender-bending has led to society's near-ubiquitous marital discord, frequent divorce, resultant poverty,[219] resultant crime,[220] dysfunctional single-parent households, and widespread human misery. This fact of life is perverse enough to be popular and popular enough to be perverse.

A parting shot: sexual promiscuity has addled the sexual revolutionaries even more than the rest of society. In early 2019's now-infamous, male-bashing, feminist Gillette commercial, the "giant razor-maker got itself into a bit of a tough scrape with an ad promoting the ideals of the #MeToo movement," allegedly "undercutting toxic masculinity."[221] Within six months of the catastrophic marketing blitz, Gillette's parent company reported "an eight billion dollar charge on its Gillette shaving business"[222] for the quarter ending on June 30 of that year. However, thanks to the short memory of the American public, Gillette seems to have recovered after that fiscal quarter. But a viewing of the commercial makes it plainly evident that the feminists running

---

[219] Isabel V. Sawhill, "How Marriage and Divorce Impact Economic Opportunity," Brookings Institute, May 6, 2014, https://www.brookings.edu/opinions/how-marriage-and-divorce-impact-economic-opportunity/.

[220] Edwin J. Fuelner, "Divorce: Ignoring the Cost," Heritage Foundation, August 28, 2000, https://www.heritage.org/marriage-and-family/commentary/divorce-ignoring-the-cost.

[221] Tovia Smith, "Backlash Erupts after Gillette Launches a New #MeToo-Inspired Ad Campaign," *NPR*, January 17, 2019, https://www.npr.org/2019/01/17/685976624/backlash-erupts-after-gillette-launches-a-new-metoo-inspired-ad-campaign.

[222] Richa Naidu and J. Soundarya, "P&G Posts Strong Sales, Takes $8 billion Gillette Writedown," Reuters, July 30, 2019, https://www.reuters.com/article/us-proctergamble-results/pg-posts-strong-sales-takes-8-billion-gillette-writedown-idUSKCN1U-P1AD.

movements like #MeToo are not even quite sure what behaviors qualify as "toxic masculinity."

Noteworthily, shortly after the two-minute commercial's one-minute mark, the ad depicts a man noticing a woman on the street, beginning to pursue her but being halted by his friend, ostensibly on moral grounds. Strangely enough, the commercial offers no explanation as to why the pursuit by a man of a woman, presumably to request a date, fits within its proscribed list of behaviors. Since the #MeToo movement doesn't condemn fornication but, rather, male sexual assertiveness, one can only assume that Gillette (and the #MeToo movement) equates "toxic masculinity" with male-initiated courtship.

One is tempted to shrug and say "the confusion runs deep" — that Gillette simply confused initiating the conversation with sexual harassment. However, one recalls that feminism hand-crafted the #MeToo movement, meaning a hatred of the male leadership implicit within male-initiated courtship. So, depending on one's level of cynicism, the Gillette debacle represents either outright or mistaken condemnation of male initiation of the conversation. Either way, it makes sense.

Romance, Human Nature, and the "Two Courtships"

One should discuss romantic relationships in two phases or "two courtships": one before and one after. There exist two related difficulties to "keeping the romance alive": chastity and maintaining the drive to impress the other.

Chastity is the more difficult challenge in the first courtship, while impression maintenance is the more difficult in the second courtship.

During the premarital courtship phase, as we saw above, the primary exercise of personal restraint inheres in the containment of sexual urges. The chaste couple in premarital courtship will abstain from sex and—whether consciously or subconsciously—will accordingly hasten to wed.

Notwithstanding the unwarranted derision of secularists, who insinuate that "religious people" typically settle for the first warm body with whom they might licitly have sex, there is certainly a nugget of truth in the proposition that sane celibates will drastically truncate the five- to ten-year premarital period during which many secularist couples "date" nowadays. Of course, those secularist couples who play house for a decade or so are almost always sexually active from the outset. Brief courtships, on the other hand, frequently involve participants who wait until marriage to begin sexual activity.

It is futile to deny the mind-body connection motivating the correlation between premarital sexual activity and its corollary, the complacent lingering outside of wedlock. An equal and opposite thing might be said about the correlation between abstinence and brief courtships. After all, the time-sensitive sexual restraint of the religious young couple forms a material complement to their formal incentive to wed quickly, informed by their vocational understanding of their own relationship. In other words, a faithful young man and woman in a promising courtship, possessed of a sacramental understanding of their rapport, will be all the more immediately motivated to wed by their sublimated physical attraction.

Whereas "waiting until marriage" to engage in sex constitutes the primary challenge of the courtship phase, this burden is eased by the fact that most young people find it the easiest period of life to keep trim, athletic, and looking and feeling their best. Human nature dictates that young people on the hunt for their spouses will effortlessly find the requisite time to exercise and care for their appearance, much more than they will do so subsequently—in old age, midlife, or even the young marriage state. To tend to one's appearance is second nature to a young person attempting to win himself a spouse.

Also according to basic human nature, this couplet of challenges reverses on a couple's wedding day. Chastity becomes comparatively easy, requiring abstinence no longer but rather adherence to a few simple sexual rules. Physical fitness and attention to personal appearance, on the other hand, will quite naturally come to be overlooked, without scrupulous self-governance. One cannot truthfully convince oneself, after all, that he is "winning" his spouse, in the literal sense, each day of his married life.

The "marital debt,"[223] as joyful an ontological guarantee as it may be for both spouses, proves counterproductive in incentivizing parties to expend great effort on their figure, charm, or appearance. On account of the natural complacency of human behavior, two otherwise happy and well-suited married people will at some point inevitably fall into the pitfall of "letting themselves go." It is a matter of *when*, not *if*—but it is altogether reversible. Restoring the romance within a married relationship is truly

---

[223] The "marital debt" is expounded by St. Paul in 1 Corinthians 7:2–5: "But since sexual immorality is occurring, each man should have sexual relations with his own wife, and each woman with her own husband. The husband should fulfill his marital duty to his wife, and likewise the wife to her husband. The wife does not have authority over her own body but yields it to her husband. In the same way, the husband does not have authority over his own body but yields it to his wife. Do not deprive each other except perhaps by mutual consent and for a time, so that you may devote yourselves to prayer. Then come together again so that Satan will not tempt you because of your lack of self-control."

God's work; marriages are called to romance, the natural bond between man and woman. Even without the scourge of feminism magnifying this manageable foible, as I will discuss below, marital romance negligence can fast become dangerously out of control.

The duration of this chapter consists in training the Catholic's concept of marriage as "the second courtship," which will do much to restore both a husband's and a wife's enthusiasm for impressing each other. As a matter of fact, the second courtship, if done properly, can be the *superior* courtship, since flirtation and intimacy during marriage do not turn out anticlimactically, as merely a blocked wish (as they do prior to marriage). In other words, a married couple who flirts together all day long can *do something about it,* unlike premarital couples. This is why I said above that the "challenge" of chastity reduces to practically nothing in marriage. Sex between licitly married spouses must be unitive and procreative. With practically no other limitations, it qualifies as not only chaste but also holy, conferring cumulative graces on the married couple with each compliant instance of the marital act.

The great delicacy lies in unifying the two challenges: married sexual rapport is considerably more sustainable when both parties keep themselves looking sharp. By the same token, making an effort to impress one another is easier when the spouses work to sustain the romance—physical and emotional—in their relationship.

What follows is an account of the most mortal singular danger to the marital will to keep romance alive.

Feminism and Bodily Identity Politics

As you've probably guessed, feminism is the culprit that crafted the most streamlined equipment for hastening the disintegration of marital romance. After all, the feminists have a trick, or at least a preliminary foray, ready at hand to dissolve every aspect of matrimonial and familial unity. As every married person already knows, romance represents a highly frangible aspect of the marital rapport, which hardly needs additional impairments in order to be counted as endangered.

The most recent feminist attack on marital romance is called the "body positivity movement," which has arisen in the obesity-beset milieu of wealthy First World nations, which has undergone an alarming spike in obesity and diabetes over the last four decades.[224] Body positivity turns a blind eye to such maladies, especially in women, and so poses a grave risk to their health.

Unsurprisingly, the movement contemporaneously arose during these same forty years, with the apparent goal of preventing the so-called fat shaming of overweight women while discouraging them from interrogating the etiology or long-term health detriments of their obesity. Ironically, the movement strongly counter-shames women who reject body positivity's complacency by embrace a regimen of diet and exercise in order to make themselves more attractive.

While feminists, radicals, and atheists view the phenomenon of shame in an anti-religious light, Christians understand that remorse for a vice such as willful overeating accrues to a sinful privation called gluttony, which can be mortal in some circumstances. Furthermore, for the Christian, feeling embarrassed about the public sight of one's gluttonous frame is naturally chastening against the continuation of the sin.

If Christianity is correct about vice and reconciliation, then body positivity is a form of relativism, since it holds that every "size" is equally healthful, physically and psychologically.

---

[224] Jay W. Richards, *Eat, Fast, Feast* (New York: Harper One, 2020), 2.

The dangerous movement's reach is expanding. According to *USA Today*, "body positivity is slowly extending beyond advertising and modeling into pop culture."[225] This means that it has moved into the culture of the household, where it can do the most damage.

In its goal of "empowering young women and letting them know they are fine the way they are,"[226] the body positivity movement flouts the wisdom of modern cardiologists, nutritionists, and psychologists. (Middle-aged and elderly women deserve "empowerment" as much as young women. This involves deserving a chance to avoid late-life heart and vascular disease, diabetes, and risk of stroke resultant from a "fine the way they are" mindset.) While it is certainly salubrious—and even helpful to diet-exercise routines—to embrace without denial or self-recrimination one's fundamental body type (for example, endomorph, ectomorph, mesomorph[227]), the body positivity movement reflexively spurns *all* prompts and expedients to female weight loss.[228] As the feminists say, "you can't have body positivity without feminism."[229] In other words, body positivity encourages complete acceptance of one's carriage and weight,

[225] Jaleesa M. Jones, "Body Positivity Has Hit the Mainstream: Now What?" *USA Today*, October 7, 2016, https://www.usatoday.com/story/life/2016/10/07/body-positivity-mainstream/91458824/.

[226] Ibid.

[227] Staff Writers, "Your Body Type—Ectomorph, Mesomorph or Endomorph?," Muscle and Strength, updated May 26, 2021, https://www.muscleandstrength.com/articles/body-types-ectomorph-mesomorph-endomorph.html.

[228] "Body Image + Body Positivity," Feminists Act!, https://www.feministsact.com/issues/body-image-body-positivity/

[229] Melissa A. Fabello, "3 Reasons Why You Can't Have Body Positivity without Feminism," Everyday Feminism, September 24,

even if medical science diagnoses that a person's problems can be avoided or amended. The movement refers to this unnatural, unhealthy goal as "body neutrality," ambitiously claiming that "body positivity is just a small step toward eventually embracing body neutrality, where bodies are accepted as-is without a positive or negative focus."[230]

Accepting your body "as is" and "without a positive or negative focus" is roughly as inane as embracing damage done to your car, as is, after a collision: if a crash has taken the car out of its original condition, the sensible goal becomes restoring the car to its original condition, rather than living with the damage. But body positivity treats human bodies as if they cannot be improved through diet and exercise. Just observe how body positivity attempts to politicize weight as a permanent political identity: the "All Womxn Project" intones weight or "size" as a protected category of special interest:

> We believe size, age, ability, gender identification or color doesn't limit us as womxn. All body shapes, genders, abilities, ages and shades deserve to be represented in fashion and the media, helping girls and womxn worldwide feel positive and confident, regardless of what they look like or whatever "flaw" they think they might have. We love an unretouched, true, natural womxn![231]

Identity politics has earned the reputation of sleazy politicking precisely because it reifies untouchable political classes out of

---

2017, https://everydayfeminism.com/2017/09/no-body-positivity-no-feminism/.

[230] Jones, "Body Positivity Has Hit the Mainstream."

[231] All Womxn Project, www.Allwomxnproject.org.

elective lifestyles or freely chosen vices. Size—unlike one's race or nationality—is not an immutable property. Mutable properties such as being unclothed, having a runny nose, and being five pounds overweight do not suffice as valid political categories because they are subject to our constant amendment. One does not feel "confident" in his appearance when he is half-dressed, possessed of a runny nose (and no tissues), or a bit bloated immediately subsequent to month-long Christmas holiday feasting. But this lack of confidence is perfectly natural. Interrogate the moral and logical relativism entailed by the notion of "confidence" regardless of one's appearance. It is absurd, even inhuman. People care about what they look like, and only a heavy dose of feminist propaganda can train them to do otherwise.

We must not absolutize citizens currently undergoing physical unfitness as a protected political class. This contradicts the morally instructive purpose of law. Ideas have consequences: so categorizing virtually guarantees that members of the unfit political class will remain unfit.

Whereas body positivity attempts to politicize weight as a special-interest political identity, everyone fluctuates in weight, to some extent. A human being of properly formed conscience—man or woman—feels self-imposed remorse after eating, say, twice as much as necessary at a given meal. It is only natural. What's more: we've all eaten gluttonously before! Body positivity advocates talk about certain kinds of women and men as if overeating-shame cycles are far less ubiquitous than they are. To overeat occasionally is human; to diet and exercise is divine! Identifying people with their proclivity toward a certain vice is evil because it makes difficult or impossible the curtailing of the bad habit.

Here is the relevance to our analysis of marital wellness: "ratchet effect" weight gain is not only bad for one's cardiology, nutrition, and psychology. It also destroys marriages. Weight gain in married life is not a matter of *if*, but *when*. Yet, if a person's weight is treated as a protected category, beyond the need or the reach of reproach—as identity politics labors to do—healthy change can never be affected.

Rather, healthy change can never be affected *unless* a loving spouse is willing to engage the party's overweight spouse in a delicate conversation. This is precisely the kind of charitable conversation that must occur, from time to time, in healthy marriages between best friends. Such a vital discussion generally has not been happening, between spouses, on account of the strain recently placed on relationships by body positivity and body neutrality.

Difficult Conversations and Thoughtful Gifts

In a loving, successful marriage, difficult conversations happen. In an unloving, unsuccessful marriage, meaningless, needlessly difficult arguments abound (and the veritably "difficult" conversations never get tended to). Among Catholic couples, aside from the one-time discussion regarding the decision to raise the family within the sacraments, the most important topic to be broached—not once but semi-regularly—comprises the set of periodic conversations regarding the revitalization of the couple's romantic intimacy. Married couples who obviate such conversations usually do so under the delusion that, even between husband and wife, certain topics may be "off-limits."

This is sheer nonsense. The most charitable conversational act a spouse can commit is the address of a volatile, yet needful romantic controversy at issue between them. He thereby risks his own temporary happiness to backlash and "guilt tripping." But marriage cannot survive without romantic candor.

To be sure, both husband and wife are responsible for expressing their own libidinal demurrers and requests. Because the marital debt binds both husband and wife, as noted above, so does this duty of communication, inclusive of preferences for a marital partner's enhancement of the other's personal hygiene, charm, sexual enthusiasm, clothing, and, last but not least, shapely figure. The duty to duly inform one's spouse of one's romantic exigencies constitutes a genuinely "gender neutral" obligation, binding on both parties—a fact that should satisfy the feminists but doesn't.

In the name of moral realism, this issue will arise most frequently in the direction of male-initiated conversations with wives about distinctly male romantic exigencies. Frequently in First World nations over the last forty years (beset with the obesity epidemic), such exigencies will periodically deliberate moderate weight loss. Notwithstanding romance's mutual, reciprocal impositions on both spouses, these healthy conversations will run afoul of feminism on account of the simple fact that they frequently contradict the imperious demands of body neutrality, which requires that no female is ever told that she is anything less than perfect. (Obviously, the feminists couldn't care less about those instances, in breach of body neutrality, of thin wives requesting their fat husbands to lose weight!)

As noted above, husbandly conversations about weight loss should be not only delicate but should also contemplate the wife's best health, given the natural disparity of body types: endomorph, ectomorph, and mesomorph. The first group naturally has more body fat and less muscle mass. The second group naturally remains slender, without much muscle or fat. The third group naturally retains a medium, "athletic," muscular frame—neither slender nor fat.

The Case for Patriarchy

Imagine an attractive young newlywed couple, both of whom are reasonably fit endomorphs on the day of their wedding. Seven years later, if both parties have gained weight, romantic exigencies will place the conversational initiative at the feet of the husband. He should say, as the head of the household, something like, "Both of us have got to get back to dieting and exercise. I know we're both stocky, and that won't change. But we should focus on being our 'best selves,' like we used to."

Many faithful wives would take this as cue enough to aggressively resume dieting and exercising. Much of the unpleasantness of the deeper conversation would be avoided. Other wives, however, might require a deeper, more difficult dive into husbandly physical requirements arising from disparate male-female sexual neurobiology. Such wives must be reminded that having a healthy marriage requires the satisfaction of these healthy urges and the deletion of immoral or unnecessary impediments to mutual attraction.

Unpleasant as it may be, such husbands would have to elect a somewhat more granular approach to the de facto romantic dangers of wifely weight gain. The deeper such husbands are required to dive by wifely resistance, the more specifically the science and theology underpinning the male sexual neurobiology should be referenced. The unpleasant conversation should be sharpened with personal details only as needed, incrementally.

Given the delicate nature of the topic, highly praiseworthy indeed is the "intuitive" husbandly expression and wifely reception of their physical or romantic difficulties.

Virtuous men, being visually focused sexual initiators, will tend vigilantly to ensuring that their physical attraction to their wives remains both sustainable and properly ordered.[232] (Virtuous men will, of course, always be attentive to their wives' collateral requests.) Their only expedient for such surety remains the difficult conversation. There is no viable substitute for it.

Nonvirtuous men, being visually obsessed sexual initiators, will fail to ensure their sustained physical attraction to their wives and will often turn to pornography or even extramarital affairs to satisfy their appetites.

Both virtuous and nonvirtuous women, being non–visually focused and non-initiators of marital sexual relations, will strongly incline toward lauding the reticence of men who refuse to have these difficult conversations. Many will even condemn men who take the controversial step of conveying these concerns to their own wives. Women must be cautioned against this inclination at all costs! The lazy husband simply won't trouble himself with the hassle of a series of necessary yet unpleasant dialogues with his wife. Charitable honesty is the hard way; pornography and extramarital affairs are, to him, the easy way out.

Virtuous wives will, in good faith, encourage and even welcome these difficult conversations, out of fealty to husbands and out of deference to the sacrament of matrimony — even if they find it impossible to empathize with the neurobiologically strong male response to visual stimuli.[233] Conversely, nonvirtuous women will err on the side of delusion and rationalization. "My husband is just as attracted to a 125-pound version of me as he is to a 175-pound or a 225-pound version of me," she'll say. This

---

[232] Emory University Health Sciences Center, "Study Finds Male and Female Brains Respond Differently."

[233] Ibid.

is the stuff of the devil's deception, and its popularity is presently harming many marriages, one at a time.

In previous chapters, we cited the near universality of pornography usage: nineteen out of twenty men have viewed it in the past six months. This tells us everything we need to know about the ubiquitous death of weaponized chastity, and the pursuant death of chaste spousal relationships. Interestingly, the liberal-minded article that cites this statistic makes a boldly austere prognostication of the relationship-crippling effects of pornography: "I predict that by the end of the 21st century, sex will finally come out of the closet — and fundamentally change what being a human being means."[234] Whereas being a human being has always meant either ordained celibacy or marital chastity in loving union, life subsequent to the surrender to a doomed relationship turns out hopeless and lonesome. Family life not lived in the community of spousal love is inhuman. In other words, if male family leaders do not resume the mantle of fighting for the good of their romantic spousal relationships — the battle is mostly waged by the prosecution of difficult conversations, after all — then the "original cell of social life" (CCC 2207) will have been all but eliminated.

One final comparison is in order. Just as loving men address their wives charitably yet directly about difficult romantic issues, good husbands proffer their wives small gifts and help with certain house chores, in love (rather than fear). Cowardly or self-interested husbands undertake such purchases and acts in a spirit of cautious self-preservation. And the caricature of "traditional" husbands — sometimes true — is that they do not undertake such acts of largesse at all. But on the contrary, the loving spouse gifts

---

[234] Brenner, "When Is Porn Use a Problem?"

from an overflowing abundance of fellow feeling and appreciation for his good wife. While — even because — it is never imposed on him as an expectation, the good husband gratefully helps his wife with chores where and when he can.

Every man secretly harbors a list of pleasant household chores to which he does not mind tending. Wives of good husbands will immediately recognize the ones that constitute their husbands' preferred tasks, opportune moments for expressing male gratitude.

The distinction between good will and bad will is an interior one, based upon a given husband's motivation, intelligible only in subtle tones. In other words, there exists no easy "tell" for the difference between a self-interested husband bringing flowers and doing dishes from self-love and he who does the same things from a selfless love. Only a man's wife will know the difference. She will judge by subtle measures, but what she will actually be calibrating is whether or not her husband loves her with a *chaste*, true love: in the marital context, a chaste love will be sexual and selfless. It cannot be faked.

Conclusion

So, what should actually be *done* about feminism? Here's what: weaponized chastity in the form of a chaste courtship, a swift engagement, a chaste "second courtship," carefully sustained marital romance, and purely motivated daily acts of marital largesse. That's what. Recall that celibacy is a nuclear weapon against feminism in the context of the single life, just as sustained, intense marital sexual attraction is thereafter.

Destroy feminism by eradicating fornication among singles to the greatest possible extent and then enlivening romance among marrieds.

In this chapter, I've explored chastity's double context of celibacy prior to marriage and selfless erotic charity thereafter. Notably, the institution of the swift engagement—after six months rather than six years—punctuates the transition between the "two courtships." A swift, seemingly lighthearted engagement period, between two serious-minded Catholics, indicates not flippancy but rather a solemnity of purpose. As such, it must be returned to in the popular culture. A speedy engagement unites the chastity of the single life and married sexual chastity in its adventurous, spontaneous, self-sacrificial approach to the joyful sacrament of marriage, which requires neither material wealth nor vast spans of time in order to be entered.

Besides all the above, weaponized chastity proves efficacious for an additional reason: twenty-first-century chaste males will never be subjected to the weaponized sexuality of feminists, who have learned to condition sex with unprincipled men upon the forced propagation of feminist ideas. Indeed, sexually incentivized male subscription to feminism has ensnared a great portion of the male population.[235] Chastity proves not only a weapon but also

---

[235] Stuart McGurk, "The Problem with Fake Male Feminists," *Gentleman's Quarterly* (United Kingdom), https://www.gq-magazine. co.uk/article/the-problem-with-fake-male-feminists. In this article, the phenomenon of feminist vetting at bars is addressed: "There's a great *Saturday Night Live* sketch, screened before the Harvey Weinstein allegations, early last year, in which a woman is alone at a bar, waiting for a friend. A guy turns up, asks if he can take the seat next to her, pre-empts her concern about it and, after she half-jokes that the whole world is full of gross guys, he makes a joke about Donald Trump with the satisfied expression of someone who has just invented cheese. Soon enough, it turns out they're both wearing the same feminist T-shirt and he asks her out, but she says no. 'OK, bitch! ... I followed all

a defense mechanism for men because it "unplugs" them from the matrix of feminist deceptions and traps. If the reader doubts this for an instant, just see what happens to feminism if even a sizable minority of single men return to the celibacy of bygone times: the toxic movement will evaporate altogether.

I've already discussed the "dangerous" proposition of encouraging young to marry early in life. To the gatekeepers of feminism, widespread youthful marriage is a terrifying prospect. The previous generation's liberals, moderates, and conservatives alike have repudiated youthful marriage mostly without even knowing why. Under the bright light of weaponized chastity, consider the ramifications of late marriage. Baby boomers—even Catholic ones—evidently care little or nothing about their offspring's unchaste approach to the long-term relationship. In other words, they've weighed prolonged unchastity against swift, sexless courtship and decisively opted for the former. Evidently, when evaluating a course of action between opposite behaviors, worldly acceptance is superior to chaste Christian obedience, in the eyes of boomers.

---

the rules!' he shouts. Cue a succession of guys, each apologising for the last, each explaining how they've just been on a march or worked for Hillary, and each exploding with fury when she won't sleep with him."

6

What Christian Patriarchy Looks Like

In this book, it has been shown that whatever else a feminist aspires to embrace, he may not be a rightly believing Christian. The demonstration has been made morally, culturally, historically, philosophically, scripturally, traditionally, and Magisterially.

Sadly, a perusal of these same disciplines readily invites the reader to two further conclusions. Firstly, the mainstream quarters of Protestant and Catholic Christianity all but abandoned the announcement of its clear teaching on femininity sometime during the late-nineteenth or early-twentieth century. Secondly, all indications are that, among the leadership of clergy and laity alike, the opportunistic conspiracy of silence on this matter will likely continue into the foreseeable future.

In other words, judging by the words and deeds of the leaders of Christianity, our faith is *ashamed* of its perennial teachings in favor of the patriarchy and against feminism. Nowhere in an examination of salvation history's priests and prophets do we find such ample evidence of deliberately buried moral teachings. In the realm of Christian doctrinal self-consciousness, the only moral teaching so universally ignored as to rival that on *sexual identity* (that is, feminism and also gender dysphoria) is that on *sexual activity*. Both of these sources of the Church's worldly embarrassment involve the anthropology of the loins.

Again, both are contemporaneous and ongoing.

A significant caveat bears mention. Nowhere in the annals of salvation history do we find a vocal majority of the people of God eagerly following the Decalogue's "hard sayings" or derivative teachings on sexual morality. Indeed, the ethics and the politics of sex are a drag. Obviously, hard sayings make for harder doings. Even in the holiest of eras, the people of God comply begrudgingly at best. This was the case even when the Church taught clearly and without hesitation. So imagine the heightened moral catastrophe that confronts us today, considering that Christianity's referees have willfully "swallowed their whistles" when observing the many flagrant fouls at play, amid the two dimensions of the sexual revolution: sexual identity and sexual activity. Not infrequently, these leaders have even *encouraged* the faithful in their feminism and in their sexual misbehaviors.

Accordingly, the only solution available to the feminism-beset layman is self-quarantine. Upon reading a book with such devastating premises as ours, the Christian is confronted with a momentous decision: "Either live how you believe, or else you will begin to believe how you live," as Archbishop Fulton Sheen taught. At the close of this final chapter, the reader will find himself in a moment of power, wherein practical change can *actually* be worked within his individual household dynamic.

In these pages, the anti-feminist Magisterial sources have been plenary. My historical documentation of the etiology of feminism has been meticulous. The teachings summarily articulated by those natural and supernatural sources have been crystal clear. However muddled up to now, the implications of those teachings have, at present, been placed within close reach of the reader. The antidote is also within reach.

In view of the well-documented malady of feminism, the remedy proves to be equally self-evident: it is "simple but not easy," as the saying goes. The reader has all the information and power he needs to elect and effectuate an individual choice that will, in a fractional way, set to rights the most fundamental problem of the laity in our post-Christian[236] popular culture—a problem prefigured even in the Original Sin. Namely, households must be rectified and healed of their cancerous feminism *one by one*. Christians, men and women of the Cross, joyfully restore Christian patriarchal order to your homes!

Since the Second Vatican Council, the Catholic laity has frequently chastened and attempted to lead the clergy, practically flipping the pyramidal hierarchy of the Church upside down. Ordinarily, this proves problematic; yet with regard to household feminism, the path to rectification proves a bit simpler than other problems facing the Christian faithful, since the hierarchs neither *themselves* head households, nor command directly the heads of households. The laity must chasten and lead *itself* away from feminism, after our leaders have ignored, encouraged, and all but endorsed it.

To the extent that such Christian leaders may opt against reversing their silence or for continuing with their misleading teachings that are complacent with the culture, they may continue along the tacitly feminist path—or they may turn from it.

---

[236] Francis X. Rocca, "Pope Francis, in Christmas Message, Says Church Must Adapt to Post-Christian West," *Wall Street Journal*, December 21, 2019, https://www.wsj.com/articles/pope-francis-in-christmas-message-says-church-must-adapt-to-post-christian-west-11576930226.

The Case for Patriarchy

They may square up and face the deuced machinations of popular feminism, or they may continue to brook foolishly such tricks and thereby help to subvert the Christological patriarchy established by God Himself. Once more, consider the common bracketing or ignoring of Ephesians 5:21–33 whenever it makes an infrequent, unwelcome appearance from the Lectionary in Mass:

> You've been there, sitting uncomfortably in the pew, waiting for the lector to read the dreaded Ephesians passage, the one that speaks the culturally anathema, "Wives be subject to your husbands …" Sometimes you notice that the offending passages have been delicately bracketed, so that only St. Paul's admonitions to the husband are going to be read, "Husbands, love your wives as Christ loved the church …" The lector gladly takes the hint, and you sigh in relief. Yet, sometimes the entire passage is read while everyone looks uncomfortably downward, counting the seconds until it's over. Once it's over, you know you're home free. Happily, no priest will ever preach on the whole passage, but will slip into the culturally comfortable preface, "St. Paul says to all of us, 'Be subject to one another out of reverence for Christ,' and so we see …" Then follows a warm meal of platitudes served on a boilerplate, perhaps with a side of nervous humor. But there is never any attempt to deal with the full passage. This neglect made me want to figure out what's really going on in the passage we dare not read aloud.[237]

[237] Benjamin Wiker, "The Key to the Dreaded Ephesians Passage," *National Catholic Register*, August 12, 2019, http://www.ncregister.com/blog/benjamin-wiker/the-key-to-the-dreaded-ephesians-passage.

Now, Jesus articulates clearly the criterion by which our spiritual leaders will be adjudged for their pedagogical noncompliance with His teachings: "If anyone causes one of these little ones—those who believe in me—to stumble, it would be better for them to have a large millstone hung around their neck and to be drowned in the depths of the sea" (Matt. 18:6, NIV). A churchman's false teaching, oriented to satisfy the ungodly craving for secular acceptance, constitutes the cardinal offense, according to Christ's admonition above. If, even at this late hour, churchmen remain unwilling to teach the gospel to a scornful world that hates its moral teachings worse than even its metaphysical teachings, then what can be said in the defense of those churchmen?

It would be far better for everyone if our moral and spiritual leaders would begin to teach against feminism's evils—and against sexual misbehavior of all sorts—in church. No doubt there. The process of amendment would be drastically accelerated. But the point of this final chapter will be that clerical permission is not *needed* for rectification in this most important domain of lay life, as it is with most other ecclesial problems seen today. (As a stark point of contrast, consider the rampant liturgical abuse on Sunday, the rampant libertinism articulated in many homilies, or the rampant homosexualism among the clergy. No amount of righteous lay anger or action can ameliorate such maladies, independent of radical clerical reform.) Feminism among the laity, conversely, can be stymied altogether by deliberate lay action. There is peculiar grace and solace in this fact.

Without devolving to a crass utopianism, society after feminism could be joyful, virtuous, robust, family-centered, and dynamic. After all, a realistic snapshot of life after recovery animates the fondest hopes and dearest motivations of the soul-sick pre-operation patient, infirm yet enthusiastically longing for a speedy recovery. Some characteristics of the post-feminist era are more predictable and some are less so. But all of them trace directly back to the overturn of feminism's perversion and subversion of the patriarchal structures of the Christian complementarity of the married vocation.

I will recur once more to a chilling prediction made in 1981 by Fatima seer Sr. Lucia dos Santos about what Satanic things will come to pass, if the world does not alter its rampant feminism: a "decisive confrontation between the Kingdom of God and Satan will take place over marriage and the family"[238]—a confrontation that may well prove to be eschatological.

Vocation No Longer to Be Mistaken for Profession

The first and best mark of the civil society that has overcome its feminism is that, in it, vocation will no longer be mistaken for profession, or vice versa. The pride in one's career—becoming careerism or professionalism when overemphasized—should be only an arrow in the male householder's vocational quiver. Building his career must remain just a means by which he attains a sufficiently stable household—with enough creature comforts but not too many—such as to focus on more important matters, such as the transmission of fatherly love and faith and morals to the offspring. After all, "when you put first things first and second things second, you get both; when you put first things second and second things first, you get neither."[239]

[238] Edward Pentin, "Cardinal Carlo Caffarra Dies at 79," *National Catholic Register*, September 6, 2017, https://www.ncregister.com/blog/cardinal-carlo-caffarra-dies-at-79-mrle8rzn.

[239] C.S. Lewis to Dom Bede Griffiths, 1951.

The first proposition describes the householder (and his household) who understands the proper relation between vocation — the "first thing" — and profession, the "second thing." The latter proposition describes our present misunderstanding of the rapport between career and family in the West. *Career* serving the soteriological ends of *family* guarantees and enhances both; *family* retrofitting and justifying *career* destroys both.

The tireless striving for his family's salvation can be the only adequate description of the layman's vocation. As noted above, most Westerners are not possessed of this point of view. Just call to mind for a moment how many people you've heard claim, Puritanically, that their career (rather than their family) is their "calling." In other words, career quickly becomes careerism, when denuded of its proper end. A man's career in the vocationally sound society could and should be time-efficient, decent-paying,[240] and low-maintenance, allowing him vivacity upon his arrival home from the workplace. In America and the West, over the last two centuries, only a minority of fathers have understood their careers in this properly ordered vocational context. Even fewer fathers have actually attained the sort of work described by this relation. A man's primary vocational duty, instruction in the virtues, begins at the *end* of the workday, rather than at the *beginning*. The real work of his calling begins precisely then.

Doubtless, such an exhausting and important daily feature in the typical Western workweek requires finesse. As King Theoden of Rohan says of the long journey to war, "It is a three-day ride and both horse and rider must arrive with strength enough to

---

[240] This is according to the social encyclicals *Rerum Novarum* (1891) by Pope Leo XIII and *Quadragesimo Anno* (1931) by Pope Pius XI.

fight." A good soldier does not arrive at the battlefield needing a nap. Energy must be conserved in clever ways throughout the journey to the primary destination. Similarly, a good father does not arrive home from work too tired to teach, play, and pray lovingly. As C. S. Lewis implied above, what is secondary must take a back seat to what is primary.

The modern nine-to-five workday slog constitutes but the prelude to a father's eventide priestly teaching office, which by morning and noontide his good wife capably filled in his stead. Winning bread proves a necessary (but not a sufficient) obligation of the Christian breadwinner, who must, like the soldier, find resourceful ways to store up energy and creativity for the late-afternoon and evening portions of his quotidian vocation. So doing proves to be simple yet not easy.

In other words, the society cured of its feminism will first — or perhaps, simultaneously — be cured of its careerism. From within a mostly male workforce (inclusive of single working women), laboring fathers will look to return lovingly to homes populated by children and wives expecting recreative, pedagogical, and spiritual refreshment from them by evening. Such a father should look to roughhouse or to play outdoors for a short period after work but before dinner. During and after dinner, he should offer quizzical educational oversight, reviewing high points in school lessons from the day. Family prayer before and after dinner should follow. Most of the evening should be consumed by this cumulative instruction. The father's intimate involvement in evening activities proves indispensable to the moral wellness of the family.

One shudders to imagine just how many professionals with titles such as *technical supervisor* and *personnel manager* return home each evening at dinnertime, attending to precisely none of the "quality control" or "professional oversight" at home that they discharged with so much special care, at work. Certainly, to the modern mind, the prospect of so doing presents a Herculean challenge. But it is nothing new.

Historically speaking, the diametrical opposite of the cheery scenario described above was and is far too common a tale, since the times of early-modern America and the English-speaking West. The spurious equation of vocation and career usually presented in the following way. In the minds of American working fathers, toiling at the behest of the "Protestant work ethic," profession and career were substituted for vocation in almost every household. (Today, this toxic substitution now happens *doubly* — to *both* working parents — in over 70 percent of households with minor children!) Long before females even dreamed of entering the workforce, the false equation happened first in the minds of working fathers. Below, I will examine the etiology of this toxic phenomenon, which proves to have been both Reformation- and Enlightenment-derived in its inception.

The Pedigree of Western Labor-Worship Exposed

Careerism became one of the most prominent features of Western feminism, especially in America. In turn, American careerism proves insidious because it is so poorly understood in its origins. To understand the new feminist manifestations of careerism that presently corrupt the popular conception of the household economy, one must understand the original problem's root cause.

In the modern era, the Protestant Reformation of the sixteenth century and the Enlightenment of the seventeenth century combined, in the domain of the workplace, to create a toxic bromide of popular labor worship. In Anglo-Saxon, Protestant places such as England and America, the so-called "Protestant work ethic"[241] was premised largely upon the inherited, Reformation view of the father's career as a replacement for what had formerly been accepted as his primary sacramental duties at home. To varying degrees, the Lutheran, Anglican, and Calvinist theologies had already dispensed with the actual grace conferred by all or most of the sacraments.

When an element so vital as *sacramentum* is suddenly removed from Christendom, a widespread psychology of replacement and dependency will instantly occur. The sixteenth century tells this tale. Nature despises a vacuum, after all: in the case of the early Americans living and toiling in the hardscrabble British colonies west of the Atlantic, labor took on an even more developed quasi-sacramental function in the popular mind.

In other words, Puritan Protestants of the English-speaking world—especially in America—attempted to funnel grace not from the sacraments, which they had spurned as Protestants, but, rather, from labor. American Puritans of the seventeenth and eighteenth centuries reified a non-Leftist "liberation theology" of labor. That sacramental substitute culminated uniquely with a phenomenon the popes came to call "Americanism," the apex admixture of the Protestant Reformation and the Enlightenment. Today's feminist careerism in America and the West owes its anthem—something like, "work hard and free yourself from all shackles"—to this first iteration of careerism writ large, an early-modern mash-up of Puritan scrupulosity with Enlightenment libertinism.[242] As much as today's feminists typically excoriate

---

[241] Ibid.

[242] See Timothy Gordon, *Catholic Republic: Why America Will Perish without Rome* (Manchester, NH: Crisis Publications, 2019), in which the full set of symptoms—religious, political, cultural, economic, familial—of this phenomenon is discussed in detail.

vestiges of what they see as "Puritanism," their ideological *sine qua non*—freedom through labor—derives exclusively from the Puritans.

In the latter half of the nineteenth century, as we have seen, feminists who were aiming to get involved in the American workforce borrowed from popular Protestant *male* presumptions at the time. More or less, these are the selfsame Protestant-Enlightenment conditions that created the "prosperity gospel," the specious view that the bountiful material conditions enjoyed by the wealthy indicate a certain favor they have found with God. In the twenty-first century, it's shocking to locate so much residual (if secularized) Puritanism within the spectrum of American Leftist ideologies, especially feminism!

For the Puritans in the young American republic, following the teachings of Luther, marriage did not constitute a sacrament but was just "a worldly thing ... like any other secular business."[243] Thus, right from the outset, the American family, insofar as it tracked one form of Protestantism or another, bore the materialist germ, stripped of its supernatural, sacramental aspects. Add to this the further fact of the widespread removal in Protestant theological circles of the ordained priesthood,[244] which ensured the disappearance of sacramental graces from daily life. As such, the sacramental fork in the road—previously forcing every Christian in Christendom to choose his calling to Heaven, either ordained or lay—virtually disappeared in North America and Northern Europe, wherever Protestantism preponderated.

---

[243] Martin Luther, *Weimar* (Weimarer Ausgabe, 1523), vol. 12, *Predigten und Schriften*, 131.

[244] This was called "the priesthood of all believers" by Luther, minimizing and desacralizing the importance of an ordained class of ministers.

The Case for Patriarchy

Without parish priests or familial domestic priests, and with no sacramental route to daily grace, the citizens of the young American republic sought to locate grace through an alternate, Puritan-Enlightenment means. Max Weber wrote the following:

> The Puritan wanted to work in calling; we are forced to do so. For when asceticism was carried out of monastic cells into everyday life, and began to dominate worldly morality, it did its part in building the tremendous cosmos of the modern economic order. This order is now bound to the technical and economic conditions of machine production which today determine the lives of all the individuals who are born into this mechanism, not only those directly concerned with economic acquisition, with irresistible force. Perhaps it will so determine them until the last ton of fossilized coal is burnt. In Baxter's view the care for external goods should only lie on the shoulders of the "saint like a light cloak, which can be thrown aside at any moment." But fate decreed that the cloak should become an iron cage.[245]

According to Weber's theory, if neither matrimonial family nor the other sacraments convey grace, then the Puritan-Enlightenment denizens of the modern order were forced to put forward *labor* as the main replacement for sacrament. Aside from the quasi-religious psychological and sociological benefits of labor pointed at by Weber, the Puritan-Enlightenment innovators of the modern West offered a version of labor in strictly materialist terms.

World Heritage Encyclopedia proffers this helpful synopsis of Max Weber's thesis: "The Reformation profoundly affected

---

[245] Weber, *The Protestant Ethic and the Spirit of Capitalism*, 181.

the [modern] view of work, dignifying even the most mundane professions as adding to the common good and thus blessed by God, as much as any 'sacred' calling. A common illustration is that of a cobbler, hunched over his work, who devotes his entire effort to the praise of God."[246] The same encyclopedia goes on to stipulate further what Weber added to this understanding of the Protestant-Enlightenment mash-up, which deified labor in the American mind:

> Weber traced the origins of the Protestant ethic to the Reformation.... The Roman Catholic Church assured salvation to individuals who accepted the Church's sacraments and submitted to clerical authority. However, the Reformation had effectively removed such assurances. From a psychological viewpoint, the average person had difficulty adjusting to this new [desacralized] worldview, and only the most devout believers or "religious geniuses" within Protestantism, such as Martin Luther, were able to make this adjustment, according to Weber. In the absence of such assurances from religious authority, Weber had argued that Protestants began to look for other "signs" that they were saved.[247]

This background investigation into Puritanism also serves to explain the confounding feminist fetishization of career. As most male breadwinners and working, single mothers would agree, there is nothing that proves to be "sexy" or "salvific" about labor. It

---

[246] *World Heritage Encyclopedia*, s.v. "The Protestant Ethic and the Spirit of Capitalism," http://community.worldheritage.org/articles/The_Protestant_Ethic_and_the_Spirit_of_Capitalism.
[247] Ibid.

proves a necessity (for laborers) and nothing more. Like Mark
Twain's character Ben Rogers, the gullible friend hoodwinked by
Tom Sawyer into whitewashing the fence on his behalf, Puritanism-
addled feminists have traded their apple and their priceless free
time for servility before petty taskmasters.

Just as the reader of *Tom Sawyer* is left to inquire whether
Rogers ever realizes that he has been "had" by Sawyer, we are left
wondering if the feminists will ever get it. Trading the homeplace
for the workplace—and more free time for less—proves to be
the raw end of the stick. But they seem none the wiser.

The Puritan-Enlightenment Woman's
Home as a Workplace?

By most measures, the Puritan component of the "American spirit"
seems less related to feminism than the secularist Enlightenment
worldview does. On the contrary, the two are intimately bound
together. In the domain of labor and the workplace, the Puritan
substitution of work for sacraments remains the most important
part of the script. By now, the popular concept of vocation—ordained and lay—has been all but lost. In the post-feminist society
of the future, vocation must be robustly recalled and reanimated.
As men come to re-embrace their late-afternoon vocation in the
home, upon the return from work, so, too, will women re-embark
upon the enthusiastic, ebullient vocation of homemaking.

When women proudly do this, the home will no longer mimic
the workplace but will shine forth as the superior environment.
In the post-feminist society of the future, therefore, the homeplace will be more celebrated—by great measures—than the
workplace.

We also saw above how, within families, the lay vocation
should be marked primarily by roles according to sex—the sexes

bodily united in sacrament. This involves two distinct parts of the family's parentage: procreation and education in faith and morals. The secondary properties of vocation usually include, as Aristotle remarks of the necessary conditions of attaining *Eudaimonia*:[248] a modicum of wealth, health, pleasure, and lifestyle accoutrements. But in neither the female nor the male domain should these secondary properties be mistaken for primary ones. Note: these latter conditions are merely secondary means by which the family typically accomplishes its veritable goal: reaching Paradise together. Vocation is merely a means of attaining Heaven, so fatherly labor and motherly homemaking turn out to be *means toward a means.*

Once more, in the anti-feminist society, the home and family must be regarded as both natural and supernatural, lest vocation be widely mistaken for profession (which is merely natural). The workplace, conversely, is only "natural" in the secondary sense of being the universal curse of Adam's sons. Yet why are so many homes — even the homes of today's stay-at-home-mothers — deliberately run like soulless workplaces? They often self-consciously mimic the workplace. The answer seems to involve the Americanist combination of home economy and an unexpected strain of feminism, which emerged furtively from the early republic's materialist admixture of Calvinism and secularism in the domicile, described above.

Too frequently (though not always), today's stay-at-home-mothering scene styles itself as a competing type of workplace. Just imagine Marge Simpson filling out her résumé, qualifying the tasks entailed by homemaking in the most "professional" way conceivable. Needlessly, the homemaker in the West is often

[248] Aristotle, *Nicomachean Ethics* 1.

unduly ashamed of her life, in the decades after the 1970s, and she constrains her characterization of her own daily routine to befit the feminist's dogmatic, Puritanical categories of professionalism. In the post-feminist society of the future, this will not be the case.

In their own advocacy, stay-at-home mothers have been shamed into coloring their sacred calling of motherhood and wifeliness as an alternative form of "career," just one among many. Such a characterization proves neither compelling nor attractive. Such homemakers forfeited their rightful property, the high ground of nature, to the feminists, who toil every moment against nature yet claim its aegis in their ungodly endeavors.

Hastily, and without considering the implications of their admission, stay-at-home mothers bought the feminist premise (borrowed from American Calvinism) that wage labor is basically sacred.

So, even within the home, the Calvinist pseudo-sacrament of labor is presently being used as a cheap surrogate in America for the real graces of one of the sacraments. It is indeed a tawdry lieutenant. As one of the seven true sacraments, matrimony produces the holy fruit of human life, which requires constant motherly instruction and oversight in children's faith and morals. To liken the sublime calling to a petty wage-earning task, as defensive stay-at-home mothers often do, proves crass and tactless. Certainly, stay-at-home mothers have only defended themselves thus as a desperate reaction (protesting too much, perhaps) against a tireless onslaught by Americanist-Calvinist feminists, who have childishly overestimated the value of a lesser commodity. In the last analysis, the most common "defense" of stay-at-home mothers ceded far too much ground to both Calvinism and feminism. And they don't even realize it.

In the English-speaking world, the culture of the Protestant work ethic absorbed by non-career mothers yielded an emergent stay-at-home feminism. Consequently, the acrimonious battle of the sexes moved not only with females into the 1970s workforce but also came to the theater of the nonworking mother's domicile. There she learned to sneer at her husband instead of admiring him. Think of the average home-products commercial described in this book's first two chapters: a trim, bright-eyed mother rolls her eyes at an overweight slouch of a husband, who perversely follows her every command.

Just as Calvinist expectations crossed with traditional masculinity and new Enlightenment notions of financial freedom to make a pseudo-religious careerism, they crossed with old and new female sensibilities to make the homeplace mimic the workplace. If the home were a workplace, she reasoned, then she, too, could call herself a "good worker." Indeed, in this new "workplace," she could even count herself "boss" over husband and children. In the decades leading to the sex revolution, the Americanist psyche of the stay-at-home mother mixed with feminist career shaming to produce the stay-at-home shrew, whose daytime household workplace would be run like a yuppie work camp.

Before the sexual revolution, a wife stood in the doorway in an apron, kissing her husband goodbye as he headed off to work, admiring his career without coveting it. After the sexual revolution, the few women who chose to stay at home decided to compete with working husbands, working women, and all the world besides by conceiving of her home as an efficient "shop." Thus the homeplace grew cold and even clinical.

In the post-feminist society, the homeplace will not be run anything like the workplace. The former will again be widely recognized as vastly superior to the latter. Similarly, the mother who heads the household in the stead of the working father will gladly return the reins to him upon his return home from work. He will be eminently worthy of his charge through his mindfulness of his vocation, which is exercised in the most important ways in the home. When the priest of the household clearly prizes the homeplace over the workplace, his lieutenant will follow suit.

Vocation or "Self-Image"?

The previous sections insinuate that in the post-feminist society, the source of so-called self-esteem will again be widely recognized as Christ. He is the source of every good thing, including our self-image.

Every serious-minded human being has been hardwired, in the image and likeness of the Creator, to care intimately about the proper cultivation of his own works and projects. There is nothing faulty in this observation. We shed blood, sweat, and tears only in arenas that we've deemed worthwhile, after all. Yet it presents a problem worthy of address for young women whose weddings are delayed for a few years. In fact, they will begin careers they never intend to complete.

For single, faithful laywomen necessitated to earn a wage by the delayed encounter of eventual husbands, professional goal setting must always be referred to the eventuation of vocational realities. The faithful young female employee should be haunted by this thought: "If and when I fall in love with a moral, noble man, both he and I will expect my career to end as soon as we are married."

This vision requires no small amount of forethought. It demands that these single women make provision in the present for an abstract future husband. Accordingly, a young woman's strict vocational mindset will be of paramount importance, in the time before meeting the appropriate suitor. As these young, unmarried women make their way in the world, embarking on their temporary careers, they must remain ever vigilant for eligible young men, whose very appearance serves as a harbinger of the end for their careers.

Even before they've met, when a young woman's husband is but an abstraction in her mind, she knows what her vocational hopes have always been. Even the unrealized notion of an eventual husband should spell, *ab initio*, a bracketed approach to career. (And that's only if she finds her career before her husband!) Being willfully oblivious to the likely timeline of locating a husband will do her no good. In the post-feminist, anti-feminist world of the future, the career of the working bachelorette will carry only short-term expectations.

Indeed, the young woman's career poses her the specific harm suffered by all who fail to manage expectations in life. Such career women will be greatly harmed by comparing themselves with young career men with whom they work, who—whether single or married—should reasonably expect to toil at their posts and develop their professional goals for the coming decades.

Especially in these relationships, the adage that "comparison is the thief of joy"[249] proves especially true. Men and women, who are utterly and essentially different, should not expect the same yield from even seemingly identical sources, like labor or exercise. I've already examined the statistical paradox that, on the average, an otherwise "successful" career causes depression and anxiety in working women, whereas such a thing brings working men great satisfaction. Similarly, testosterone-building exercise

---

[249] Kathryn Albig, "Comparison Is the Thief of Joy," Active Christianity, https://activechristianity.org/comparison-is-the-thief-of-joy.

proves to fortify and perfect male fertility, while it depletes and damages female fertility.

Given the nature of human habit-formation,[250] any woman's career—even a licit one in the life of a single woman who must earn for herself a justifiable wage in the meantime—proves perilous. Daily habit always threatens to addict a human being to his routine. Whatever else a woman's career benefits may be, they may always pose sufficiently alluring to her such as to risk the indefinite continuation, past her wedding day, of her career. She must be willing to drop, at a moment's notice, the various projects of good will entailed by her career. If a young working woman cannot with full enthusiasm throw herself into her career as a young man would, shouldn't we characterize her identification with her salaried post in a fundamentally different way than his?

Of course we should! In the society that has outlived feminism, workplaces and universities full of young people will again be recognized as mostly male environments, to be entered temporarily by job- or education-seeking females in search of males.[251]

---

[250] In the *Nicomachean Ethics*, books 2 and 3, Aristotle describes how pleasure in a given field or excellence will grow with repetition and improvement.

[251] In the 1970s, because post-Christian, feminist society no longer afforded young people the appropriate occasions for meeting spouses, women began to enter the male domains after graduation from high school. Given that many young women are only half-hearted feminists at best, they frequently meet, court, and marry a husband encountered at university or at a first professional workplace. Accordingly, the anti-feminist society must restore all the wholesome occasions for young men and women to encounter one another. Young women should not have to enter universities (unless they have independently planned to do so) or workplaces simply to meet men.

Only those women who are not yet nuns or wives will typically enter therein, although the university has much more to offer the stay-at-home wife than the workplace does. This means that female career proficiency is *natural* to the extent that habitual improvement in the virtues is to be expected, but *unnatural* to the extent that the female vocation (whether ordained or lay) will, as an eventuality, divert her permanently from her short-lived profession. This paradox must be navigated with the purest motivation and circumspect discernment—with neither chauvinism nor feminism.

But what should *not* be regarded disparately between the sexes is their primary source of "self-esteem," identity in Jesus Christ. This remains true even if accidental properties of the female and male vocations—such as skillful cooking (female) or the perquisites of a "cool career" (male)—prove to be a minor, blameless source of pride. For both sexes, the *primary* source must always be Christ, through proficiency in one's sacramental vocation. Truly, vocation is one's path to Paradise.

Although careerism is vastly less unnatural in men than in women, we have seen the ghastly, unnatural effects of the substitution of career for vocation in both.

Of course, for men, career partially constitutes the vocation, whereas for women, it does not. For a woman, the career prior to wifely motherhood proves wholly extraneous to her vocation, a proposition that will surely distress many young women: it merely sustained her until she met a husband. Yet here may be found an unexpected source of "equalization" between the sexes, the quarry ever sought by feminists: the male career, too, proves mostly extraneous to his vocation. The main component of a man's career overlapping with his vocation is his *paycheck*, which is sufficient to the task as long as it pays the bills. The more important share of the male vocation resides at home, after work, as stated above. Whether through a "sexy" career or a gritty one, the labor a given householder does to earn his wage matters not.

Various, somewhat arbitrary conditions produce a fortunate householder getting to spend more time with his family than other working men: short work hours, the ability to work from home, successful investment, and so on. The main point is that male workers lucky enough to spend a greater portion of their work week at home with family enjoy an *enhanced* (not a *diminished*) means to perfect their vocation. The exception proves the rule: the Calvinist deification of labor and the "prosperity gospel" reflect a deep Americanist misunderstanding (and even nullification) of vocation.

Frugality Recalled after False Vocations Die

So, evidently, consumerist materialism lies near to the heart of the pseudo-vocation that cross-fertilized feminism in Western civilization sometime in the middle of the nineteenth century. As seen above, its antidote will be a widespread, renewed understanding of true vocation. In the post-feminist society of the future, immediately after the renewal of our sense of Christian calling, widespread materialism reasonably should be expected mostly to die out as well.

Frugality will prevail after worldly possessions have been relegated to their proper place in society: a mere means to the end of vocational family. Creature comforts are necessary only to the extent that they guide and facilitate the proper learning of natural and supernatural virtue in the home, as instructed by mothers and fathers. Proof for this claim may be found in sociological studies that have repeatedly found that per capita happiness rates rise linearly with increased income, yet only to a certain moderate extent,[252] peaking around the $105,000 salary in America, after which point happiness drops precipitously again.

Such sociological studies vindicate not only the above idea of profession in service of vocation (over against vocation in service of profession) but also the presently unsung virtue of *frugality*. My analysis will hardly be the first to connect the single-wage household to virtuous frugality, or the double-wage household to vicious consumerism. After all, the Church taught this quite clearly in the late-nineteenth and early-twentieth centuries. But my analysis may rightly be seen as among the first in the twenty-first century to hearken back to the Church's teaching on the value of the economic virtue.

In his encyclical *Rerum Novarum*, Pope Leo XIII makes these connections explicit within Church teaching:

> If a workman's wages be sufficient to enable him comfortably to support himself, his wife, and his children, he will find it easy, if he be a sensible man, to practice thrift, and he will not fail, by cutting down expenses, to put by some little savings and thus secure a modest source of income. Nature itself would urge him to this.[253]

Note Pope Leo's careful connection of male wage-earning ("to support himself, his wife, and his children") to *virtue* ("if he be a sensible man"), to *prudential economy* ("to practice thrift"), and to *natural law* (which "would urge him to this"). A single household

---

[252] Josh Hafner, "Does Money Equal Happiness? It Does, but Only Until You Earn This Much," *USA Today*, February 26, 2018, https://www.usatoday.com/story/money/nation-now/2018/02/26/does-money-equal-happiness-does-until-you-earn-much/374119002/.

[253] Leo XIII, *Rerum Novarum*, no. 46.

income proves to be the means by which the father provides for his home economy. Pope Leo's clarion call was renewed by Pope Pius XI in *Quadragesimo Anno*:

> In the first place, the worker must be paid a wage sufficient to support him and his family. That the rest of the family should also contribute to the common support, according to the capacity of each, is certainly right, as can be observed especially in the families of farmers, but also in the families of many craftsmen and small shopkeepers. But to abuse the years of childhood and the limited strength of women is grossly wrong. Mothers, concentrating on household duties, should work primarily in the home or in its immediate vicinity. It is an intolerable abuse, and to be abolished at all cost, for mothers on account of the father's low wage to be forced to engage in gainful occupations outside the home to the neglect of their proper cares and duties, especially the training of children. Every effort must therefore be made that fathers of families receive a wage large enough to meet ordinary family needs adequately.[254]

Note how Pius carefully balances the need for reasonable fatherly wages with domestic motherly work. He weighs the need for filial or wifely help around the family farm or family shop with a caution against the father's overuse of workplace aid from unpaid family workers—not least due to the fatal opportunity cost to mothers in their household duties. He sees a need both for an employer's generosity and the employee's thrift. Together, all this insinuates frugality. If an employer pays a fair wage, a householder

[254] Pius XI, *Quadragesimo Anno*, no. 71.

should be able to cover his family's expenses through shrewd fiscal management. The post-feminist society shall be marked by such frugality.

Head of Home, Head of State

Virtuous male leadership, recall, is instantiated by the repopularization of the cardinal virtues.

In regard to justice, the post-feminist society will be marked by local and familial laws centering on the disposition of *fairness*, not *equality*. Justice allocates to each what he deserves; equality allocates too much to some and too little to others—giving the perfect amount to almost no one. In the post-feminist society, juridical remedies at law will be stern but not harsh.

Once again, winners will be winners and losers will be losers. Fairness will be the law of the land: to the victor shall go the spoils. In Little League tournaments, trophies will be distributed only to champions, rather than to everyone. Not every mother's little boy will play the same amount of innings in the tournament; however, plenty of fathers will be on hand to teach the less-skilled Little Leaguers how to improve their throwing and catching. So-called grade inflation in high schools and colleges will no longer exist.

Within the family, of course, the father's just judgment on matters of dispute will be final and fair. Mothers will advise and support the decisions of their husbands on these disputed matters. They will not (as they too often do in our era) undermine the decisions of fathers in front of children. Fathers will be heeded, as they will be just; they will be just, as they will be heeded. Fatherly prudence will be the hallmark of the post-feminist society.

Speaking of prudence, the post-feminist society will in all corners witness fathers being consulted about snap judgments once more. Alongside justice, the reader should recall that prudence is one-half of the couplet of "ruler's virtues." The Christian household economy plainly dictates that the ruler's virtue of prudence does not pertain to mothers, which shocks our modern countrymen. In the post-feminist society, if a child falls ill on a Sunday, he will consult his *father*—not his mother—about whether he is too sick to attend Mass. Only this configuration of authority squares with the one established by all the chapters of this book. The Christian father is priest of the *ecclesiola*. Real-time decisions of on-the-fly moral calculus fall to prudential judgment calls, which must be rendered by the agent properly disposed for extemporaneous riddle solving.

In regard to temperance, fathers of the post-feminist era will lead their families away from dependency on bodily pleasures—which is to say, toward moral and intellectual rectitude, which carry their own pleasures. These men will usher in an era of "weaponized chastity," disabling Jezebels from empowerment. Such fathers will advise their college-bound offspring against the dangers of drinking, smoking, and fornication. (Advice of this kind is offered infrequently in our era).

Moreover, they will lead their sons and daughters by example. If society is ever to return to an era of virtue, in which the bodily pleasures do not have the last word over mankind's will, then household fathers must habituate the overcoming of the bodily pleasures—most especially those of touch and taste. In reality, this requires that the ills of fornication, unchastity, gluttony, and radical insobriety will once again become objects of opprobrium.

Such objects must find themselves frequently in the sermons of household fathers. In our current society, mothers generally tend to this, if at all. As such, the ills of intemperance are ineffectively guarded against in our day. Conversely, weaponized chastity will safeguard the post-feminist society against the furtive return of feminism, which perennially stalks Christendom for the ambush signal of forfeited self-quarantine.

In regard to fortitude, the era after feminism will everywhere be recognizable by its excellence in this manliest of virtues. Post-feminism, fathers will be heard referring the practice of all the other virtues back to exercises in courage. Are we brave enough to be just? Are we brave enough to be temperate?

The manly concept of "struggling" or "fighting" will be restored as a literal and figurative reference for most every situation in life. Children will willingly tune in to such lessons, once mothers stop attempting to be the messengers, as is the case in our feminist era. Fathers will teach their sons the art of fighting once more: how to do it, when to do it, and when not to do it. Our era of feminism is the era of pacifism, in which the young are brainwashed to the fatalist effect that only "bad guys" fight back, ever.

Feminism and Our Lady of Fatima

The late Cardinal Carlo Caffarra, one of the holiest men of our age, spoke on May 19, 2017 to the Rome Life Forum about issues centrally important to feminism. Cardinal Caffarra, one of the four "dubia cardinals," was well-known within the Church for having "helped to found the Pontifical John Paul II Institute for Studies on Marriage and the Family in 1981."[255] The academic

---

[255] Edward Pentin, "Cardinal Caffarra: Satan Is Hurling at God the Ultimate and Terrible Challenge," *National Catholic Register*, May 20, 2017, http://www.ncregister.com/blog/edward-pentin/ cardinal-caffarra-satan-is-hurling-at-god-the-ultimate-and-terrible-challen.

life of Caffarra's cardinalate centered on sacramental matrimonial expertise.

Although the term "feminism" makes no appearance in Cardinal Caffarra's speech at the Rome Life Forum, its contents convey some of the all-time subtlest diagnoses, prognoses, and remedies for the scourge of feminism. Because he died four short months after delivering it, his uncommonly insightful speech turned out to be one of his very last. Arguably, it was his most important. (This book has referred to it in several of its chapters.)

Before turning to his remarks, it behooves us to offer a final word about their startling context. The context appears to be eschatological. Quoting a 1981 letter written to him by Fatima seer Sr. Lucia dos Santos, upon his foundation of the Institute, Cardinal Caffarra framed our present era of history *eschatalogically*: "There will come a time when the decisive confrontation between the Kingdom of God and Satan will take place over marriage and the family,"[256] as Sr. Lucia wrote him. (She added in subsequent remarks to the cardinal that advocates of Christian marriage and family "will undergo trials and tribulations" in this final era.)

Recalling all this, Caffarra shared earnestly with the Rome Life Forum attendees that his speech had been "based on these words of Sister Lucia, and therefore on the conviction that what Sister Lucia said in those days are being fulfilled in these days of ours."[257] Having been "etched in the heart [of the] Church's leading expert on marriage and the family,"[258] this connection between ongoing familial destruction and eschatology chastens today's vigilant opponent of feminism. His Eminence maintained

---

[256] Pentin, "Cardinal Carlo Caffarra Dies."
[257] Ibid.
[258] Ibid.

until his dying day that the ongoing feminist attack on the family marked the beginning of the end of the world.

Also, in his Rome Life Forum speech, Cardinal Caffarra described "the ultimate and terrible challenge" posed against God by the devil, a final assault upon creation itself. When, under such bedeviled human agency, the widespread relations between man and woman have been fundamentally realigned, an "anti-creation" will have been unleashed upon the world, signaling Caffarra's prediction about the last era's unfurling of creation. Careful analysis reveals that this force of "anti-creation" means *feminism* (easily more so than it means "LGBT"), attacking the complementary and procreative means by which parents cooperate with God to co-author and co-educate their offspring.

Cardinal Caffarra then develops the concept of anti-creation as an attack on what he calls two pillars of creation: the "first being the transformation of the crime of abortion into a legal and subjective right" and the second being the denial of the "truth of marriage, [rejecting] the mind of God the Creator with regard to marriage."[259] Caffarra notes how the anti-creation expresses the following Satanic anthem: "I am demonstrating to [God] that I [Satan] am capable of constructing an alternative to your creation. And man will say it is better in the alternative creation than in your creation."

Although Cardinal Caffarra trains all his Rome Life Forum speech's fire on abortion, contraception is an important aspect of the "abortive mindset." From first- to fourth-wave feminism, weaponized abnegations of the female reproductive power—namely, abortion and contraception—proved indispensable to the foremost goal of de-domesticating women. Not surprisingly, in all four

---

[259] Pentin, "Cardinal Caffarra: Satan Is Hurling."

waves of feminism, the feminists tacitly or explicitly encouraged promiscuous and contraceptive sex, heightening the movement's emphatic preclusion of virtuous marital procreation. Satan's anti-creation curtails the first pillar's "human cooperation in the Creative act of God"[260] via a gradual estoppage of authentic matrimonial sexual activity. Although Satan employed multiple modes of effectuating this estoppage in the popular mind, feminism's most deadly assault on the sacrament inhered in sexualizing premarital life and desexualizing marital life.

The second proposition warned against by Cardinal Caffarra employs language that denigrates Christian matrimony by "denying entirely the truth of marriage."[261] Certainly, the false ennobling of "homosexual marriage" is the target upon which the cardinal trained most of his fire in the 2017 speech. Yet Caffarra also implicitly condemns the illogic of the *original* transgenderism — feminism — wherein Christian men began, before and during heterosexual marriage, to believe they may function like women and vice versa.

Perhaps more than the LGBT movment, confusion of the so-called gender roles *within marriage* denies the godly truth of sacramental sexuality. Only this heterosexual form of transgenderism proved capable of disintegrating Christian marriage at the staggering, precipitous volume we have seen recently. Anyway, while Cardinal Caffarra's second pillar treats almost exclusively of the vitiation of marriage in terms of homosexuality, far fewer Catholic laymen are touched by these temptations. In other words, for the laity, the marital falsehoods of the LGBT movement present a less immediate, more abstract problem than

---

[260] Ibid.
[261] Ibid.

heterosexual feminism, which corrupts and destroys no small number of sacramental and natural marriages.

All of Cardinal Caffarra's points about the disintegration of Christian marriage apply with equal or greater rigor to Satan's imposition of non-transgendered sexual dysphoria—that is, sexual role reversal, of husbands acting like wives and vice versa. This means, of course, that each of the eschatological dangers His Eminence spoke of apply with special force to feminism.

In the post-feminist society of a brighter day, the procreative and marital fonts of Christian complementarity will be restored to society. They shall be that society's proof against all evil.

Conclusion

In the society outlasting feminism sometime in the future, which will arise like a phoenix from its ashes, a man with an expecting wife will no longer tell you, "We are pregnant." In that healthier, merrier day to come, men would not stand for such a thing—and neither would women. As a matter of fact, this pregnancy neologism "we are pregnant" self-sufficiently proves the point that feminists want to commandeer whatever is male, abandoning or reallocating to males whatever is female. Even as it seeks to destroy the patriarchy, feminism eschews femaleness and idolizes maleness—an idolization that, of course, does not mitigate their *ressentiment* and misandry.

After all, female fecundity presents the paradigm instance of what *ought* to be popularly conceived as "girl power." If feminism truly centered on celebrating the feminine, which its advocates claim—and which this book has shown to be an abject lie—then feminists would never say of their husbands that "we are pregnant." They would show their own pride in being the unique, sex-specific, nonandrogynous conduit of life.

The Case for Patriarchy

In the post-feminist society, vocation will be understood to enliven and enable people's existence rather than draw against the vivacity of their day-to-day lives. A vibrant culture of life will abide. Vocation is life, to use the old adage. Human identity will not be popularly reducible to practical or economic functionalism; this hackneyed critique of capitalism would be far more aptly leveled against feminism and Calvinism. As such, congregants at dinner parties will not blithely discuss their jobs in hopeless tones like soulless drones; instead, they will discuss their Church, their families, and their adventures together. They will tell jokes. They will share stories.

Male or female, what you do for a living is not who you are. Your unique identity lies in the Redeemer. It is evidenced by the particular, contingent qualities of your vocation—married or ordained or celibate-in-waiting. That alone is "who you truly are." More important still, it is who you will be, since it is your path to Heaven.

In the post-feminist society, there will be no such thing as "man caves." What else but a man cave emblemizes the lonely retreat into hibernation by the modern male from the joyful and central command of his family's life? The man cave constitutes an actual retreat to the literal and figurative fringes of his family's living space, hiding away from his wife whatever remnants of his masculinity she has not yet chipped from his character like so much marble pillaged by Vandals from the Coliseum. Nathaniel Hawthorne wrote that "physiognomy," the outward appearance of a thing, should be taken as offering some insight into its character.

The physiognomy of the husband and father in the feminist era is the enervated and hamstrung slouch, retreating on his heels in defeat, to his man cave, with a visibly broken spirit. He is not welcome abroad in daylight in the very house he provides. In the anti-feminist era yet to come, male householders will be barrel-chested hobbyists, whose wives and children engage in the milieu of their provider's hobbies as in the robust days of old. To no small extent, the family life should revolve around the wholesome, community-building, protective, outdoor hobbies of the father, such as hunting, fishing, camping, hiking, and so on.[262]

In the post-feminist society, no "veteran" husbands will cynically admonish fearful newlywed husbands to heed their wives' orders, as if by imperious decree. No "happy wife, happy life." Such a spurious proposition of marital logic sells short both husbands and wives. This false wisdom—predicated upon a false notion of happiness—flatters no one: it makes Hitler out of wives and Chamberlain out of husbands.

In that healthier, merrier day to come, husbands and wives will love each other passionately. The "battle of the sexes" will be definitively ended. Single couples in love will dream without partaking of loving one another passionately. They will anticipate with holy joy and trepidation what unknown adventures might come of their love and their life. Marriage will be restored to its rightful throne amid secular life. The family will once more gain its rightful recognition as the font of all culture.

The culture that it creates will bring with it Christendom once again. And with Christendom will come an appreciation for the kingship of the social reign of Christ, King of the Patriarchy!

---

[262] This also means, gentlemen, that most nights should be spent at home with the family, not at the pub!

About the Author

Timothy J. Gordon, J.D., Ph.L., M.A., studied the philosophy of Aristotle and Thomas Aquinas in pontifical graduate universities in Rome, taught it at Southern Californian colleges, and then went on to law school. He holds degrees in literature, history, philosophy, and law. He resides in Southern Mississippi with his large family, writing, teaching, and speaking on philosophy and theology.

For leisure, he wears the furs of endangered species, eats preservative-rich and plastic-wrapped foods, and adamantly refuses to recycle. In these dark times in the Church and the world, he lives by this maxim of G. K. Chesterton: "Solemnity flows out of men naturally, but laughter is a leap. It is easy to be heavy: hard to be light." *Risus est bellum.*

CRISIS Publications

Sophia Institute Press awards the privileged title "CRISIS Publications" to a select few of our books that address contemporary issues at the intersection of politics, culture, and the Church with clarity, cogency, and force and that are also destined to become all-time classics.

CRISIS Publications are *direct*, explaining their principles briefly, simply, and clearly to Catholics in the pews, on whom the future of the Church depends. The time for ambiguity or confusion is long past.

CRISIS Publications are *contemporary*, born of our own time and circumstances and intended to become significant statements in current debates, statements that serious Catholics cannot ignore, regardless of their prior views.

CRISIS Publications are *classical*, addressing themes and enunciating principles that are valid for all ages and cultures. Readers will turn to them time and again for guidance in other days and different circumstances.

CRISIS Publications are *spirited*, entering contemporary debates with gusto to clarify issues and demonstrate how those issues can be resolved in a way that enlivens souls and the Church.

We welcome engagement with our readers on current and future CRISIS Publications. Please pray that this imprint may help to resolve the crises embroiling our Church and society today.

Sophia Institute Press® is a registered trademark of Sophia Institute.
Sophia Institute is a tax-exempt institution as defined by the
Internal Revenue Code, Section 501(c)(3). Tax I.D. 22-2548708.